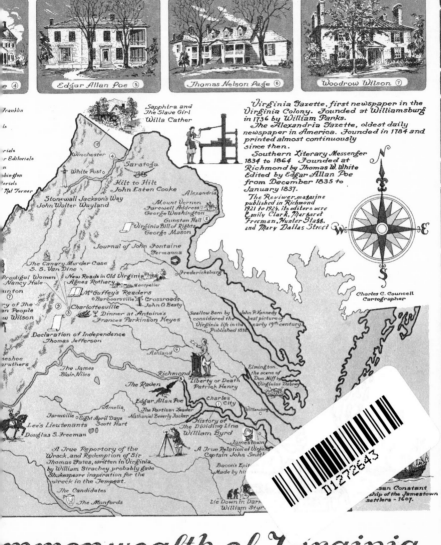

Edgar Allan Poe ⑤

Thomas Nelson Page ⑥

Woodrow Wilson ⑦

Sapphira and
The Slave Girl
Willa Cather

Virginia Gazette, first newspaper in the
Virginia Colony. Founded at Williamsburg
in 1736 by William Parks.

The Alexandria Gazette, oldest daily
newspaper in America. Founded in 1784 and
printed almost continuously
since then.

Southern Literary Messenger
1834 to 1864. Founded at
Richmond by Thomas W. White.
Edited by Edgar Allan Poe
from December 1835 to
January 1837.

The Reviewer, magazine
published in Richmond
1921 to 1924. Its editors were
Emily Clark, Margaret
Freeman, Hunter Stagg,
and Mary Dallas Street

Franklin

Editorials

Nat Turner

Winchester ④
White Post
Saratoga
Hilt to Hilt
John Esten Cooke
Alexandria
Stonewall Jackson's Way
John Walter Wayland
Mount Vernon
Farewell Address
George Washington
Gunston Hall
Virginia Bill of Rights
George Mason
Germanna
Journal of John Fontaine
Fredericksburg
The Canary Murder Case
S. S. Van Dine
New Roads in Old Virginia
Nancy Hale   Agnes Rothery
Montpelier
Prodigal Women
McGuffey's Readers
Barboursville   Crossroads
Charlottesville   John O. Beaty
Dinner at Antoine's
Frances Parkinson Keyes
Declaration of Independence
Thomas Jefferson
Swallow Barn by
John P. Kennedy
considered the best picture of
Virginia life in the early 19th century.
Published 1832
Ashland
Elmington
the scene of Don Miff
by Virginius Dabney
The James
Blair Niles
Richmond
Liberty or Death
Patrick Henry
The Raven
Edgar Allan Poe
Charles City
Williamsburg
Amelia
The Partisan Leader
Nathaniel Beverly Tucker
Farmville   Eight April Days
Scott Hart
Lee's Lieutenants
Douglas S. Freeman
History of
The Dividing Line
William Byrd
Jamestown
A True Repertory of the
Wreck, and Redemption of Sir
Thomas Gates, written in Virginia
by William Strachey, probably gave
Shakespeare inspiration for the
wreck in the Tempest.
The Candidates
The Munfords
A True Relation of Virginia
Captain John Smith
Bacon's Epit
Made by hi
Lie Down in Dar
William Sty

Charles C. Councell
Cartographer

Susan Constant
ship of the Jamestown
settlers - 1607.

Commonwealth of Virginia

 nger ⑧

 Ellen Glasgow ⑨

Sherwood Anderson ⑪

 Willa Cather ⑫

Welford Dunaway Taylor

Maurice Duke

VIRGINIA AUTHORS
Past and Present

VIRGINIA AUTHORS
Past and Present

Welford Dunaway Taylor
General Editor

WITH

Maurice Duke, *Bibliographical Editor*

AND

Mary Marcy Councell, *Compiler and Editor*
Katharine Groseclose Sieg, *Assistant Editor*
Rubye Lee Norris, *Assistant Editor*
Lucille Portlock, *Compiler*

1972

VIRGINIA ASSOCIATION OF TEACHERS OF ENGLISH

Copyright © 1972 by Virginia Association of Teachers of English

Library of Congress Catalog Card Number: 72-77884

PRINTED IN THE UNITED STATES OF AMERICA
BY THE WILLIAM BYRD PRESS, INC.,
RICHMOND, VIRGINIA

Distributed by
THE
VIRGINIA ASSOCIATION OF TEACHERS OF ENGLISH

To the late

RINALDO C. SIMONINI, JR.

this book has been dedicated for his long years of devoted service
to the Virginia Association of Teachers of English, as member,
president, and editor of the *Virginia English Bulletin,* and for
his unselfish work and the guidance he gave during this book's
embryonic stage.

INTRODUCTION

During the preparation of the ensuing volume, I was frequently asked whether "all Virginia writers" would be included. The answer was always a hasty "no," followed by an explanation which should be perfectly obvious to anyone who has given the subject serious thought: Any attempt to treat all Virginians who have published writing of any sort would be doomed from the start. Not only would indefinable numbers and sparse material render such an undertaking impracticable, but its scholarly plausibility would be highly questionable. If one stretches the definition of "Virginia author" to include everyone from the Pulitzer Prize-winning biographer to the gossip columnist in a country weekly, he has made his task both impossible and ridiculous. Selectivity is the obvious recourse.

This volume is offered, therefore, as a guide for studying those authors whose work has interested and/or influenced the reading public of the Commonwealth as a whole. Writers have been deemed Virginians either by birth or adoption (which means having lived a substantial amount of time in Virginia and having reflected this experience in their work). In short, I have sought to make what to me seemed the most meaningful limitations of a subject of infinite vastness. My ultimate aim has been to compile a "who's who" of Virginia authors past and present.

I am well aware that my selections—or anyone's, for that matter—will be questioned by some. As in all situations where individual criteria are exercised, one can never hope to please everyone. Hopefully, though, this is but the first of many future efforts.

I am also aware that I am omitting a large number of dedicated, talented writers who have made significant achievements within a limited sphere. It is with sincere regret, for instance, that it was necessary to omit many writers of purely local history, several of whom have produced definitive works on a number of Virginia localities. Once again, one could never hope for completeness, and variation within the genre would require selection anyway. Still, there may well have been another *Natural History and Antiquities of Selbourne* or some village Shakespeare who has gone unsung here. Such regrettable sins of omission are solely mine.

A large portion of this volume had been intended for publication early in the 1960's, but for various reasons was forced to remain in manuscript. I was offered the job of editing and updating in June, 1970, by the Virginia Association of Teachers of English. In assuming responsibility for all selections, I was likewise given categorical freedom in making them, for which I am sincerely grateful.

From the original manuscript—meticulously compiled by Mary M. Councell, Katherine G. Sieg, and Rubye Lee Norris—I deleted some three dozen figures. I edited the sketches on those remaining (something over two hundred) in order to achieve consistency of tone and point of view, and finally added some seventy-five new writers, many of whom have achieved prominence since the original manuscript was completed.

"A Research Guide to Virginia Writers," which did not appear in the original version, was written by Maurice Duke, Associate Professor of English, Virginia Commonwealth University. He also edited the bibliographical selections following each sketch, greatly increasing the book's value as a reference tool.

The result is not meant as the final word on the subject of Virginia writers and writing. Hopefully, it will become but one of many touchstones in this area. It appears at a time when regional distinctions are becoming obscured by the advancing march toward a thoroughly national consciousness. However, it is offered in the belief that as this drive continues, Americans in general will feel more sharply than ever the need of identifying with differing features of their land, especially at the State level. This assumption is being borne out by recent publications of this sort in other states and by the growing curricula of regional literatures in a variety of American universities. So, to students of Virginia authors and to those who would honor America's myriad local distinctions, this volume is offered—not as a statement of culmination, but in the hope of stimulation.

University College,
The University of Richmond,   W.D.T.
February 4, 1972

A RESEARCH GUIDE
TO VIRGINIA WRITERS

Because regional American literature parallels the move-
ments of American literature as a whole, many nationally
oriented reference works will be useful to the researcher working
on Virginia writers. The field of American reference bibliography
at large, its history, present state, and future needs, has been
admirably surveyed by G. Thomas Tanselle in "The State of
Reference Bibliography in American Literature," appearing in
Resources for American Literary Study, Vol. 1, No. 1 (Spring
1971). In this study, which systematically presents and discusses
the major reference tools in American literature, Professor
Tanselle mentions several works central to Virginia writers
whose reputations go beyond state lines and regional boundaries.

Chief among reference tools is the comprehensive *Literary
History of the United States* (2 vols.) by Robert E. Spiller, and
others, which covers literary trends and individual writers, and
includes a selective bibliography for each. A more comprehensive list, however, can be found in the annual *Publication of the
Modern Language Association (PMLA)* bibliography, a work
which yearly lists all major scholarship done on American, and
other, writers during the preceding year. In addition to the
PMLA, the annual *Modern Humanities Research Association*
publication is also valuable. Sometimes more inclusive than
the *PMLA,* this volume includes references to book reviews and
has been indexed since 1922. A handy reference work, containing materials appearing in many major periodicals, is readily
accessible in Lewis Leary's *Articles on American Literature 1900-
1950* (1954) and *Articles on American Literature 1950-1967*
(1970). Also central is *American Literary Scholarship: An Annual,* published each year by Duke University Press. Under the
editorship of J. Albert Robbins, this book contains valuable
essays on secondary literature, some of which centers on Virginians. The book is indexed, making it more useful.

Apart from information about those Virginia writers whose
reputations have reached the national level, little to aid the

researcher working on the Commonwealth's authors will be
found in the above volumes. Turning to works about Southern
literature, however, one finds considerably more material. Two
of the central works on Southern writers before the twentieth
century, containing significant information about those from
Virginia, is E. A. Alderman, and others, *The Library of Southern Literature* (1907-1923) and James Wood Davidson's *The
Living Writers of the South* (1869). Both these works are better
known for their breadth rather than depth of coverage, but
they do contain considerable information about little-known
authors. The standard literary history of Southern literature,
however, is still Jay B. Hubbell's (*q.v.*) *The South in American
Literature, 1607-1900* (1954), whose bibliography contains count-
less references to three centuries of Virginia writers. More recent,
and more specifically a reference tool, is *A Bibliographical
Guide to the Study of Southern Literature* (1969) edited by Louis
D. Rubin, Jr. (*q.v.*). This is a book which cannot be overlooked
by anyone working in the field of Southern literature. Divided
into two parts, General Topics and Individual Writers, it covers
all the significant criticism on Southern writing and writers,
including many from Virginia. Important to note is the fact
that this volume is continually brought up to date by the "Annual Checklist on Southern Literature," appearing in each spring
issue of the *Mississippi Quarterly*. *Southern Literary Culture: A
Bibliography of Masters' and Doctors' Theses* (1955) edited by
Clyde H. Cantrell and Walton R. Patrick, lists theses on Southern culture as well as individual authors, many of them Virginians. This important work is currently being updated by the
Society for the Study of Southern Literature.

Two of the central tools for research in Virginia history,
much of which revolves around literary figures, is Earl Gregg
Swem's (*q.v.*) *A Bibliography of Virginia* (5 vols.) (1916-1955, and
1965), and Lester J. Cappon's (*q.v.*) *Bibliography of Virginia History Since 1865* (1930). Another important source, focusing exclusively on Virginia writers, is a section of Clarence Gohdes'
*Literature and Theater of the States and Regions of the U.S.A.;
an Historical Bibliography* (1967). Containing the titles of just
under 150 articles about Virginia writers, writing, and theater,
the book is an invaluable tool for the serious scholar. Early
Virginia literature is well covered, and carefully documented, in
The Literature of Virginia in the Seventeenth Century (1946,
rev. 1968) by Howard Mumford Jones. Other information can

often be obtained from the libraries of the State's newspapers, obituaries of minor authors often proving to be invaluable sources of biographical, and sometimes critical, information. A list of Virginiana at the Virginia State Library is currently being prepared for publication. When available, this will be a welcome addition to the resources for the study of Virginia literature. Other works about the Commonwealth's writers appear in the individual reference sections throughout the present volume.

The serious student of Virginia literature should be aware of the myriad materials to be found in the Commonwealth's libraries. The College of William and Mary, Sweetbriar, Washington and Lee, Hampden-Sydney, Randolph-Macon, Hollins, and others, hold significant materials by Virginia writers who number among their graduates. The Alderman Library at the University of Virginia has long been collecting materials by and about the State's writers, and their effort, coupled with the fact that many nineteenth century Virginia male writers studied at the University, makes it central to a study of local authors. (The University of Virginia's recent brochure, *The Virginia Author, 1819-1969,* University of Virginia Library (1969), lists the works of many Virginia writers.) Another major repository is the Lipscomb Library at Randolph-Macon Woman's College, which has a collection of writings by Virginia women. In Richmond, the James Branch Cabell Library at Virginia Commonwealth University is actively collecting materials by and about Virginia writers. Begun by the late N. Harvey Deal, Librarian, and the Associates of the James Branch Cabell Library, under the leadership of Mrs. Cabell, the project is well under way, that institution having made significant strides in collecting Virginiana. (For detailed information see *The Cabellian,* Vols. I, II, and III). The Sargeant Memorial Room of the Norfolk Public Library, the Library of the Virginia Historical Society, the Jones Memorial Library at Lynchburg, and the Virginia State Library are also central to a study of Virginia's writers. Manuscripts and letters relating to those Virginia writers who have enjoyed a reputation outside the state can often be located with the aid of *American Literary Manuscripts* (1960) and *The National Union Catalog of Manuscript Collections.*

*   *   *

Having joined the project to prepare *Virginia Authors: Past and Present* after almost all the spade work was done, my task has been largely one of excising and shaping rather than re-searching and compiling. The sections titled Books, and Re-sources, following the brief biographical sketch on each author were, for the most part, compiled several years ago by Mary Marcy Councell, Katharine Groseclose Sieg, and Rubye Lee Norris. I have let their work stand as they completed it, with the exception of deleting some of the references to materials which I felt would not be available to most readers, or references to materials which seemed to me marginally informative. In some cases, I have made slight additions in order to bring sections up to date. The reader should be warned, however, that the reference sections are not meant to be complete lists of criticism on the authors. Especially is this the case when dealing with authors whose reputations are so great that to list all that has been written about them would fill separate volumes. Hopefully, the materials listed in the reference sections will be significant enough to lead the reader to other published material about the author of his interest. In the case of many minor authors, how-ever, no secondary body of literature exists, and in such instances the reference sections include only the material from which the writer of the biographical sketch took his or her material. Also, the sections titled Books, although sometimes complete, often omit some authors' titles, the intent being to give a generous sampling rather than a complete listing.

I should like to express my special thanks to the three members of the original committee who prepared most of the manuscript. To Professor Albert M. Lyles, Chairman of the English Department at Virginia Commonwealth University, who was able to lighten my duties so that this book could be completed, I owe a special debt of gratitude. My thanks also go to my colleague, Professor M. Thomas Inge, for his sound suggestions, and to my wife, and professional colleague, Anne, who for months has heard me sing of heretofore unsung Virginia writers.

Virginia Commonwealth University   M.D.
March, 1972

ACKNOWLEDGMENTS

Whatever the strengths of this volume, they are to a large degree the result of enlightened and unselfish aid from the following persons: my wife, Carole, who has the patience of ten average scholars' wives; to Mrs. Lucille Portlock and her dedicated staff of the Sargeant Memorial Room of the Norfolk Public Library; to Milton Russell and the staff of the Virginia State Library; to Miss Kathleen Francis of the Boatwright Memorial Library of the University of Richmond; to the Executive Committee of the Virginia Association of Teachers of English, most especially to Mrs. Frances Wimer, Mr. Wayne Bowman, Mr. Hal F. Paris, and Professor Foster B. Gresham; to the Virginia Education Association and its Executive Secretary, Dr. Robert F. Williams; and finally to my old friends Maurice Duke, Rubye Lee Norris, and Baylor Blackford.

The contributions of those cited in the following acknowledgement, while benefiting me greatly, were more keenly sensed by the compilers of the first draft of this manuscript. I therefore include their detailed statement of gratitude, altering it only by the addition of "the late" before several names:

February 4, 1972   W.D.T.

The editors extend their thanks to all members of the Virginia Association of Teachers of English who assisted in compiling this material.

Special appreciation is due librarians who have been unfailingly helpful in compiling a list of Virginia writers. Among these are the late N. Harvey Deal and his co-workers and Mr. Francis L. Berkeley, Jr. of Alderman Library at the University of Virginia; the late Dr. Carrol Quenzel of Mary Washington College; Miss Ellen Coolidge Burke of the Alexandria Library; Mrs. Florence R. Robertson of the Danville Library; Mrs. Jane B. Shaw of the Falls Church Library; Mrs. Bettie V. Griffith of the Wallace Library, Fredericksburg; Miss Lottie Driver of the Newport News Library; Mrs. Katherine T. Taylor of the Richmond Public Library; the late Miss Mary C. Brown of the Sargeant Memorial Room, Norfolk Public Library; Mr. Harold Sander and Mr. Philip S. Ogilvie of the Roanoke Public Library; and Mr. C. Vernon Eddy of Handley Library.

Further help has come from Miss Ethel Joyner and Miss Blanch Mays, librarians at Washington-Lee High School, and Miss Evelyn Thornton, County Supervisor of School Libraries, Arlington.

Still further help was given by Mr. and Mrs. Robert Whitton, who made their private collection of Virginiana accessible, and Mrs. Anita Heffner, who opened her file of Virginia authors to the editors. Miss Margaret Carpenter, editor of the *Virginia Authors' Yearbook,* gave valuable suggestions. The late Dr. George Harding Foster of Washington and Lee University called together a group of people to help with the list from the Lexington area.

Others to whom the editors are indebted include the late Dr. Earl Gregg Swem, Librarian Emeritus of William and Mary; the late Dr. James Southall Wilson, former Poe Professor of English, University of Virginia; Dr. Charles Herbert Huffman, former Professor of English, Madison College; and Dr. Louis Glenn Locke, Director of Humanities, Madison College; and Charles C. Councell, artist, who designed the "Literary Map of the Commonwealth of Virginia."

M.M.C.
K.G.S.
R.L.N.

June, 1963

A KEY TO INITIALS

Approximately two-thirds of the biographical sketches were written by Mrs. Councell or by one of the contributors whose help she solicited. All sketches followed by initials can be identified by the following key. Unsigned sketches were written either by the general editor or by one of the original contributors who preferred to remain anonymous. All authors are listed alphabetically by last name.

R.H.B.: RUTH H. BLOUNT
G.B.C.: GERTRUBE B. CLAYTOR
C.C.C.: CHARLES C. COUNCELL
M.M.C.: MARY M. COUNCELL
B.P.D.: BETTY PAGE DABNEY
L.T.D.: LUCILLE T. DICKERSON
C.D.E.: CECIL D. EBY
M.E.: MURRELL EDMUNDS
P.W.E.: POCAHONTAS WIGHT EDMUNDS
F.F.: FITZGERALD FLOURNOY
S.H.: SOPHIE HILTON
C.H.H.: CHARLES H. HUFFMAN
L.G.L.: LOUIS GLENN LOCKE
N.L.P.: NORWOOD L. PINDAR
D.B.S.: DOROTHY B. SCHLEGEL
K.G.S.: KATHARINE G. SIEG
R.C.S.: RINALDO C. SIMONINI, JR.
M.O.S.: MARGARET OLCOTT STETSON
T.P.W.: THEO PAGE WALLER
R.J.W.: RUTH JONES WILKINS

VIRGINIA AUTHORS
Past and Present

VIRGINIA AUTHORS

ANDERSON, SHERWOOD (1876-1941), short story writer, poet, novelist, and writer of non-fiction, was born in Camden, Ohio, but spent much of his youth in Clyde, the town which served as a setting for *Winesburg, Ohio*. One year at Wittenberg College gave him his only formal education after he was fourteen. He served in Cuba during the Spanish-American War. Later he became manager of a paint factory in Elyria, Ohio, but his rebellion against industrial civilization made him forfeit his job and head for Chicago. Here he lived with his brother Karl, later a well known painter.

The "Chicago group"—including Carl Sandburg, Theodore Dreiser, Floyd Dell, and others—was influential in having his first books published; but not until his masterpiece *Winesburg, Ohio* was published in 1919 did he receive the attention (often controversial) of the critics. With *Dark Laughter* he reached a high level of fame and material success. It was his only book to approximate a best seller.

In the late 'twenties Sherwood Anderson migrated to Marion, Virginia, where he bought two papers, one Republican, the other Democratic. *Hello Towns!* (1929) is a collection of his articles written for both papers. *Nearer the Grass Roots,* written the same year, gives his reason for retirement—to be "in close and constant touch with every phase of life in an American community every day of the year."

He lived over his print shop for a while, though he had built a stone and log house on Ripshin Creek, twenty-two miles from Marion, near the North Carolina border. In 1933 he married Eleanor Copenhaver of Marion, a national Y.W.C.A. executive, and became increasingly interested in the plight of the then non-unionized worker in the South. He died in Colon, Panama, and is buried in Marion.

BOOKS: *Windy McPherson's Son,* 1916; *Marching Men,* 1917; *Winesburg, Ohio,* 1919; *Poor White,* 1920; *The Triumph of the Egg,* 1921; *Many Marriages,* 1922; *Horses and Men,* 1923; *A Story Teller's Story,* 1924; *Dark Laughter,* 1925; *Sherwood Anderson's Notebook,* 1926; *Tar: A Midwest Childhood,* 1926; *Hello Towns!* 1929; *Perhaps Women,* 1931; *Death in the Woods,* 1933; *No Swank,* 1934; *Puzzled America,* 1935; *Kit Brandon,* 1936; *Hometown,* 1940; *Sherwood Anderson's Memoirs,* 1942; *Letters,* 1953; *Sherwood Anderson Reader,* 1947; *The Portable Sherwood Anderson,* 1949; Welford Dunaway Taylor, ed. *The Buck Fever Papers,* 1971.

REFERENCES: Kunitz and Haycraft, *Twentieth Century Authors,* 1943 and Supplement, 1955; James D. Hart, *Oxford Companion to American Literature,* 1965; James Erwin Scheville, *Sherwood Anderson: His Life and*

Work, 1951; Irving Howe, *Sherwood Anderson*, 1951; David D. Anderson, *Sherwood Anderson: An Introduction and Interpretation*, 1967. See also Robert E. Spiller, *et al., Literary History of the United States*, 1965 (bibliography).

ANDREWS, MARIETTA MINNEGERODE (1869-1931), poet, novelist, illustrator, and writer of non-fiction, was born in Richmond. Her early art studies took her to Washington, D. C., Paris, and Munich; and she spent the majority of her life in Washington, where her husband, Eliphalet Fraser Andrews, was director of the Corcoran School of Art. While leading an active life as an artist (primarily a portraitist), she wrote several books of poetry which she illustrated (e.g. *Out of the Dust* (1920)). The influence of painting is also reflected in her collection of prose sketches, *From My Studio Window* (1928). In addition to her novels, she was well known for her *George Washington's Country* (1930), a historical-geographical work which demonstrates her active interest in history and the preservation of historic shrines.

BOOKS: *Songs of a Mother*, 1917; *Out of the Dust*, 1920; *The Cross Triumphant*, 1921; *The Darker Drink*, 1922; *The Voice of the Wilderness*, 1922; *Memoirs of a Poor Relation*, 1927; *My Studio Window*, 1928; *Scraps of Paper*, 1929; *The Seventh Wave*, 1930; *George Washington's Country*, 1930; *Many Waters*, 1931.

REFERENCES: *Who Was Who in America*, Vol. 1, 1897-1942; Richmond *Times-Dispatch*, Aug. 8, 1931.

ANDREWS, MATHEW PAGE (1879-1947), writer of non-fiction, a native of Shepherdstown, West Virginia, took his A.B. degree at Washington and Lee University in 1901; A.M., 1902; and Litt.D., 1924. After graduating from college he became a teacher in private schools in Winchester, Virginia, 1902-04, and Baltimore, 1904-11. He was never married.

In 1923 he was editorial adviser in the Chronicles of America series of the Yale University Press. He was chairman of the Baltimore City George Washington Bi-Centennial Committee in 1932, and of the Maryland Ter-Centenary Committee of Baltimore in 1934.

A lecturer as well as a writer, he was interested mainly in the Colonial period of American history. He wrote a history of Virginia, one of Maryland, a United States history, and other books. (M.M.C.)

BOOKS: *The Birth of America*, 1920; *Women of the South in War Times*, 1924; *Virginia: The Old Dominion*, 1937; *The Soul of the Nation: Founding of Virginia and Projection of New England*, 1943; *Social Planning of Frontier Thinkers*, 1944; *Ye Fountain Inn Diary: George Washington's Inn Site*, 1948.

REFERENCES: *Who's Who in America*, Vol. 25, 1948-49; *Who Was Who in America*, Vol. 2. See also Swem's *Virginia Historical Index*, Vol. 1, 1934.

AVARY, MYRTA LOCKETT (1857-1946) a native of Halifax, Virginia, and later a resident of Atlanta, Georgia, wrote for periodicals and journals and published several books. In addition she was the editor of a number of Civil War diaries. (C.H.H.)

BOOKS: *Dixie After the War*, 1906; *Joel Chandler Harris and His Home*, 1913; *A Diary from Dixie* (as written by Mary Boykin Chestnut), 1905; ed., *A Virginia Girl in the Civil War, 1861-1865*, 1903; ed., *Recollections of Alexander H. Stephens*, 1910.

REFERENCES: Armistead C. Gordon, Jr., *Virginian Writers of Fugitive Verse*, 1923.

BAGBY, GEORGE WILLIAM (1828-1883), editor and humorist, was born in Buckingham County, Virginia. After being educated at Prince Edward Court House, at Edgehill School, Princeton, N. J., and at the University of Pennsylvania (for medicine), he began to practice medicine, but soon gave it up for writing. He wrote first for Lynchburg papers and then managed one, *The Express*, of which he was part owner. After it failed, he contributed to numerous others in various parts of the country. In 1860, he succeeded John R. Thompson as editor of the *Southern Literary Messenger*.

Scorning the sentimental writing of the period, he sought work of solid merit. He encouraged writers to write about things familiar to them, and soon followed suit himself by adopting native Virginia dialect in his "Letters of Mozis Addums to Billy Ivvins," which ran serially in the *Messenger* (Feb. to Dec., 1858) and which brought him fame. Both during the Civil War and after, he worked on a variety of newspapers, mainly Virginian. After the war, he added lecturing to his activities and became famous for his "Old Virginia Gentleman" and "Virginia Negro" presentations. He also served as State Librarian for three administrations.

BOOKS: *John M. Daniel's Latch Key*, 1868; *What I Did with My Fifty Million: By Mozis Addums*, 1874; *Meekins's Twinses*, 1877; *Selections from the Miscellaneous Writings of Dr. George Bagby* (2 vols.), 1884-85; *The Old Virginia Gentleman* (ed. with introduction by Thomas Nelson Page), 1910.

REFERENCES: Kunitz and Haycraft, *American Authors 1600-1900*, 1938; J. B. Hubbell, *The South in American Literature* (bibliography), 1954; Joseph Leonard King, *Dr. George Bagby: A Study of Virginian Literature, 1850-1880*, 1927; Louis D. Rubin, Jr., ed., *A Bibliographical Guide to the Study of Southern Literature*, 1969. See also Swem's *Virginia Historical Index*, Vol. 1, 1934.

BAILEY, TEMPLE (1887-1953), novelist and short story writer, was born in Petersburg, Virginia, and was educated in private schools in Richmond. Further education came from special college courses. Her forbears were New Englanders rather than Virginians.

Miss Bailey was a prolific and popular writer of a romantic fiction which was considered quite expert of its kind. One of her critics said of her that she could not write an uninteresting story. She was John Wanamaker's favorite author. Whenever she published a new novel, he would order 150 or 200 copies to give to his friends.

Her serials were in so much demand that she found herself writing them as they were published, although she disapproved of this practice. She preferred writing short stories and thought her writing was at its best in them. Her books, including reprints, have sold an estimated 3,000,000 copies. (M.M.C.)

BOOKS: *Judy*, 1907; *Glory of Youth*, 1913; *Contrary Mary*, 1914; *Mistress Anne*, 1917; *Adventures in Girlhood*, 1917; *The Tin Soldier*, 1919; *The Trumpeter Swan*, 1920; *The Gay Cockade*, 1921; *The Dim Lantern*, 1922; *Peacock Feathers*, 1924; *The Holly Hedge*, 1925; *The Blue Window*, 1926; *Wild Wind*, 1930; *So This is Christmas*, 1931; *Little Girl Lost*, 1932; *Enchanted Ground*, 1933; *The Radiant Tree*, 1934; *Fair as the Moon*, 1935; *I've Been to London*, 1937; *Tomorrow's Promise*, 1938; *The Blue Cloak*, 1941; *The Pink Camelia*, 1942; *Red Fruit*, 1945.

REFERENCES: Kunitz and Haycraft, *Twentieth Century Authors*, 1942, and *First Supplement*, 1955; *Saturday Evening Post*, Nov. 15, 1919; *Publishers' Weekly*, June 24, 1933; *Saturday Review*, April 11, 1936; New York *Times*, July 8, 1953.

[BALCH], EMILY CLARK (1892-1953), editor and fiction writer, was born in Richmond, Virginia, and grew up there. In 1924 she married Edwin Swift Balch of Philadelphia and lived in the "Quaker City" until her death in 1953.

She is best known as one of the founders and editors of *The Reviewer*, a literary magazine published in Richmond from 1921 to 1924. Mrs. Balch's account of this literary adventure is given in *"The Reviewer*—An Experiment in Southern Letters," which forms the introductory chapter of *Innocence Abroad* (1931). Other editors of the magazine were James Branch Cabell, who edited three issues (Oct.-Dec., 1921), and Paul Green, who continued the publication through 1925 from Chapel Hill, North Carolina.

Although its original purpose was to encourage writing in the South, *The Reviewer* published contributions from many of the leading American authors of the time. It introduced a number of brilliant young authors, including Southerners Julia Peterkin, DuBose Heyward, and Paul Green.

Emily Clark was the author of two books. She also contributed essays to the *Virginia Quarterly Review*, the *American Mercury*, the *Smart Set*, and other magazines. Three of the essays she wrote for the *Virginia Quarterly Review* were on James Branch Cabell, Ellen Glasgow, and Du Bose Heyward.

In 1953 Mrs. Balch left two-thirds of her estate in perpetual trust to the Rector and Visitors of the University of Virginia. She directed that the income from the fund be used for the purpose of "stimulating appreciation and creation in American literature." Both the English Department of the University and the *Virginia Quarterly Review* share the beneficence. Thus far the English Department has used its share to bring to the University, as writers in residence, such persons as William Faulkner and Katherine Anne Porter. The *Virginia Quarterly Review* has established literary contests, varying the type each year. (M.M.C.)

BOOKS: *Innocence Abroad,* 1931; *Stuffed Peacocks,* 1927.

REFERENCES: Francis C. Rosenberger, *Virginia Reader,* 1948; University of Virginia Alumni Fund, *University Topics,* Vol. 2, No. 2, April, 1956; James D. Hart, *Oxford Companion to American Literature,* 1956; Gerald Langford, ed., *Ingénue Among the Lions: Letters of Emily Clark to Joseph Hergesheimer,* 1965; Maurice Duke, "The Reviewer: A Bibliographical Guide to a Little Magazine," *Resources for American Literary Study,* Vol. 1, No. 1 (Spring 1971).

BARLOWE, M. ARTHUR (also **BARLOW**), (*c.* 1550-1620), writer of non-fiction, was the captain of one of two ships sent out in 1584 under a license granted to Walter Raleigh by Queen Elizabeth "to discover, search, find out, and view such remote, heathen, and barbarous lands, countries, and territories, not actually possessed of any Christian prince, nor inhabited by Christian people. . . ." The explorers sailed along the North American coast, and on their return Captain Barlowe wrote an account of the expedition so enthusiastic as to prompt Queen Elizabeth to confer knighthood on Walter Raleigh and name the vast western lands Virginia. Although Captain Barlowe did not set foot on land now the state of Virginia, the new possession did include that territory. (M.M.C.)

BOOKS: The account was first published in Richard Hakluyt's *Divers Voyages touching the Discoverie of America,* 1582; in recent times, in "The First Voyage to Roanoke," Old South Leaflets, General Series, Vol. 4, No. 92, Boston, 1898; "Barlow's description of the North Carolina Coast" in *The Ocean Highway: New Brunswick, New Jersey to Jacksonville, Florida,* a Federal Writers' Project, 1938; also in *Sir Walter Raleigh and his Colony in America,* ed. by Increase Niles Tarbox, 1884, The Prince Society. A copy can also be found in *Virginia Reader* (see below).

REFERENCES: *Dictionary of American Biography,* Vol. 1, 1928; Francis Coleman Rosenberger, *Virginia Reader,* 1948. See also Swem's *Virginia Historical Index,* Vol. 1, 1934.

BARNUM, FRANCES COURTENAY BAYLOR (1848-1920), novelist and poet, was born of Virginian parentage in Fayetteville, Arkansas. She lived most of her adult life in Virginia, particularly in Lexington and Winchester, and wrote articles published in such magazines as *Lippincott's, Atlantic Monthly,* and the *Princeton Review.* Two of her poems that have been widely republished are "Kind Words to Virginia" and "The Last Confederate." From 1886 to 1900 she published eight books, mainly novels. *On Both Sides,* published in 1886, went through eight editions in one year. *Juan and Juanita,* published first in 1888, was republished in 1926 and again in 1930. (C.H.H.)

BOOKS: *On Both Sides,* 1886; *Behind the Blue Ridge,* 1887; *A Shocking*

Example, and Other Sketches, 1889; *Juan and Juanita*, 1888; *Claudia Hyde*, 1894; *Miss Nina Barrow*, 1897; *The Ladder of Fortune*, 1899; *A Georgian Bungalow*, 1900.

REFERENCES: Armistead C. Gordon, Jr., *Virginian Writers of Fugitive Verse*, 1923.

BARR, STRINGFELLOW (1897-   ), writer of non-fiction, novelist, American educator and world federationist, was born in Suffolk, Virginia. When he was fifteen, he attended Tulane University for one year and then returned to Virginia to take his B.A. and M.A. degrees at the University of Virginia.

Two years in the army in World War I were followed by two years at Balliol College, Oxford University, as a Rhodes Scholar. For work in modern history he received a B.A. degree with honors in 1921. That same year he married Gladys Baldwin, a theology student at King's College, London.

He returned to the United States in 1923, spent a year in Asheville, N. C., and then accepted an assistant professorship in history at the University of Virginia. Subsequently, he became an associate and then a full professor. His teaching was interrupted by a year's leave from the University to become a member of a committee which Robert Hutchins, then President of the University of Chicago, had set up to investigate the undergraduate curriculum of American colleges and universities.

After a year of research, he accepted the presidency of St. John's College in Annapolis, Maryland, where he introduced a four-year, all-required curriculum, based on the study of the great books of Western Civilization from the Greeks to the present, and including intensive training in mathematics and laboratory sciences. He resigned from St. John's College in 1946 to start a similar college in Massachusetts, plans for which were later abandoned. In 1948 he was made president of a new organization, the Foundation for World Government.

Another association with Virginia came in 1951 when he returned to the University of Virginia as Visiting Professor of Political Science, while retaining his presidency of the Foundation for World Government. (M.M.C.)

BOOKS: *Mazzini: Portrait of an Exile*, 1935; *Pilgrimage of Western Man*, 1949; *Let's Join the Human Race*, 1950; *Citizens of the World*, 1952; *The Kitchen Garden Book*, 1956; *Purely Academic*, 1958; *The Will of Zeus*, 1961; *The Three Worlds of Man*, 1963; *The Mask of Jove*, 1966.

REFERENCES: *Twentieth Century Authors*, First Sup., 1955; *Leaders in Education*, 3rd ed., 1948; *Directory of American Scholars*, 3rd ed., 1957; *Who's Who in America*, Vol. 31, 1960-61; *Newsweek*, Dec. 23, 1946; B. Kalb *Saturday Review*, Dec. 13, 1952; Richmond *Times-Dispatch*, July 31, 1949.

BARRINGER, PAUL BRANDON (1857-1941), writer of non-fiction, was born in Concord, North Carolina, but lived most of his adult life in Virginia. He was graduated in medicine from the University of Virginia, studied in New York and aboard, and practiced at Davidson, North Carolina. In 1888 he became Professor of Physiology and Materia Medica at the University of Virginia, and served as Chairman of the Faculty from 1896 to 1903. He was President of Virginia Polytechnic Institute from 1907 to 1913. He also served as President of the Medical Society of Virginia. Among his books were *The American Negro, His Past and Future* (1900) and his memoirs, which were published posthumously. (C.H.H.)

BOOKS: *The American Negro: His Past and Future*, 1900; ed., *University of Virginia: Its History, Influences, Equipment*, etc. 1904; *The Natural Bent* (memoirs of Dr. Paul B. Barringer), 1949.

REFERENCES: Armistead C. Gordon, Jr., *Virginian Writers of Fugitive Verse*, 1923; Richmond *Times-Dispatch*, Aug. 7, 1947. See also Swem's *Virginia Historical Index*, Vol. 1, 1934.

BEATY, JOHN OWEN (1890-1961), novelist and non-fiction writer, educator and biographer-critic, was born at Crow, West Virginia, of Virginia parents. Orphaned at an early age, he was reared at "Aspengrove," his mother's ancestral home in Greene County. After receiving a B.A. in Romance languages at the University of Virginia, he went on to earn a Ph.D. in English and comparative literature at Columbia and did further study in Montpellier, France.

Of his long, varied career he writes: "From study, teaching, travel, and observation, came many many fugitive pieces, and a dozen books, which collectively have gone through more than a hundred printings and editions."

"*John Esten Cooke: Virginian*, is a biography of a famous novelist. *Image of Life* examines twentieth century literature in its relation to our heritage of Christian civilization. *Race and Population*, written after a tour of twenty-nine countries, was an unheeded prophecy of World War II. *Swords in the Dawn*, a historical novel of the founding of England, was published—and enjoyed high acclaim—in America, England, and Australia."

"I served in England and France in World War I; assigned, in World War II, to the General Staff in the Pentagon, I reached the rank of Colonel of Military Intelligence. This experience is reflected in the book, *The Iron Curtain Over America*."

"*Crossroads: A Novel of the Twentieth Century South* (1956) shows Virginia people neither as dashing cavaliers and fainting ladies nor as degenerate and violent scoundrels, but just as they are—with utmost fidelity to the facts of character and time and place."

Among his academic honors, Dr. Beaty lists first his long tenure as chairman of the English Department at Southern Methodist University. He retired from academic life in 1957.

BOOKS: *Facts and Ideas* (with Ernest E. Leisy and Mary Lamar), 1930; *An Introduction to Poetry* (with J. B. Hubbell), 1936; *An Introduction to Drama* (with J. B. Hubbell), 1927; *John Esten Cooke: Virginian*, 1922; *Image of Life*, 1940; *Swords in the Dawn*, 1937; *The Iron Curtain Over America*,

1951; *Crossroads: A Novel of the Twentieth Century South,* 1956.

REFERENCES: *Who's Who in America,* Vol. 27, 1952-53, and later; *Who's Who in the South and Southwest,* 1956 and later; Richmond *Times-Dispatch,* Oct. 30, 1949.

BEATY, JOSEPHINE POWELL (1896-   ), poet, was born in New York City and educated at Veltin and at Barnard College (A.B. 1919). In 1920, she married John Owen Beaty (*q.v.*) and has lived for many years in Virginia. She has published poems in a number of magazines and is included in several anthologies. Her poems have won both state and national prizes and have been collected into two books.

BOOKS: *Milestones,* 1951; *Tapestries,* 1953; *For Us the Living Reverie,* 1964; *The Road to Jericho,* 1965.

BELITT, BEN (1911-   ), poet and prose writer, came with his Ukraine mother and Virginia stepfather to Lynchburg when he was ten. Two teachers at Lynchburg's E. C. Glass High School recognized his talent for writing early and helped cultivate it. With the help of scholarships, he was able to complete both B.A. and M.A. degrees at the University of Virginia. Here he wrote poems, articles and reviews for numerous Virginia papers and national magazines (e.g. *Poetry, Nation,* and *New Outlook*).

In 1936 he was given the job of editorial assistant of *Nation,* beginning what he calls an "unforgettable apprenticeship in the practical and professional aspects of magazine reporting. . . ." under Joseph Wood Krutch, who encouraged him to try his hand at various genres. He has taught for many years at Bennington College in Vermont. His honors include the Shelley Memorial (shared with Charlotte Wilder, 1936) and a Guggenheim grant (1946).

BOOKS: *The Five-Fold Mesh,* 1938; *Four Poems by Rimbaud: The Problem of Translation,* 1947; *Wilderness Stair,* 1955.

REFERENCES: Kunitz and Haycraft, *Twentieth Century Authors, First Supplement,* 1955; *Who's Who in America,* Vol. 3, 1959-60; Francis Colman Rosenberger, *Virginia Reader,* 1948; George Kumler Anderson and Eda Lou Walton, *This Generation,* 1931.

BEVERLEY, ROBERT (1673-1722), historian, was born on a plantation in Middlesex County, Virginia. His father, also Robert Beverley, was a prominent political figure in early Virginia.

Educated in England, young Beverley returned to Virginia upon the death of his father. He became a scrivener in the provincial secretary's office, and because of notable achievements here he was recommended for service as clerk of the Legislative Committee. By 1696 he had been given further responsibilities as clerk of the General Court, clerk of the Council, and clerk of the General Assembly. As a freeholder he was qualified to become a Burgess; he served in the House of Burgesses from 1699-1706.

In 1697 he married Ursula Byrd, sister of William Byrd II. She died a

year later and he did not marry again. Litigation over an estate he had
bought took him to England for a year and a half. While there he was asked
by his bookseller, Richard Parker, to observe the section on Virginia and
Carolina in John Oldmixon's *The British Empire in America*. He found that
the account contained "most strange and untrue Parts" and wrote his *History and Present State of Virginia* to correct the misrepresentations. Because
of its simplicity and directness, his book has remained for two centuries a
"significant source." A second book, *An Abridgment of the Public Laws of
Virginia*, was first published in 1722, the year of his death. (M.M.C.)

BOOKS: *History and Present State of Virginia*, London, 1705, 1722;
Richmond, 1855; with Introduction by Louis B. Wright, 1947; *The Abridgment of the Public Laws of Virginia*, London, 1722, 2nd ed., 1928.

REFERENCES: *Dictionary of American Biography*, Vol. 2, 1929; Kunitz
and Haycraft, *American Authors 1600-1900*, 1938; J. B. Hubbell, *The South
in American Literature 1607-1900*, 1954; Louis D. Rubin, Jr., ed., *A Bibliographical Guide to the Study of Southern Literature*, 1969.

BLACKFORD, CHARLES MINOR (1833-1903), writer of non-fiction
born in Fredericksburg, Virginia, received his college education at the University of Virginia, where he took his degree in law. In 1861 he entered the
Confederate Army and was made captain in the Second Regiment of Virginia
Cavalry.

After the war he made his home in Lynchburg, Virginia, where he
became a distinguished lawyer and a prominent citizen, interested in intellectual and civic projects. He was one of those citizens responsible for the
Centennial Celebration of 1886, for the first efforts to establish a public
library in the city, and for the organization of Holcombe Hall Association
to provide lectures on scientific and literary subjects. He himself was one
of the speakers.

After the destruction by fire of the Rotunda at the University of Virginia, he was a member of a committee to seek funds to further the restoration.

He was the author of several books of an historical nature. His war
letters were compiled and privately printed by his wife, under the title,
Memoirs of the War Between the States. These letters, abridged and edited
by his grandson, Charles Minor Blackford, III, himself a writer, were published again in 1947. (M.M.C.)

BOOKS: *Trials and Trial of Jefferson Davis*, 1901; *Campaign and Battle
of Lynchburg, Virginia*, 1901; *Memoirs of the War Between the States* 1894-
96, 1947.

BLACKFORD, (LT. COL.) WILLIAM WILLIS (1831-1905), biographer,
was born in Fredericksburg, Virginia, and educated as an engineer. This
skill, plus his ability as a horseman (learned during his boyhood from the
llaneros in South America), made him a valuable asset to the staff of General J. E. B. Stuart, where he served as first Adjutant and later as Chief

Engineer. He and his brother Charles Minor Blackford (*q.v.*) were two of five brothers who served in the Confederate Army, despite the fact that their mother was an ardent abolitionist and sent her slaves to Liberia. He wrote numerous letters concerning his war experiences (as did his brother) (*q.v.*), some of which have been reprinted and quoted by historians. His most important writing, however, is his *War Years with Jeb Stuart*, written probably during the 1880's, but not printed until 1945. Of this book Douglas Freeman remarked: "Every line of this narrative has the 'feel' of the Cavalry Corps of the Army of Northern Virginia."

BOOK: *War Years with Jeb Stuart*, 1945.

REFERENCE: *Encyclopaedia of Virginia Biography*, Vol. 5, 1915.

BLAIR, JAMES (1655-1743), Scottish-born clergyman, who came to Virginia in 1685, was one of the most influential men in the colony. A member of the Governor's Council and the representative of the Bishop of London for Virginia, he gave his greatest service to Virginia when he founded the College of William and Mary in 1693. He became its first president and continued in that office until his death. In 1740-1 he also acted as governor of the colony. (C.H.H.)

BOOKS: With Henry Hartwell and Edward Chilton, in 1697, *The Present State of Virginia, and the College*. (The report was first published in London in 1727. In 1940 it was republished as the first volume of the Williamsburg Restoration Studies.)

REFERENCES: James D. Hart, *The Oxford Companion to American Literature*, 1965; Francis Coleman Rosenberger, *Virginia Reader*, 1948; *Dictionary of American Biography*, Vol. 2, 1929; Daniel Esten Motley, *Life of Commissary James Blair*, 1901; Samuel R. Mohler, *Churchman, Educator, and Politician of Colonial Virginia*, 1944; Edgar Legare Pennington, *Commissary Blair*, 1936; Louis D. Rubin, Jr., ed., *A Bibliographical Guide to the Study of Southern Literature*, 1969; Parke Rouse, Jr., *James Blair of Virginia*, 1971.

BLANTON, WYNDHAM BOLLING (1890-1960), physician and historian, was born in Richmond and spent most of his life there. After receiving his M.D. from Columbia University, he did advanced study at the Universities of Berlin and Edinburgh. While his publication in the technical aspects of medicine was active, his best known writings are the volumes on *Medicine in Virginia* (1930-33)—one volume for each of the first three centuries of Virginia's existence. They have come to be regarded as the definitive work on the subject.

BOOKS: *Medicine in Virginia in the Seventeenth Century*, 1930; *Medicine in Virginia in the Eighteenth Century*, 1931; *Medicine in Virginia in the Nineteenth Century*, 1933.

REFERENCE: *Who Was Who*, Vol. 2, 1961-1968.

BOND, NELSON SLADE (1908-), short story writer, playwright, and writer of non-fiction, settled in Roanoke, Virginia, in April, 1939, after having lived and worked variously in Philadelphia, Pa., Halifax, N. S., and Augusta, Ga. While a student at Marshall College, Huntington, W. Va., he met and married Betty Gough Folsom of that city.

After working as an engineer (for which he was originally trained), an instructor of electrical engineering, and a public relations director, he turned to writing.

In 1937 Bond became a full-time free-lance writer, producing since more than 500 short stories and articles for national magazines. He started writing for radio in the early 1940's, in 1943 winning the annual "Dr. Christian Award" for a contest script. He was a pioneer in television; in 1947 his *Mr. Mergenthwirker's Lobblies* was the first three-act play ever to be telecast over a TV network. This script has since been televised in the United States, Canada, Great Britain, Belgium, Holland, Germany, France, Italy and Australia. In all, Bond's radio scripts number more than three hundred; his TV dramas more than fifty. Turning to the stage in the 1950's he has created two three-act plays continuously in use by college and community theaters.

Bond acknowledges he has "very little patience with the writer who, under the guise of creating high art, fails to communicate with his audience." He believes the writer must tell his story as clearly and as beautifully as his ability to use words permits, and let posterity judge the results.

Bond's short stories appear in more than forty anthologies and school texts. (M.M.C.)

BOOKS: *Mr. Mergenthwirker's Lobblies and Other Fantastic Tales*, 1946; *The Thirty-first of February*, 1949; *Exiles of Time*, 1949; *Lancelot Biggs: Spaceman*, 1950; *No Time Like the Future*, 1954; *Mr. Mergenthwirker's Lobblies*, 1957; *State of Mind*, 1958; *Animal Farm: A Fable in Two Acts*, 1964; *Nightmares and Daydreams*, 1968.

REFERENCES: Roanoke *World-News*, May 2, 1939; January 7, 1944; July 13, 1945; January 17, 1952. Roanoke *Times*, June 10, 1943; July 15, 1949. Richmond *Times-Dispatch*, June 19, 1949; Aug. 20, 1950; Margaret H. Carpenter, *Virginia Authors' Yearbook*, 1956, 1957, 1958.

BOSHER, KATE LEE LANGLEY (1865-1932), who sometimes wrote under the name "Kate Cairns," was born in Norfolk and was educated at the Norfolk College for Young Ladies. Yet in her novels and stories she exemplifies the sentimental characteristics of many of her female contemporaries to only a slight degree. A dedicated suffragette, she viewed the world of the Reconstruction South with a rather objective eye. A good example is her most popular novelette, *Mary Cary* (1910), which features an intrepid little orphan girl who acts with pluck and speaks her mind freely. Still, like her contemporary realist William Dean Howells, she tended to show the "smiling" aspects of life.

BOOKS: *Bobbie*, 1899; *Mary Cary*, 1910; *Miss Gibbie Gault*, 1911; *House of Happiness*, 1912; *The Man in Lonely Land*, 1913; *How It Happened*, 1914;

People Like That, 1915; *Kitty Canary,* 1917; *His Friend: Miss Mac Farlaine,* 1918.

REFERENCES: *Who Was Who,* Vol. 1, 1897-1942; Richmond *Times-Dispatch,* July 29, 1932.

BOSWORTH, ALLAN RUCKER (1901-   ), prolific novelist and short story writer, is a native of San Angelo, Texas. He settled in Roanoke, Virginia, after a varied career as newspaperman (on several California newspapers), Naval officer (in Japan during World War II), and free-lance writer. Though he has published about five hundred stories in pulp magazines and about one-fifth as many in American popular magazines, he is probably best known for his novels. These tend to reflect his Texas background (e.g. *Sancho of the Long Long Horns* (1947)) or his experiences in the Orient (e.g. the award-winning *The Lovely World of Richi-San* (1960)).

BOOKS: *Sancho of the Long Long Horns,* 1947; *The Lovely World of Richi-San,* 1960; *The Crows of Edwina Hill,* 1961; *New Country,* 1962.

REFERENCE: *Contemporary Authors,* 4.

BOYKIN, EDWARD CARRINGTON (1889-   ) of Charlottesville has written or edited numerous books on Virginia or Southern topics and characters. One of the most unusual was the ninth book, *Victoria, Albert and Mrs. Stevenson,* a collection of letters written by Mrs. Sally Coles Stevenson, wife of Andrew Stevenson, a Richmond lawyer and politician, who served as U. S. Minister to the Court of St. James. (M.M.C.)

BOOKS: *The Autobiography of George Washington, 1753-1799,* 1935; ed., *Facsimiles of Famous American Documents and Letters,* 1934; *The American History Quiz Book,* 1940; *The Home Book of Quizzes, Games, and Jokes,* 1941; ed., *The Wisdom of Thomas Jefferson,* 1941; ed., *Living Letters from American History,* 1942; *The Second American History Quiz Book,* 1942; *Shrines of the Republic: A Treasury of Fascinating Facts about the Nation's Capitol,* 1953; *Congress and the Civil War,* 1955; *Ghost Ship of the Confederacy,* 1957; ed., *Victoria, Albert and Mrs. Stevenson,* 1957; *Sea Devil of the Confederacy,* 1959; *Beefsteak Raid,* 1960; *The Wit and Wisdom of Congress,* 1961.

REFERENCE: Charlottesville *Daily Progress,* March 14, 1957; Margaret H. Carpenter, *Virginia Authors' Yearbook,* 1958.

BROWN, ALEXANDER (1843-1906), historian, was born in Glenmore, Nelson County, Virginia. He was educated by a private tutor and in public schools. He spent the years 1860 and 1861 at Lynchburg College. He left to enter the Confederate Army, serving 1861-65.

After the war he established a mercantile business which he continued for fifteen years. He became a farmer as well in 1872.

His first marriage, in 1873, was to Caroline Augusta Cabell, who died in 1876. Ten years later, in 1886, he married Sarah Randolph. They lived in Norwood, Virginia. (C.H.H.)

BOOKS: *New Views of Early Virginia History*, 1886; *The Genesis of the United States*, 1890; *The Cabells and Their Kin*, 1896; *The First Republic in America*, 1898; *The History of Our Earliest History*, 1898; *English Politics in Early Virginia History*, 1901.

REFERENCES: *Who Was Who in America*, Vol. 1, 1942. See also Swem's *Virginia Historical Index*, Vol. 1, 1934.

BROWN, ALEXANDER CROSBY (1905-   ), novelist, historian, and newspaper editor, was born in Rosemont, Pennsylvania. After attending Yale and William and Mary, he set out with several college classmates on a 30,000-mile trip around the world in a thirty-three-ton schooner. It took twenty-seven months to complete the trip. His interest in nautical matters is well displayed in the majority of his writings (e.g. *The Old Bay Line 1840-1940*, (1940) and *Women and Children Last* (1961)). He is presently literary editor of the Newport News *Daily Press*.

BOOKS: *Horizon's Rim*, 1936; *The Old Bay Line, 1840-1940; Newport News' 325 Years*, 1946; *The Dismal Swamp Canal*, 1946; *Women and Children Last*, 1961.

REFERENCES: *Contemporary Authors*, 2; *Virginia Lives*.

BROWN, REV. DR. JOHN (1771-1850), was a leader in the German Reformed Church in Rockingham and adjacent sections from 1800 to 1850. So salubrious was his influence that it won for him the tender sobriquet of "Father Brown." He was born near Bremen, Germany, July 21, 1771. He died in Bridgewater, Rockingham County, in 1850, and is buried in Friedens Church cemetery.

In 1818 "Father" Brown published a book addressed to the German people of Rockingham, Augusta, and adjoining counties. In 1830 he published a brief treatise on the Christian religion. (C.H.H.)

BOOKS: *Schreiben an Die Deutchen Einewohner von Rockingham and Augusta, und den benachbarten Counties*, 1818.

BRUCE, PHILIP ALEXANDER (1856-1933), poet, biographer and historian, the son of Charles and Sarah (Seddon) Bruce, was born at "Staunton Hill," Virginia. He was graduated from the University of Virginia in 1876. He married Betty T. Taylor, October 19, 1896; and they had one daughter, Phillipa Alexander. Their home was in Charlottesville.

Dr. Bruce, a Virginia historian, held honorary degrees from Harvard (1879), Washington and Lee (1908), and the College of William and Mary (1909). (C.H.H.)

BOOKS: *The Plantation Negro as a Freeman*, 1889; *Economic History of Virginia in the Seventeenth Century*, 1895, 1935; *The Rise of the New South*, 1905; *Social Life in Virginia*, 1907; *Robert E. Lee*, 1907; *Institutional*

History of Virginia in the Seventeenth Century, 1910; *Pocahontas and Other Sonnets*, 1912, pub. by author; *Brave Deeds of Confederate Soldiers*, 1916; *History of the University of Virginia*, 1920-22; *History of Virginia*, 1924; *Virginia: Rebirth of the Old Dominion*, 1929; *The Virginia Plutarch*, 1929.

REFERENCE: *Who Was Who in America*, Vol. 1, 1942. See also Swem's *Virginia Historical Index*, Vol. 1, 1934.

BRUCE, WILLIAM CABELL (1860-1946), biographer and historian, brother of Philip Alexander Bruce (*q.v.*), received his early education in Norwood, Virginia. After a year at the University of Virginia, he studied law at the University of Maryland. In 1887 he became a member of Fisher, Bruce, and Fisher law firm and retained his connection with the firm until 1910, with the exception of the five years from 1903 to 1908, when he was head of the Law Department of the City of Baltimore. He was a member of the Maryland Senate from 1894 to 1903.

While at the University of Virginia, Bruce was co-editor of the *University of Virginia Magazine* and a member of the Jefferson Literary Society. In competition with Woodrow Wilson and others, he won the medal as the best debater of the Society. He also won the award for the best essay submitted in competition.

His most noted writing is *Benjamin Franklin: Self-Revealed*, which won the Pulitzer prize for biography in 1918. (M.M.C.)

BOOKS: *Benjamin Franklin: Self-Revealed* (2 vols.) 1917; *Below the James*, 1918; *John Randolph of Roanoke* (2 vols.) 1922; *Recollections*, 1931; *Imaginary Conversations with Franklin*, 1933; *Additional Selections from the Speeches, Addresses, Etc. of William Cabell Bruce*, 1928.

REFERENCES: *Who Was Who in America*, Vol. 1, 1942; James D. Hart, *The Oxford Companion to American Literature*, 1965; Boston *Transcript*, Nov. 21, 1917; *Literary Digest*, Dec. 15, 1917; New York *Times*, Jan. 6, 1918; *Outlook*, Dec. 5, 1917; *Review of Reviews*, Jan. 18, 1918; *The Times Literary Supplement*, Jan. 10, 1918. See also Swem's *Virginia Historical Index*, Vol. 1, 1934.

BRYAN, DANIEL (1795-1866), merchant, lawyer, colonel in the War of 1812, was also a poet and the author of several books. He was born in Rockingham County and attended Washington College (now Washington and Lee University) in Lexington, Virginia, from which he was graduated in 1807.

From 1826 to 1851 he was postmaster in Alexandria, Virginia. He died in Washington, D. C., December 22, 1866. (C.H.H.)

BOOKS: *The Mountain Muse*, 1813; *The Appeal for Suffering Genius*, 1826; "*Edwardian Rhymes*," 1904; *The Lay of Gratitude* (poems occasioned by the recent visit of Lafayette to the United States) 1826; "Thoughts on Education in Connection with Morals" (a poem recited before the literary and philosophical society of Hampden-Sydney College, September, 1828), 1830.

REFERENCES: John W. Wayland, *History of Rockingham County, Virginia,* 1912; F. V. N. Painter, *Poets of Virginia,* 1907; J. B. Hubbell, *The South in American Literature,* 1954. See also Swem's *Virginia Historical Index,* Vol. 1, 1934.

BRYAN, JOSEPH, III (1904-   ), writer of various genres of non-fiction, was born in Richmond and educated at Princeton (B.A., 1927). He has held editorial positions on the *Saturday Evening Post, Town and Country,* and the Richmond *News Leader.* He served in World War II under Admiral Halsey and was co-author of *Admiral Halsey's Story* (1947). He has published articles in virtually every important national magazine. His essays have embraced many subjects, but one of his abiding interests is history, especially that of his native region.

BOOKS: *Naming Quintuplets,* 1935; with Philip Reed, *Mission Beyond Darkness,* 1945; *Admiral Halsey's Story,* 1947; *Aircraft Carrier,* 1954; *The World's Greatest Showman: The Life of P. T. Barnum,* 1954; *The Sword Over the Mantel,* 1960; *The Civil War and I: A Personal Family Memoir,* 1960.

REFERENCES: *Virginia Lives,* Richmond *Times-Dispatch,* June 14, 1945.

BRYANT, ARTHUR HERBERT (1917-1956), promising young author of two published novels and two still unpublished, was killed in a racing accident in England in 1956. The next year the British Racing Association held a trophy race in his honor. The Avon Tire Company established a trophy to be given each year to the American most deserving of it in world wide competition.

An Alexandrian by birth, Arthur Bryant attended Episcopal High School and later the University of Virginia, graduating in 1940.

He enlisted in the Navy in 1940 and served in a PT Squadron. He later became Commander of the destroyer *Larson,* and under his command it was awarded the Navy "E." Following his naval service, he became an aide on the NATO Staff in London.

Both of Commander Bryant's novels received praise from James Branch Cabell. *Double Image* covers twenty-four hours in a tourist camp on the northeast coast of Florida. *The Valley of St. Ives* is set in hunting country. (M.M.C.)

BOOKS: *Double Image,* 1947; *The Valley of St. Ives,* 1949.

REFERENCES: Warfel, *American Novelists of Today,* 1951; Richmond *Times-Dispatch,* Feb. 20, 1949. Obituary, *Publishers' Weekly,* May 28, 1956.

BRYANT, BERNICE (1908-   ), writer of juvenile stories and plays, was born in St. Louis, Missouri and is now a resident of Strasburg, Virginia. She began writing playlets at the age of nine, but soon gave them up. After attending the University of Illinois and Northern Illinois Normal School and becoming a mother and housewife, she resumed writing. "This came about after talking to someone who wrote for children. She not only wrote but sold. Maybe I could be the same. Almost immediately I sat down and rewrote one of my little plays. I sent it to the *Normal Instructor*. Two weeks later came a Check (deserves capitals) and a letter asking for more. And so I wrote more, and more, and more."

Mrs. Bryant credits her young daughter as being the inspiration for her plays. She has also written several books, of which *Trudy Terrill: Eighth Grader* is her favorite. " 'Trudy' has done all kinds of things," she says "—has been serialized by the Methodist Book Concern, chosen as the best book of the year for girls by the National Federation of Press Women, translated into several languages, rewritten for radio and school plays, and has taken me to dozens of autographing parties."

BOOKS: *Yammy Buys a Bicylce*, 1940; *Pedie and the Twins*, 1945; *Future Perfect*, 1944; *Trudy Terrill: Eighth Grader*, 1946; *Trudy Terrill: High School Freshman*, 1947; *Misbehavior*, 1948; *Fancy Free*, 1949; *Follow the Leader*, 1950; *Dan Morgan*, 1952; *P's and Q's*, 1953; *Party ABC's*, 1954; *Let's Be Friends*, 1954; *Miss Behavior: Popularity, Poise, and Personality for the Teen-Age Girl*, 1960; *George Gershwin: Young Composer*, 1965.

REFERENCE: Vertical File, The Handley Library, Winchester, Virginia.

BRYDON, GEORGE McCLAREN (1875-1963), was born in Richmond, and spent most of his long career here as Historiographer and Registrar of the Episcopal Diocese of Virginia (1922-1963). He was educated at Roanoke College and the Virginia Theological Seminary and served various pastorates and as missionary to Japan before he began his definitive church histories. Most famous among these is *Virginia's Mother Church* (1947-52) (2 vols.), which treats the Episcopal Church in Virginia from Jamestown to 1814.

BOOKS: *The Established Church in Virginia and the Revolution*, 1930; *The Clergy of the Established Church in Virginia and the Revolution*, 1933; *Days in the Diocese of Virginia*, 1935; *The Episcopal Church Among the Negroes of Virginia*, 1937; *New Light Upon the History of the Church in Colonial Virginia*, 1941; *Virginia's Mother Church and the Political Conditions Under which it Grew*, 1947; *The Colonial Churches in Virginia*, 194?; *The Church of England in England and her Oldest Daughter, the Protestant Episcopal Church of Virginia*, 1957; *Religious Life of Virginia in the Seventeeth Century; the Faith of Our Fathers*, 1957.

REFERENCES: Margaret H. Carpenter, *Virginia Authors' Yearbook*, 1956, 1958; Richmond *Times-Dispatch*, Sept. 27, 1963.

BUXBAUM, MARTIN ["MARTIN NOLL"] (1913-   ), was born in Richmond and has worked as an editor, a free-lance photographer and (currently) as director of communications for a Washington restaurant chain. All the while he has written poetry which he has collected into several anthologies (e.g. *Whispers in the Wind* (1966) and *The Underside of Heaven* (1963)). He has won numerous awards, including the George

Washington Medal of Honor and Maryland poet of the Year. He currently makes his home in Bethesda, Maryland.

BOOKS: *Rivers of Thought*, 1958; *Bux's Scrapbook*, 1960; *The Underside of Heaven*, 1963; *Table Talk for Family Fun*, 1964; *The Unsung*, 1964; *What Every Young Bridegroom Should Know*, 1966; *Whispers in the Wind*, 1966; *Around Our House*, 1968; *Once Upon a Dream*, 1970.

REFERENCES: *Who's Who of International Poets; Contemporary Authors*, 17-18.

BYRD, RICHARD EVELYN (1888-1957), non-fiction writer, born in Winchester, Virginia, was the brother of Senator Harry F. Byrd, Sr. and a direct descendant of William Byrd II (*q.v.*). An aviator and U. S. Navy officer, he is remembered mainly as a polar explorer. He told of his experiences in five books, all best sellers. In addition to the American editions, there were translations into many foreign languages. He was the subject of many articles and biographies. (M.M.C.)

BOOKS: *Skyward*, 1928; *Little America*, 1930; *Discovery*, 1935; *Exploring with Byrd*, 1937; *Alone*, 1938.

REFERENCES: Fitzhugh Green, *Dick Byrd—Air Explorer*, 1928; Coram Foster, *Rear Admiral Byrd and the Polar Expeditions*, 1930; Guernsey Van Riper, *Richard Byrd: Boy Who Braved the Unknown*, 1958; Michael Gladych, *Admiral Byrd of Antarctica*, 1960; Alfred Steinberg, *Admiral Richard E. Byrd*, 1960; Alden Hatch, *The Byrds of Virginia*, 1969; Kunitz and Haycraft, *Twentieth Century Authors*, 1942; *Current Biography*, 1956; *National Geographic*, Oct., 1947; *Newsweek*, Dec. 16, 1946; *Time*, April 28, 1947; New York *Times*, March 12, 1957. See also Swem's *Virginia Historical Index*, Vol. 1, 1934.

BYRD, WILLIAM, II (1674-1744), diarist, born at Westover Plantation on the James River in Virginia, was the son of William Byrd I, planter and president of the Council of State. His mother, Mary Horsmanden (Filmer) Byrd, was the daughter of a Cavalier officer who came to Virginia during the English Civil Wars.

William Byrd II attended a grammar school in Essex, England; traveled in Holland and France; and returned to England. Instead of going to one of the universities, he read law in London at the Middle Temple from 1692 to 1695. He was admitted to the bar, but never practiced.

When he returned to Virginia after an absence of twelve years, he was at once elected to the House of Burgesses. He still spent much time in England on business for the colony. In 1698 he was made agent and in 1706, receiver-general of Virginia, succeeding his father who had died in December, 1704. He became a councilor in 1708, and in the last year of his life succeeded Commissary Blair as President of the Council.

In 1728 he helped determine the dividing line between Virginia and North Carolina and recorded his experiences with the surveying party. About 1730 be built a great house, and by 1733, needing money, he devised the plan of dividing some of his land into city lots and selling them for a higher price than he could get for a piece of farming land. His lots sold, and thus he is credited with the founding of Richmond. He also founded Petersburg.

A few of his poems and a pamphlet or two were published in London during his lifetime, but not until 1841 was the first of his important writing published. Since then other diaries and records have come to light and been published. (M.M.C.)

BOOKS: *The Westover Manuscripts* ("History of the Dividing Line Between Virginia and North Carolina," "A Journey to the Land of Eden," "A Progress to the Mines") 1841; *A History of the Dividing Line and Other Tracts* (2 vols.), ed. by T. H. Wynne, 1866; *The Writings of "Colonel William Byrd of Westover in Virginia, Esqr.,"* ed. by John Spencer Bassett, 1901; *William Byrd's Histories of the Dividing Line*, ed. by William K. Boyd, 1929; *William Byrd's Natural History of Virginia*, ed. by Richmond Croom Beatty and William J. Mulloy, 1940; *The Secret Diary of William Byrd of Westover, 1709-1712*, ed. by Louis B. Wright and Marion Tinling, 1941; *Another Secret Diary of William Byrd of Westover* (trans. and collated by Marion Tinling), ed. by Maude Howlett Woodfin, 1942; *The London Diary, 1717-1721, and Other Writings*, ed. by Louis B. Wright and Marion Tinling, 1958.

REFERENCES: J. B. Hubbell, *The South in American Literature 1607-1900*, 1954 (bibliography); Richmond Croom Beatty, *William Byrd of Westover*, 1932, rev. ed. with new preface by M. Thomas Inge, 1970; Louis D. Rubin, Jr., ed., *A Bibliographical Guide to the Study of Southern Literature*, 1969. See also Swem's *Virginia Historical Index*, Vol. 1, 1934.

CABELL, JAMES BRANCH (1879-1958), author of novels, short stories, histories, poems, and memoirs, was born on April 14, 1879, in Richmond, Virginia. In 1898 he graduated with Phi Beta Kappa honors from the College of William and Mary, where he had been an instructor in French and in Greek while still an undergraduate. Except for brief flings at newspaper work in Richmond and in New York from 1899 to 1901, at coal mining from 1911 to 1913, and at genealogical research, which led to the publication of three books of family history between the years 1907 and 1915, Cabell devoted his entire life to *belles lettres*.

As early as 1902 Cabell began publishing short stories and articles in contemporary magazines. By 1919 he had, in addition, published a dozen books, which had attracted little attention, until the indictment of *Jurgen* (1919) by the New York Society for The Suppression of Vice (1920) won him international fame.

Cabell's work gained a new richness and depth after his character Manuel had taken on full proportion in *Figures of Earth* (1921). For most of the next decade Cabell strove to harmonize all of his current and even his preceding work with his new purpose—the composition of an allegory of human thought on three levels: that of the average individual; of the typical Virginian; and of humanity considered in its entirety. The Storisende Edition of the *Biography of the Life of Manuel* (1927-1930) may well be, as Cabell wrote in *Preface to the Past* (1936), "the most ambitiously planned literary work which has ever come out of America."

In addition to his genealogies and to his monumental *Biography of the Life of Manuel*, Cabell published two trilogies of fiction, three of history and memoirs, and eleven miscellaneous works, termed by him x, y, & z. Exclusive of the *Biography*, the group which is, perhaps, the most deserving of fame is the trilogy, *Smirt* (1934), *Smith* (1935), and *Smire* (1936), an allegory of the intellectual life of the author.

Cabell died at his home in "Richmond-in-Virginia" of a cerebral hemorrhage on May 5, 1958, leaving behind him fifty-two volumes. (D.B.S.)

BOOKS: *The Eagle's Shadow*, 1904; *The Line of Love*, 1905; *Gallantry*, 1907; *The Cords of Vanity*, 1909; *Chivalry*, 1909; *The Soul of Melicent*, 1913; *The Rivet in Grandfather's Neck*, 1915; *From the Hidden Way*, 1916; *The Certain Hour*, 1916; *The Cream of the Jest*, 1917; *Beyond Life*, 1919; *Jurgen*, 1919; *Domnei*, 1920; *The Jewel Merchants*, 1921; *Figures of Earth*, 1921; *The Lineage of Lichfield*, 1922; *The High Place*, 1923; *Straws and Prayer-Books*, 1924; *The Silver Stallion*, 1926; *The Music from Behind the Moon*, 1926; *Something About Eve*, 1927; *The White Robe*, 1928; *The Way of Ecben*, 1929; *Sonnets from Antan*, 1929; *Some of Us: An Essay in Epitaphs*, 1930; *These Restless Heads*, 1932; *Special Delivery: A Packet of Replies*, 1933; *Smirt: An Urban Nightmare*, 1934; *Ladies and Gentlemen*, 1934; *Smith: A Sylvan Interlude*, 1935; *Preface to the Past*, 1936; *Smire: An Acceptance in the Third Person*, 1937; *The King Was in His Counting House*, 1938; *Hamlet Had an Uncle*, 1940; *The First Gentleman of America: A Comedy of Conquest*, 1942; *The St. Johns: A Parade of Diversities*, 1943; *There Were Two Pirates*, 1946; *Let Me Lie*, 1947; *Quiet Please*, 1952; *As I Remember It*, 1955; Padraic Column and Margaret Freeman Cabell, eds. *Between Friends: Letters of James Branch Cabell and Others*, 1962.

REFERENCES: Louis D. Rubin, Jr., *No Place on Earth: Ellen Glasgow, James Branch Cabell and Richmond-in-Virginia*, 1959; Joe Lee Davis, *James Branch Cabell*, 1962; Arvin R. Wells, *Jesting Moses: A Study in Cabellian Comedy*, 1962; Desmond Tarrant, *James Branch Cabell: The Dream and the Reality*, 1967; Edgar E. MacDonald, "The Glasgow-Cabell Entente," *American Literature*, Vol. 41, No. 1 (March 1969); Edgar E. MacDonald, "Cabell's Hero: Cosmic Rebel," *Southern Literary Journal*, 2 (Fall 1969); Edgar E. MacDonald, "Cabell's Richmond Trial," *Southern Literary Journal*, 3 (Fall 1970); Maurice Duke, "James Branch Cabell's Personal Library," *Studies in Bibliography*, Vol. 23 (1970); Louis D. Rubin, Jr., ed., *A Bibliographical Guide to the Study of Southern Literature*, 1969. See also *The Cabellian* and *Kalki*, publications devoted entirely to the study of Cabell.

CABELL, MARGARET ANTHONY (1814-1882), the author of a book about Lynchburg, was a contributor to *The Southern Literary Messenger* when Edgar Allan Poe was editorial assistant. Her book on Lynchburg, published in 1858, contained a variety of information about the early years of the city's history.

Dr. Asbury Christian (*q.v.*) said that Mrs. Cabell, though born "in the twilight of Quakerism," exemplified its virtues. Her book, true to the conditions of her day, was not intended for publication, but for the entertainment of her children. It was not the custom for women's names to appear in print at that time, and Mrs. Cabell, though but forty-three years old, signed her sketches "the oldest inhabitant."

Her men, the early residents of Lynchburg, are all handsome and brave, and her women fair and virtuous. The authenticity of her sketches had never been questioned, and books published since her day have accepted her work as historically accurate. Genealogies have been based upon it and local boundaries have been fixed by it. That she would be one of Lynchburg's best known authors apparently never occurred to Margaret Anthony Cabell as she penned her intimate stories of Lynchburg's early life. (R.H.B.)

BOOK: *Sketches and Recollections of Lynchburg by the Oldest Inhabitant*, 1858.

REFERENCES: Manuscript Collection of Biographies of Lynchburg Writers at the Jones Memorial Library, Lynchburg, Virginia. An index of the *Recollections* was compiled by William Frederick Holcombe, and published in *Bulletin of the Virginia State Library*. Vol. 13, No. 3.

CAPERTON, HELENA LEFROY (1878-1962), short story and nonfiction writer, was born of an Irish father and a Virginia mother. During her youth she lived in her grandfather's home in County Down, North Ireland.

After 1920, when she started writing, she had many stories and articles published. In 1930 the O. Henry Award was given "The Honest Wine Merchant," and the O'Brien *Anthology of the Best Short Stories of 1930* gave "The Lost Governess" a star rating. In 1950 *Legends of Virginia* was published by Garrett and Massie in Richmond. Of this volume James Branch Cabell pointed out the authenticity of "The Honest Wine Merchant" and added that truth is quite ofen stranger than fiction.

Dorothy Parker, who wrote "A Few Words" at the beginning of another of her books, *Like a Falcon Flying*, said "I do not know the words for Mrs. Caperton's stories. They are strange, swift, tense, emotional . . . all these. But there is more about them. There is a wildness, a fierce rush of drama, a long spreading terror, a passionate championship of the lovely and the innocent and then a sudden curious tenderness."

Mrs. Caperton also wrote book reviews for the Richmond *Times-Dispatch*, the Louisville *Courier-Journal*, and the Louisville *Times*. (M.M.C.)

BOOKS: *Like a Falcon Flying*, 1943; *Legends of Virginia*, 1950.

REFERENCES: Richmond *Times-Dispatch*, Mar. 26, 1950; Introduction to *Legends of Virginia*; Margaret H. Carpenter, *Virginia Authors' Yearbook*, 1957, 1958.

CAPPON, LESTER JESSE (1900-   ), historian and bibliographer, though born in Milwaukee, has spent much of his professional life in Virginia and methodizing the study of his adopted state. He is perhaps best known for his compendious *Bibliography of Virginia History Since 1865* (1930), but he has also edited *The Adams-Jefferson Letters* (1959), and published numerous monographs on phases of Virginia history, one of the most notable being *Virginia Newspapers, 1821-1935: A Bibliography* (1936).

BOOKS: *Bibliography of Virginia History Since 1865*, 1930; *Virginia Newspapers, 1821-1935: A Bibliography*, 1936; *New Market, Virginia: Imprints*, 1942; *A Plan for the Collection and Preservation of World War II Records*, 1942; *The Collection and Preservation of World War Records*, 1942; *Virginia Gazette Index, 1736-1780*, 1950; *Genealogy: Handmaid of History*, 1957; *Reference Works and Historical Texts: War Records in the States, 1941-1943; American Genealogical Periodicals: A Bibliography with a Chronological Finding List*, 1962.

REFERENCE: *Virginia Lives*.

CARLSON, NATALIE SAVAGE (1906-   ), writer of juveniles, was born in Winchester, Virginia, but has lived a good part of her life near the sea—in Norfolk and currently in Newport, Rhode Island—with her husband, a Rear-Admiral. She has also lived in France for three years and has made numerous trips to French Canada. Her stories show a strong French influence (e.g. *The Talking Cat and Other Stories of French Canada* (1952) and *Carnival in Paris* (1962). In 1966 she was the United States' nominee for the International Hans Christian Andersen Award.

BOOKS: *The Talking Cat, and Other Stories of French Canada*, 1952; *Alphonse: that Bearded One*, 1954; *Wings Against the Wind*, 1955; *Sashes Red and Blue*, 1956; *The Happy Orpheline*, 1957; *Hortense: the Cow for a Queen*, 1957; *The Family Under the Bridge*, 1958; *The Tomahawk Family*, 1960; *Evangeline: Pigeon of Paris*, 1960; *Old Murders Never Die*, 1960; *The Song of the Lop-Eared Mule*, 1961; *Carnival in Paris*, 1962; *A Pet for the Orphelines*, 1962; *Jean-Claude's Island*, 1963; *School Bell in the Valley*, 1963; *The Letter on the Tree*, 1964; *The Orphelines in the Enchanted Castle*, 1964; *The Empty Schoolhouse*, 1965; *Sailor's Choice*, 1966; *Ann Aurelia and Dorothy*, 1966; *Chalou*, 1967; *Luigi of the Streets*, 1967; *Befana's Gift*, 1969; *Marchers for the Dream*, 1969; *The Half Sisters*, 1970.

REFERENCE: *Contemporary Authors*, 4.

CARPENTER, FRANCES (1890-   ), writer of children's stories, was born in Washington, D. C., but spent "more than sixty summers on the Blue Ridge, where our house looked across the Shenandoah Valley towards Winchester." She was graduated from Smith College, but claims that an even greater influence upon her youth was her close relationship with her father, journalist Frank G. Carpenter. "Together, my father and I crossed many seas, and from him I acquired my love of far countries which has made the writing of geographical books for the elementary schools such a pleasure to me. As the wife of my foreign service husband, W. Chapin Huntington, I continued these travels, and we were living in Paris when our two daughters were born. During our subsequent family journeys in Europe, I gathered much of the source material and discovered the illustrators for my folk tale books, *Tales of a Swiss Grandmother, Tales of a Basque Grandmother,* and *Tales of a Russian Grandmother.*

"My love for Virginia was the motivation for my book, *Pocahontas and her World,* published at the time of the Jamestown celebration [1957]; and my deep interest in my native city resulted in *Holiday in Washington* which followed it. My fondness for the pets we had at our home on the Blue Ridge is reflected in my *Wonder Tales of Horses and Heroes* and *Wonder Tales of Dogs and Cats,* and my enthusiasm for ocean travel is responsible for my *Wonder Tales of Seas and Ships,* published in 1959."

BOOKS: *Ourselves and Our City,* 1928; *The Ways We Travel,* 1929; *Tales of a Basque Grandmother,* 1930; *Our Little Friends of Eskimo Land,* 1931; *Tales of a Russian Grandmother,* 1933; *Our Little Friends of the Arabian Desert,* 1934; *Our Little Friends of the Netherlands,* 1935; *Our Little Friends of Norway,* 1936; *Our Little Friends of China,* 1937; *Our Little Neighbors at Work and Play,* 1939; *Our State Flags,* 1937; *Tales of a Swiss Grandmother,* 1940; *Our South American Neigabors,* 1942; *The Pacific: Its Lands and Peoples,* 1944; *Canada and Her Northern Neighbors,* 1946; *Tales of a Korean Grandmother,* 1947; *Children of Our World,* 1949; *Wonder Tales of Dogs and Cats,* 1955; *Pocahontas and Her World,* 1957; *Wonder Tales of Seas and Ships,* 1959; *African Wonder Tales,* 1963; *South American Wonder Tales,* 1969; *The Story of Korea,* 1969.

REFERENCES: *Who's Who in America,* Vol. 31, 1959-60; Margaret H. Carpenter, *Virginia Authors' Yearbook,* 1956, 1957, 1958.

CARPENTER, MARGARET HALEY (1917-   ), poet, biographer, and editor, writes: "A native of Virginia, I have lived most of my life in Norfolk and am a graduate of Westhampton College, University of Richmond. I edited the *Virginia Authors' Yearbook* (1956, 1957, 1958) and have been a guest editor of *The Lyric.* While engaged in research for a book about Sara Teasdale, I became interested in the work of Marion Cummings, poet and philosopher, to whom Sara Teasdale dedicated her second book, and I edited *Poems* by Marion Cummings. I also edited David Morton's last book, *Journey into Time,* published after his death. I collaborated with William Stanley Braithwaite on his *Anthology of Magazine Verse for 1958,* my part being to make a selection of representative poems from his previous anthologies (1913-1929), which were included as the second section of the 1958 anthology. In 1960 my authoritative biography of Sara Teasdale was published, for which I was allowed to use the previously unpublished, fascinating letters of Vachel Lindsay to this poet.

"My poetry has appeared in periodicals in England, Canada, and the United States, and I have been fortunate enough to win a number of prizes, including the Arthur Davison Ficke Award of the Poetry Society of

America (co-winner) and the Greenwood Prize of the Poetry Society of Great Britain. Besides creative writing, painting and music are my other most absorbing interests."

BOOKS AND PAMPHLETS: *Sara Teasdale: A Biography*, 1960; ed., *Poems* by Marion Cummings, 1957, privately printed; ed., *Journey into Time*, 1958; ed., *Virginia Authors' Yearbook*, 1956, 1957, 1958; co-editor with William Stanley Braithwaite, *Anthology of Magazine Verse for 1958; A Gift for the Princess of Springtime*, 1964.

REFERENCES: *Who's Who of American Women*, Vol. 1; *Harper's Magazine*, Jan. 1961; *Norfolk Virginian-Pilot* and *Portsmouth Star*, Sept. 18 and Nov. 20, 1960; Richmond *News-Leader*, Nov. 23, 1960; St. Louis *Globe-Democrat*, Nov. 20, 1960; New Haven, Conn., *Register Magazine*, Dec. 4, 1960; *Library Journal*, Dec. 15, 1960; Chicago *Daily News*, Dec. 24, 1960; Wichita, Kan., *Eagle*, Dec. 25, 1960; Charlotte (N. C.) *Observer*, Jan. 8, 1961; Pittsburgh *Press*, Jan. 29, 1961.

CARUTHERS, WILLIAM ALEXANDER (1802-1846), novelist, was born in Lexington, Virginia, where there were strong bonds with the North. The economic and social structure of the Valley of Virginia of that period was partially responsible for the anti-slavery views he gave voice to in his novels. He was of the independent and strong-willed Presbyterian Scotch-Irish who settled early in the Valley.

From 1817 to 1820 he was a student enrolled in Washington College (later to become Washington and Lee University) in Lexington. In 1821 he enrolled in the School of Medicine of the University of Pennsylvania. He graduated from there in 1823. Shortly afterward he married Miss Louise Gibson, a planter's daughter, from Whitemarsh Island, Georgia. He returned, after his marriage, to Lexington where he lived until he suffered a reversal of fortune in 1829. Almost penniless he moved his family to New York and there entered the medical profession. He served well during the cholera epidemics of that era and at the same time began work on his first novel. In 1843, *The Kentuckian in New York* was published. It is through this novel that Dr. Caruthers is best revealed.

The Kentuckian was quickly followed the next year by *The Cavaliers of Virginia*. In it are royalists, rebels, Indians, frontiersmen and all the colorful figures of that colonial period. Particular attention was paid to Nathaniel Bacon, a forgotten figure in Southern literature.

Caruthers' third and last novel was published after his departure from New York to Savannah, Georgia. Published by an obscure press in Wetumpka, Alabama, it enjoyed neither the publicity nor the distribution of his earlier novels. This book, *The Knights of the Horse-Shoe*, despite its lack of popularity, was the best constructed of the author's works. In it he honors Alexander Spotswood, another forgotten character in Southern history. As the title suggests, it deals with the western expedition to the Blue Ridge.

Caruthers attracted a brief flurry of enthusiasm among his contemporaries and readers. However, the political substance of his writings was not such that a Southerner of the times would praise. To the people of the North he was a Southerner, writing in a period when all things Southern were regarded as inferior, or biased, or both. Only in the last few years has he been regarded as an author worthy of a prominent place in Southern literature.

Caruthers died in 1846. He lies in a lost and unmarked grave. In his relatively short productive period he had authored only three novels and a few short articles. But he had pointed the way to a new literature—a literature rich with a new untreated folklore and tradition. Upon his foundation was to be constructed a new literature of substance and quality. (C.H.H.)

BOOKS: *The Kentuckian in New York: Or, The Adventures of Three Southerners*, 1834; *The Cavaliers of Virginia*, 1837; *The Knights of the Horse-Shoe*, 1845, 1882, 1970.

REFERENCES: Curtis Carroll Davis, *Chronicler of the Cavaliers: A Life of the Virginia Novelist, Dr. William A. Caruthers*, 1953; J. B. Hubbell, *The South in American Literature*, 1954 (bibliography); Louis D. Rubin, Jr., ed., *A Bibliographical Guide to the Study of Southern Literature*, 1969. See also Swem's *Virginia Historical Index*, Vol. 1, 1934.

CATHER, WILLA SIBERT (1873-1947), editor, drama and music critic, poet, and novelist, was born at "Willowshade," in Bear Creek Valley near Winchester, Virginia, but by the time she was twelve, her parents had settled with some relatives in a little colony northwest of Red Cloud, Nebraska. Here she came to know the land and the people from whom the majority of her fiction would be derived.

After four years at the new University of Nebraska, she wrote as a free-lance critic for some months before joining the editorial staff of Charles Axtell's *Home Monthly* magazine in Pittsburgh. Within a year she was managing editor. Before publishing *April Twilights*, her first book, in 1903, she had worked on the *Daily Leader* (Pennsylvania's largest newspaper) and had taught school for a few years. The poetic volume *April Twilights* was followed in 1905 by a volume of short stories, *The Troll Garden*, containing the celebrated "Paul's Case," which showed her resentment of the West. While living in Boston and serving on the staff of *McClure's* (1906-1912), she made friends of many local literati, including Sarah Orne Jewett and Ferris Greenslet (a reviewer of *April Twilights*), who led her interests back to the Nebraska of her youth. *Alexander's Bridge*, her first novel, was serialized in *McClure's* in 1912 and proved to be a prelude to *O Pioneers!*, which established her reputation as a novelist of the first order.

After resigning from *McClure's* in 1912, she spent the next fifteen years as a resident—with her friend Ellen Lewis—of Greenwich Village, where she proceeded to write nine novels and to hold her famous Friday afternoon at-homes. She also made occasional trips to Nebraska during this period, and these furnished her with material for perhaps her two best Nebraska novels, *My Antonia* (1918) and *Death Comes for the Archbishop* (1927). *One of Ours* (1922), which reflects her reaction to World War I, won her the Pulitzer

Prize. *A Lost Lady,* published the next year, is often considered her most structurally perfect novel.

After a period of spiritual searching following the War, she was confirmed an Episcopalian, along with her parents. This heightened religious consciousness is reflected in *The Professor's House, My Mortal Enemy,* and *Death Comes for the Archbishop (q.v.).*

Between 1932 and 1940, Willa Cather published four books: *Obscure Destinies, Lucy Gayheart, The Song of the Lark,* and *Sapphira and the Slave Girl.* "Old Mrs. Harris," a short story in the first of these, recounts the author's memories of her family's move from the South to the West. And the last is a novel recreating life in the Bear Creek Valley of her childhood. While writing the novel in the spring of 1938, she returned for the last time to its setting. Though she had prepared a "Library Edition" of her works during 1937-38, she added *Sapphira and the Slave Girl* to these twelve volumes in 1941. For the remaining six years of her life she wrote little, though she remained active physically and socially.

BOOKS: *April Twilights,* 1903; *The Troll Garden,* 1905; *Alexander's Bridge,* 1912; *O Pioneers!,* 1913; *My Antonia,* 1918; *Youth and the Bright Medusa,* 1920; *One of Ours,* 1922; *A Lost Lady,* 1923; *My Mortal Enemy,* 1926; *Death Comes for the Archbishop,* 1927; *Shadows on the Rock,* 1931; *Obscure Destinies,* 1932; *Lucy Gayheart,* 1935; *Not Under Forty,* 1936; *Sapphira and the Slave Girl,* 1940; *The Old Beauty and Others,* 1948; *Willa Cather on Writing,* 1949; *Writings from Willa Cather's Campus Years,* 1950; *Five Stories,* with article by Geo. N. Kates on Willa Cather's last unfinished and unpublished Avignon story, 1956; *Early Stories,* selected with commentary by Mildred R. Bennett, 1957.

REFERENCES: Rene Rapin, *Modern American Writers,* 1930; Alexander Porterfield, *Willa Cather,* 1927; Elizabeth Moorhead Vermorchen, *These Two Were Here: Louise Homer and Willa Cather,* 1950; Josephine Lurie Jessup, *The Faith of Our Feminists: A Study in the Novels of Edith Wharton, Ellen Glasgow, and Willa Cather,* 1950; David Daiches, *Willa Cather: A Critical Introduction,* 1951; Edith Lewis, *Willa Cather Living: A Personal Record,* 1953; E. K. Brown and Leon Edel, *Willa Cather: A Critical Biography,* 1953; Elizabeth Shepley Sergeant, *Willa Cather: A Memoir,* 1953; Ruth Franchere, *Willa,* 1958. See also Robert E. Spiller, *et al., Literary History of the United States.*

CHAMBERS, LENOIR (1891-1970), editor and biographer, was a native of Charlotte, North Carolina. He attended Woodberry Forest School, the University of North Carolina (B.A., 1914), and the Columbia School of Journalism. After working on many North Carolina and Virginia newspapers, he became editor of the Norfolk *Virginian-Pilot* in 1950 and held the post until his death. A series of editorials he wrote concerning the school crisis of 1959 won him the Pulitzer Prize. His biography, *Stonewall Jackson* (1959) has become a standard work on its subject.

BOOKS: *Stonewall Jackson* (2 vols.), 1959; *Salt Water and Printer's Ink: Norfolk and its Newspapers, 1865-1965,* 1967.
REFERENCE: *Who's Who in the South and Southwest,* Vol. 6.

CHASE, RICHARD (1904-   ), a nationally known folklorist, is also a lecturer, teacher, author, and at one time was a part-time farmer near Charlottesville. He majored in botany and was graduated from Antioch College in Ohio, with a B.S. degree.

It was a chance visit to the Pine Mountain Settlement School in the Kentucky Cumberland Mountains that determined his life work. Here he heard his first ballad. From then on, he says, he was aware everywhere he went of "something relating to our heritage of English-American ballads, songs, folk-hymns, tales, singing games [and] country dances."

He has been a consultant to recreation leaders and taught dances and folk games in schools from Georgia to Maine. In Virginia he was associated with the White Top Folk Festival and the Virginia Writers' Project, W. P. A. He was also the Virginia representative of the Country Dance Society. His hobbies are folk crafts, botany, and making and playing bamboo shepherd's pipes, which he also uses in teaching folk songs.

He travels extensively, collecting material, teaching and making talks. For several summers he has directed summer-long Folk Festivals at Boone, North Carolina, and taught a Folk Arts Workshop at Appalachian State Teachers College. (M.M.C.)

BOOKS: *Old Songs and Singing Games,* 1938; ed., *The Jack Tales,* 1943; ed., *Grandfather Tales,* 1948; compiler, *Hullaballoo and Other Singing Folk Games,* 1949; *Jack and the Three Sillies,* 1950; *Wicked John and the Devil,* 1951; ed., *American Folk Tales . . . as Preserved in the Appalachian Mountains and Elsewhere,* 1956; *Billy Boy,* 1966.
REFERENCES: Richmond *Times-Dispatch,* May 1, 1949; Richard Walser, *Picturebook of Tar Heel Authors,* 1957.

CHILDS, JAMES RIVES (1893-   ), fiction and diplomatic report writer, was born in Lynchburg, the son of John William and Lucy Howard (Brown) Childs. He was graduated from Randolph-Macon College in 1912, took his M.A. degree at Harvard in 1915, and was graduated from the Army War College in 1917. On August 13, 1922, he married Georgina de Brylkine.

After working as a newspaper reporter, he served in World War I, and later, in 1923, became a free lance writer. In November of the same year he entered the American Consular Service and for a period of many years served variously in Jerusalem, Bucharest, Cairo, Teheran, Tangier, Saudi Arabia, Yemen, and Ethiopia. (M.M.C.)

BOOKS: *Reliques of the Rives,* 1929; *Before the Curtain Falls,* 1932; *The Pageant of Persia,* 1936; *Escape to Cairo* (by Henry Filmer, pseud.), 1938; *The Evolution of British Diplomatic Representation in the Middle East,* 1939; *American Foreign Service,* 1948; *The Descendants of William*

Christopher Rives, 1954; *Casanoviana: An Annotated World Bibliography of Jacques de Seingalt and of Works Concerning Him*, 1956; *Casanova: A Biography Based on New Documents*, 1961; *Diplomatic and Literary Quests*, 1963; *Foreign Service Farewell*, 1969.

REFERENCES: Richard Clement Wood, ed. *Collector's Quest: The Correspondence of Henry Miller and J. Rives Childs, 1947-1965*, 1968. Edgar E. MacDonald, "The J. Rives Childs Collection of Henry Miller at Randolph-Macon College," *Resources for American Literary Study*, Vol. 1, No. 1 (Spring 1971). See also the Reference Collection of Biographies of Lynchburg Writers at the Jones Memorial Library, Lynchburg, Virginia; *Who's Who in America*, Vol. 30, 1958-59.

CHRISMAN, ARTHUR BOWIE (1889-   ), story-teller, was born at "West Brook," a farm one mile north of White Post, Virginia. His parents, Isaac Arthur and Mary Louise (Bryarly) Chrisman, were both descendants of early colonial settlers, one of whom was Joosten Hite who, in 1732, with other members of the family, completed Virginia's first settlement west of the Blue Ridge.

He learned to read and write when he was very young, and had as early companions two fascinating story-tellers. A man skilled in the lore of wild animals was one of these; the other was a former Indian fighter with marvelous stories of adventures in the West. Both told tales tirelessly to the eager young listener. A later influence came to him from "a wise and kindly man of China," whom he met in Los Angeles, and who aroused his interest in Chinese life and literature.

Although Arthur Chrisman began early to tell stories to the children on the farm, and was a seasoned story-teller, his first writing submitted for publication met with the usual rejection. His first published book, *Shen of the Sea*, 1926, was awarded the Newbery Medal, given annually for "the most distinguished contribution for American literature for children." (M.M.C.)

BOOKS: *Shen of the Sea*, 1925; *The Wind That Wouldn't Blow*, 1927; *Treasurers Long Hidden*, 1941.

REFERENCES: Kunitz and Haycraft, *The Junior Book of Authors*, 1951; Kunitz *Living Authors*, 1931; Kunitz and Haycraft, *Twentieth Century Authors*, 1942; "Newbery Medal Books, 1922-1955," *Hornbook*, 1955.

CHRISTIAN, W[ILLIAM] ASBURY (1866-1936), historian, the son of Dunscombe and Cornelia Burton Christian, was born in Lynchburg. He was educated at Randolph-Macon College and Vanderbilt University. His books were about Virginia. (L.T.D.)

BOOKS: *Lynchburg and Its People*, 1900; *Marah: Story of Old Virginia*, 1903; *Richmond: Her Past and Present*, 1912.

REFERENCES: Reference Collection of Biographies of Lynchburg Writers at the Jones Memorial Library, Lynchburg, Virginia.

CLAY, HENRY (1777-1852), orator, was born in Hanover County, Virginia. He became secretary to the clerk of the Virginia High Court of Chancery in 1795, read law under Chancellor George Wythe, and was admitted to the bar in 1797. That same year he went west to Kentucky and settled in Lexington, where he soon gained political prominence. After filling out two unexpired terms in the United States Senate, he was elected to the House of Representatives and became its first prominent Speaker. He was an unsuccessful candidate for the Presidency in 1824, but the next year he became Secretary of State under John Quincy Adams. In 1830 he became a member of the Senate and, with the exception of a brief period or two, served as a Senator the rest of his life.

Again in 1832 and 1844 he was candidate for the Presidency, but was defeated each time. Warned in 1839 that his public attack on Abolitionism would hurt him politically, he is said to have replied, "I had rather be right than be President."

Some of his notable orations are: "On the Greek Revolution" (1824); "Defense of the American System" (1832); "Compromise of 1850" (1850); and "Farewell to the Senate." (M.M.C.)

BOOKS: James B. Swain, ed., *The Life and Speeches of Henry Clay*, 1843; Calvin Colton, ed., *The Works of Henry Clay* (6 vols.); James F. Hopkins, and others, eds., *The Papers of Henry Clay*, 1959-61.

REFERENCES: *Dictionary of American Biography*, Vol. 4, 1930; Carl Schurz, *Life of Henry Clay*, 1887; Bernard Mayo, *Henry Clay*, 1937; Glyndon Garlock Van Dusen, *The Life of Henry Clay*, 1937; Gamaliel Bradford, *As God Made Them*, 1929; Gerald W. Johnson, *America's Silver Age: The Statecraft of Clay—Webster—Calhoun*, 1939.

CLAYTON, JOHN BELL (1907-1955), novelist and short story writer, was born Craigsville (Augusta County) and attended schools in Churchville and Staunton. He attended the University of Virginia (1924-1928). He then became a reporter for The *Daily Progress* of Charlottesville (1929-32) and served as managing editor (1938-40). During the 1930's he worked as a free-lance writer, and after 1940 he became a staff writer for the Scripps-Howard News organization in Washington and later wrote for the Philadelphia bureau of the United Press and the San Francisco *Examiner*.

Though the author of three novels, he was more honored as a writer of short stories, many of which were collected in the posthumous volume *The Strangers Were There*. Numerous stories were set in Virginia and some had appeared in *Colliers, The American Mercury, Esquire, Discovery, Harper's Magazine*, and *A New Southern Harvest*, edited by Robert Penn Warren. One, "The White Circle," received the O. Henry Memorial Award in 1947.

BOOKS: *Six Angels on My Back*, 1952; *Wait, Son, October is Near*, 1953; *Walk Toward the Rainbow*, 1954; *The Strangers Were There*, 1957.

REFERENCES: Charlottesville *Daily Progress*, May 29, 1957; Margaret H. Carpenter, *Virginia Authors' Yearbook*, 1958.

CONWAY, MONCURE DANIEL (1832-1907), novelist and writer of non-fiction, was born near Falmouth, Virginia, across the Rappahannock from Fredericksburg. He was an alien in his own country. Early in his life he became an abolitionist, a transcendentalist, and a Unitarian, and after a time a freethinker.

He studied at Fredericksburg Academy, but said that the most important part of his education came from listening to a discussion of cases in the law courts and in his own home. At Dickinson College in Pennsylvania, his greatest interest was in literature. However, since libraries were inadequate and contemporary writers were not taught at Dickinson, he did not find copies of Emerson, Hawthorne, Channing, George Sand, and Goethe until later. These authors were to make a profound impression on him.

After he was graduated from Dickinson at seventeen, he began to search for a satisfactory way of life. He studied law for a time in Warrenton but gave that up to become a Methodist circuit rider in Maryland. This, too, proved unsatisfactory, and he decided to study at Harvard Divinity School.

Here he met the major New England writers, but was especially impressed by Emerson, noting in his diary on the day of their meeting: "The most memorable day of my life: spent with Ralph Waldo Emerson!"

After his graduation in 1854, he held pastorates in the Unitarian Church in Washington, D. C., from which he was soon dismissed because of his anti-slavery sentiments, and in Cincinnati, where his freethinking congregation allowed him to preach in defense of Thomas Paine. He continued to campaign for abolition and drifted into literature by becoming editor of the *Dial* for 1860 and an associate editor of the *Commonwealth* in 1862. The latter assignment brought him back to Massachusetts, where Wendell Phillips succeeded in persuading him to go to England to lecture for the Union cause. Becoming disappointed with the growing respect for war in the North, he decided to remain in England as pastor of the liberal South Place Chapel in Finsbury. Many of his sermons were published. In all he was the author of more than seventy books and pamphlets. His *Life of Thomas Paine*, in two volumes, published in 1892, is considered his best work. It was followed by a comprehensive four-volume edition of *The Writings of Thomas Paine*. In 1909 a selection of Conway's work was published under the title *Addresses and Reprints: 1850-1907*. His seventy books and pamphlets are listed in this volume. (M.M.C.)

BOOKS: *Free Schools in Virginia*, 1850; *The Rejected Stone: Or Insurrection vs. Resurrection in America by a Native Virginian*, 1861; *The Earthward Pilgrimage*, 1874; *Idols and Ideals*, 1877; *Demonology and Devil-Lore*, 1879; *A Necklace of Stories*, 1880; *Thomas Carlyle*, 1881; *Lessons for the Day*, 1882; *Emerson at Home and Abroad*, 1882; *Pine and Palm*, 1887; *Prisons of Air*, 1891; *Life of Nathaniel Hawthorne*, 1890; *Life of Thomas Paine* (2 vols.), 1892.

REFERENCES: J. B. Hubbell, *The South in American Literature 1607-1900* (bibliography), 1954; Francis Coleman Rosenberger, *Virginia Reader*, 1948; James D. Hart, *Oxford Companion of American Literature*, 1965;

Mary Elizabeth Burtis, *Moncure Conway, 1832-1907*, 1952. See also Swem's *Virginia Historical Index*, Vol. 1, 1934.

COOKE, JOHN ESTEN (1830-1886), novelist, biographer, and historian, was born near Winchester, reared in the Valley of Virginia, and later moved to Richmond. He was educated at Charlestown Academy and by a private tutor. At sixteen he left school to study law in his father's office. His heart, however, was set on writing.

He served in the Civil War under J. E. B. Stuart and later under Lee. After the War he married and settled at "The Briars" in Clark County. He had a very successful married life and reared three children, all of whom became famous.

A disciple of Cooper, he wrote of early America—particularly the pre-Civil War South. But he wrote too much for his own reputation, and he soon realized that literary history had passed him by. Several of his articles were accepted by *Harper's Magazine* and the *Southern Literary Messenger*.

He was a poetic romanticist whose keen sense of drama was overweighed by a rather cloying charm, but his books are well grounded; he knew his colonial and Revolutionary history and every foot of the Valley as well as every inhabitant. The Shenandoah Valley is the background of most of his novels. This knowledge makes his *History of Virginia* perhaps his most lasting work.

After the death of his wife, a deep note came into his writing, and it lost the dashing spirit which had been one of its chief attractions.

Richard Henry Stoddard wrote: "His books have the charm of elegant comedy, the pathos of pastoral tragedy, sparkles of wit, flashes of humor, and everywhere the amenities of high breeding." (C.H.H.)

BOOKS: *Leather Stocking and Silk*, 1854; *The Virginia Comedians*, 1853, 1854, 1855; *Henry St. John, Gentleman*, 1859; *Life of Stonewall Jackson*, 1863, 1966; *Surry of Eagle's Nest*, 1866, 1894, 1937; *Wearing of the Gray*, 1867; *Mohun*, 1869, 1893, 1896, 1936; *Hilt to Hilt*, 1869, 1893, 1896; *Hammer and Rapier*, 1870, 1898; *The Heir of Gaymount*, 1870; *A Life of General Robert E. Lee*, 1871; *Stories of the Old Dominion*, 1879; *The Virginia Bohemians*, 1880; *Virginia: A History of the People*, 1883, 1891, 1903.

REFERENCES: Kunitz and Haycraft, *American Authors 1600-1900*, 1938; *Dictionary of American Biography*, Vol. 4, 1930; J. B. Hubbell, *The South in American Literature 1607-1900* (bibliography), 1954; John O. Beaty, *John Esten Cooke*, 1922; Oscar Wegelin, *A Bibliography of the Separate Writings of John Esten Cooke, of Virginia, 1830-1886*, 1941; Louis D. Rubin, Jr., ed., *A Bibliographical Guide to the Study of Southern Literature*, 1969. See also Swem's *Virginia Historical Index*, Vol. 1, 1934.

COOKE, PHILIP PENDLETON (1816-1850), the older brother of John Esten Cooke (*q.v.*), was a poet and story writer. Born near Martinsburg, Virginia (now West Virginia), he grew up in the Shenandoah Valley. He was educated at Martinsburg Academy and the College of New Jersey (now Princeton) from which he was graduated in 1834, at the age of seventeen. He read law with his father and was admitted to the bar in 1836, when he was not yet twenty. He married in 1837.

Some of his poetry from college days appeared in the *Knickerbocker Magazine* before he was graduated. He had several serials running in current magazines. Yet he was primarily a Southern gentleman with a busy social life. In 1845 he moved to a plantation near Ashby's Gap, Virginia. Here he wrote poems describing his surroundings and in 1847 published a volume of them. It was his only published volume; although the unfinished historical novel, *The Chevalier Merlin,* which ran as a serial, was intended to be published in book form when completed. He died at the age of thirty-three.

His best-known poem, "Florence Vane," which was set to music and became a parlor favorite, was translated into several languages. This work was quite sentimental. His stories, as yet uncollected, were better, being vivid bits of whimsy and satire. (C.H.H.)

PRINCIPAL WORK: *Froissart Ballards and Other Poems,* 1847.

REFERENCES: J. B. Hubbell, *The South in American Literature* (bibliography), 1954; James D. Hart, *Oxford Companion to American Literature,* 1965; *Dictionary of American Biography,* Vol. 4, 1930; John D. Allen, ed., *Philip Pendleton: Poet, Critic, Novelist,* 1969; Louis D. Rubin, Jr., ed., *A Bibliographical Guide to the Study of Southern Literature,* 1969.

COTTON, JOHN (fl. 1676), of Queen's Creek near Williamsburg, is believed to have been the author of "The Burwell Papers," also called "The History of Bacon's and Ingrim's Rebellion." The manuscript, now in the library of the Virginia Historical Society, gives an account of Nathaniel Bacon's rebellion in 1676. Also included in "The Burwell Papers" are two poems expressing entirely opposite views of the rebel leader: "Bacon's Epitaph, Made by His Man" and "Upon the Death of G. B. [General Bacon]." The "Epitaph," which is really an elegy, has been considered the best American poem written in the seventeenth century. (M.M.C.)

REFERENCES: J. B. Hubbell, *The South in American Literature 1607-1900,* 1954; James D. Hart, *The Oxford Companion to American Literature,* 1965; Armistead C. Gordon, *Virginian Writers of Fugitive Verse,* 1923; Louis D. Rubin, Jr., ed., *A Bibliographical Guide to the Study of Southern Literature,* 1969.

CROCKETT, LUCY HERNDON (1914-   ), author of children's books and adult novels, writes: "I was born in Honolulu. As the daughter of an army officer I grew up on various military posts in the States and in various countries abroad. I received a haphazard education at schools in Venezuela, Switzerland, England, and this country, forfeiting college to follow my father, first to Puerto Rico, where he served as adviser to the Governor, and then to the Orient, where he was adviser to the Governor General of the Philippine Islands."

In 1936, she was diverted from her intent to become a commercial artist into the writing and illustrating of three children's books: *Lucio and his Nuong: A Tale of the Philippine Islands; That Mario;* and *Capitan: The Story of an Army Mule.* The first was one of thirty books chosen for an international graphic arts show at the Metropolitan Museum of Art, and the second won the *Herald Tribune* Spring Festival Award.

She was twice in the Pacific theater during World War II and covered the occupation as a correspondent. These assignments took her to New Caledonia, the Solomon Islands, Manila and various spots in Japan and Korea. These experiences inspired *Popcorn on the Ginza; Teru: A Tale of Yokohama;* and *Pong Choolie, You Rascal!* Perhaps her most famous adult novel is her first, *The Magnificent Bastards* (1954), a story of Marines and a Red Cross woman in the South Pacific which was later made into a Paramount film called *The Proud and the Profane. Kings Without Castles* (1957) was the result of an in-depth journey through Spain in 1954.

BOOKS: *Capitan: The Story of an Army Mule,* 1940; *That Mario,* 1940; *Popcorn on the Ginza: An Informal Portrait of Postwar Japan,* 1949; *Teru: A Tale of Yokohama,* 1950; *Pong Choolie, You Rascal!,* 1951; *The Magnificent Bastards,* 1954; *Kings Without Castles,* 1957; *The Year Something Almost Happened in Pinoso,* 1960.

REFERENCES: *Wilson Library Bulletin,* May, 1953; *Current Biography Yearbook,* 1953; Margaret H. Carpenter, *Virginia Authors' Yearbook,* 1958.

DABNEY, ROBERT LEWIS (1820-1898), a Presbyterian theologian, teacher, and historian, was born in Louisa County, Virginia, one of eight children. He attended Hampden-Sydney College in 1836-37, taught school the next year, and then finished his undergraduate work at the University of Virginia.

After further study at the Virginia Union Theological Seminary he became a minister, serving first as a rural missionary and later as the pastor of Tinkling Spring Church. During the Civil War he served as a chaplain with his friend and idol, Stonewall Jackson.

From 1853 to 1883, save for the war years, he taught at the seminary from which he was graduated, preached at a local chapel, and from time to time conducted courses at Hampden-Sydney. He was a well-known commentator in Presbyterian publications.

Before the war he opposed secession; but after it started, he looked upon the North as wicked and the South as having a purely Christian nature. After the South's defeat he still maintained this belief and until his death entertained plans for a mass migration of the South to Brazil or to Australia.

The latter part of his life was spent in Texas. From 1890 until his death he was infirm and totally blind, but remained active. (M.M.C.)

BOOKS: *Life and Campaigns of Lieutenant-General Thomas J. Jackson,* 1866; *Defense of Virginia and the South,* 1867; *The Christian Soldier,* 1863; *A Memorial of Lieutenant Colonel John T. Thornton,* 1864; *Sacred and*

Rhetoric (lectures on preaching, printed for students), 1870; *Parental Obligation*, 1880; two courses of lectures which appeared in *Christ Our Penal Substitute*, 1898, all printed in Richmond by The Presbyterian Committee of Publication; *Syllabus and Notes of the Course of Systematic and Polemic Theology*, 1871; *The New South; Practical Philosophy*, 1897.

REFERENCES: *Dictionary of American Biography*, Vol. 1, 1928; Thomas Carey Johnson, *The Life and Letters of Robert Lewis Dabney*, 1903; *In Memoriam, Robert Lewis Dabney, born March 5th, 1820; died, January 3rd, 1898*, Knoxville, 1899, University of Tennessee Press. See also Swem's *Virginia Historical Index*, Vol. 1, 1934.

DABNEY, VIRGINIUS (1835-1894), lawyer, teacher, and novelist, was born at "Elmington," his father's plantation in Gloucester County, Virginia. He spent his childhood in Virginia and Mississippi, but returned to Virginia for college at the University in Charlottesville.

Following the Civil War, in which he was a captain, he gave up the practice of law to teach and to write. He founded the Loudoun School in Middleburg, Virginia, and taught later in preparatory schools in Princeton and New York. He was a member of the editorial staff of the New York *Commercial Advertiser* and also acted as literary adviser to several prominent publishing houses.

His first novel, *The Story of Don Miff*, told of the social order evolving from the post-war period. It had its setting at "Elmington," where later Thomas Dixon wrote several of his novels of Southern life. Dabney's story went through four editions in six months. His second novel, *Gold That Did Not Glitter*, was not as popular as its predecessor. (M.M.C.)

BOOKS: *The Story of Don Miff*, 1886; *Gold That Did Not Glitter*, 1889.

REFERENCES: *Dictionary of American Biography*, Vol. 5, 1930; Francis Coleman Rosenberger, *Virginia Reader*, 1948. See also Swem's *Virginia Historical Index*, Vol. 1, 1934.

DABNEY, VIRGINIUS (1901-   ) newspaper editor and non-fiction writer, was educated at home by an aunt and by his father, Dr. Richard Heath Dabney, a professor of history and Dean of the Graduate School of the University of Virginia. Significantly, this education, which lasted until he was thirteen, did not include instruction in either English grammar or Latin. Dr. Dabney believed that it was far more effective to learn languages by reading them than by learning laborious rules. His assumptions were correct, as his student learned English, French, German and Greek by this method. The fact that upon entering Episcopal High School he was placed in fourth-year English, thus skipping all the grammar courses, testifies to the success of his father's theory, as do the many honors (including the Pulitzer Prize) which have come to his son.

Of his career, Virginius Dabney writes: "After finishing my formal schooling, I taught French for a year at Episcopal High. While there I engaged in the task of trying to decide on my life's work, and Father asked

36   VIRGINIA AUTHORS

if I had ever considered journalism. I hadn't but the idea appealed to me. I got a job as a cub reporter in Richmond, and have been there ever since.

"A few years after joining the staff of the Richmond *News Leader* I began writing for magazines. In 1926, I sold an article on Virginia to the *American Mercury,* then in its heyday under the editorship of H. L. Mencken. Three years later, the University of North Carolina Press invited me to write a book on *Liberalism in the South.* It appeared in 1932.

"I then produced a biography of Bishop James Cannon, Jr., the premier politico-ecclesiastic in American history, but was unable to get it published then, as the Bishop was suing people right and left who were writing about him. The book, rewritten and expanded, appeared in 1949 after his death.

"Some lectures I gave at Princeton University in 1939-40 on the New South led Appleton-Century to ask me to write *Below the Potomac: A Book About the New South.* This was published in 1942."

BOOKS: *Liberalism in the South,* 1932; *Below the Potomac: A Book About the New South,* 1942; *Dry Messiah: The Life of Bishop Cannon,* 1949; Introduction to *The University of Virginia: Thirty-Two Wood Cuts* by Charles W. Smith, 1937; *Virginia: The New Dominion,* 1971.

REFERENCES: *Who's Who in the South and Southwest,* Vol. 3, 1956; *National Cyclopedia of American Biography,* 1952; *Current Biography Yearbook,* 1949; Kunitz and Haycraft, *Twentieth Century Authors, First Supplement,* 1955; J. Connors, "Vee Dabney Says," *Editors and Publishers,* July 20, 1957; *Saturday Review,* April 16, 1949; M. H. Carpenter, *Virginia Authors' Yearbook,* 1956, 1957, 1958.

DANIEL, JOHN WARWICK (1842-1910), political writer and orator, was born in Lynchburg. He was graduated with honors from the Lynchburg Military College and matriculated at the Locust Grove Academy in Albemarle County under the famous Latinist George Long. A hip wound received in the Battle of the Wilderness on May 5, 1864, gave him the sobriquet of the "lame lion of Lynchburg."

After studying law under John B. Minor at the University of Virginia, he became his father's law partner in 1866. He later served in the Virginia House of Delegates (1868-72), Senate (1874-81), U.S. House of Representatives (1885-87), and Senate (1886-1910). While his *Law of Attachments under the Code of Virginia* (1869) is primarily a compilation, it met a genuine need and has been consistently used as a standard authority in the Virginia courts. His masterful treatise on *Negotiable Instruments* (1876) was the result of eight years of work. (R.H.B.)

BOOKS: *Law of Attachments under the Code of Virginia,* 1869; *Negotiable Instruments,* 1876; *Speeches and Orations of John Warwick Daniel,* compiled under the direction of the Joint Committee on Printing, Washington, D. C., 1911.

REFERENCES: Manuscript Collection of Biographies of Lynchburg Writers at the Jones Memorial Library, Lynchburg, Virginia; *Memorial Addresses on the Life and Character of John Warwick Daniel,* compiled under the direction of the Joint Committee on Printing, Washington, D. C., 1911.

DAVIS, ARTHUR KYLE (1897-   ), ballad collector and professor emeritus of English at the University of Virginia, was born in Petersburg, Virginia, where his father was the president of Southern College for more than fifty years.

Dr. Davis has a diploma from Balliol College of Oxford University where he was a Rhodes scholar. He took his A.B., his M.A., and his Ph.D. degrees at the University of Virginia. He has been the archivist of the Virginia Folklore Society since 1924. (M.M.C.)

BOOKS: *Traditional Ballads of Virginia*, 1929; *Folk Songs of Virginia*, 1949; *More Traditional Ballads of Virginia*, 1960; *Matthew Arnold's Letters: A Descriptive Checklist*, 1968.

REFERENCES: *Who's Who in America*, Vol. 31, 1960-61; *Who's Who in the South and Southwest*, Vol. 3, 1956; Richmond *Times-Dispatch*, Dec. 25, 1949.

DAVIS, BURKE (1913-   ), novelist, journalist, historian and biographer, was born in Durham, North Carolina. He received his degree in journalism from the University of North Carolina in 1937 and subsequently worked as a reporter and as a public relations official for Colonial Williamsburg. Since 1960, however, writing has become his vocation. He considers *They Called Him Stonewall* (1954), a book published before he became a full-time writer, his favorite non-fictional production. The majority of his many titles have been historical, the most recent being *The Campaign That Won America: The Story of Yorktown* (1970). *They Called Him Stonewall; Gray Fox: Robert E. Lee and the Civil War* (1956); and *To Appomatox* (1959) all received the Most Distinguished Book of the Year award of the American Library Association.

BOOKS: *Yorktown*, 1952; *They Called Him Stonewall*, 1954; *Gray Fox: Robert E. Lee and the Civil War*, 1956; *Jeb Stuart: The Last Cavalier*, 1957; *To Appomattox*, 1959; *Our Incredible Civil War*, 1960; *The Cowpens-Guilford Courthouse Campaign*, 1962; *Marine!: The Life of Lt. Gen. Lewis B. (Chesty) Puller*, 1952; *Appomattox*, 1963; *The Summer Land*, 1965; *The Billy Mitchell Affair*, 1967; *A Williamsburg Galaxy*, 1968; *Get Yamamoto*, 1969; *The Billy Mitchell Story*, 1969.

REFERENCES: *Contemporary Authors*, 1; Richmond *Times-Dispatch*, April 5, 1970.

DAVIS, DANIEL WEBSTER (1862-1913), poet and historian, a native of North Carolina, moved with his parents to Richmond after the Civil War. There he was graduated from high school with honors in 1878. Two years later he became a teacher in a Richmond school and remained in the teaching profession until 1885, when he became a preacher. He wrote two books of verse as well as some prose. His best known book is *Weh Down Souf*, which mainly follows the plantation tradition. (C.H.H.)

BOOKS: *Idle Moments*, 1895; *Weh Down Souf, and Other Poems*, 1897; (co author) *The Industrial History of the Negro Race of the United States*, 1908.

REFERENCES: James Weldon Johnson, *The Book of American Negro Poetry*, 1922, 31, and 59.

DAVIS, JOHN (1774-1854), bookseller, traveler, and novelist, was born in England but spoke of the United States as the country of his literary birth. Material for his novels was collected on a walking trip through fifteen states during a period of four and one-half years. Davis, a romantic observer of American life, said that he "entered with equal interest, the mud-hut of the Negro and the log-house of the planter." His novel *The First Settlers of Virginia* (1805) includes the first fictional treatment of Pocahontas. In 1817 he republished the Pocahontas story separately. Most of his American books went through more than one edition. (M.M.C.)

BOOKS: *The Farmer of New Jersey*, 1800; *The Wanderings of William*, 1801; *The Post Captain* (4th ed.), London, 1805; *The First Settlers of Virginia*, 1805; *Walter Kennedy*, 1808; *Travels of Four Years and a Half in the United States*, 1802; *Captain Smith and Princess Pocahontas: An Indian Tale*, 1817.

REFERENCES: James D. Hart, *The Oxford Companion to American Literature*, 1965; Max J. Herzberg, *The Reader's Encyclopedia of American Literature*, 1962; Thelma Kellogg, *The Life and Works of John Davis*, 1924.

DAVIS, PAXTON (1925-   ), writer of novellas, writes: "I was born in North Carolina in 1925, attended public schools in Winston-Salem, spent a year at the Virginia Military Institute. I served three years in the Army in World War II, after which I was graduated in 1949 from The Johns Hopkins University, and worked for four years as a newspaper reporter in North Carolina and Virginia. Since 1953 I have been a member of the faculty of Washington and Lee University, Lexington, where I am Associate Professor of journalism."

Mr. Davis recalls that he was very slow to begin writing, but that in the summer of 1954, "I sat down and at last got started. The story came out of my two years as a medical sergeant in the China-Burma-India Theatre in World War II. . . ." The next summer he did a second novella-length story which was published with the first as *Two Soldiers* (1956).

He summarizes his attitude toward his writing as follows: "All I can say is that I write because I enjoy doing it—I enjoy doing it daily—and I can't imagine doing anything else. . . ."

BOOKS: *Two Soldiers*, 1956; *The Battle of New Market*, 1963; *One of the Dark Places*, 1965; *The Season of Heroes*, 1967.

DENNIS, WESLEY (1903-   ), writer and illustrator of juvenile fiction, came to the horse country near Warrenton, Virginia, to paint some of the horses of Walter Chrysler and decided he wanted to stay. He found a place to his liking, and there he lives today with his family, surrounded by his farm on which he has many kinds of animals, chiefly horses.

His desire to become an artist was as great as his love for horses, and he studied in Boston and in Paris, and then did some advertising art.

His first book was written soon after his marriage. While he and his wife were in Santa Fe, they met the juvenile editor of Viking Press. On their return to New York, he called on the editor to see if she had a book for him to illustrate. The editor suggested that he write a book and illustrate it. *Flip* was the book he wrote. It was immediately successful and was followed by other books about the entrancing pony.

Flip also led to the happy collaboration of Wesley Dennis and Marguerite Henry. Dissatisfied with the artist her publisher had chosen to illustrate *Justin Morgan Had a Horse*, she cast about for one of her own choosing. When she came upon *Flip*, she was delighted with what she called that artist's ability to see "beyond hide and hair and bone." There was no doubt that he loved the animals he drew and that he could give them personality. He illustrated the book, and since then they have collaborated successfully on several other books.

In all, Dennis has written or illustrated more than ninety books. (M.M.C.)

BOOKS: *Flip*, 1941; *Flip and the Cows*, 1942; *Flip and the Morning*, 1951; ed. and illustrator, *Palomino and Other Horses*, 1950; *Portfolio of Horses*, 1952; *Portfolio of Horse Paintings*, 1964; *Tumble: the Story of a Mustang*, 1966.

REFERENCES: Falmouth *Enterprise*, Aug. 17, 1956; *Sunday Star Magazine*, Wash., D. C., Jan. 11, 1959; Margaret H. Carpenter, *Virginia Authors' Yearbook*, 1957, 1958.

DILLON, GEORGE (1906-1968), poet, was born in Florida, moved about frequently as a youth, and was thus given the impetus to begin writing. Upon entering the University of Chicago (1923), he found companionship among other students with similar inclinations. The group gave readings and with the proceeds started *The Forge*, a literary magazine. He soon became associate editor of *Poetry* and published his first collection, *Boy in the Wind*, in 1927. With the aid of a Guggenheim Fellowship, he travelled widely in Europe and North Africa, but spent much time in Paris, gaining the mastery of French which would produce *Flowers of Evil* (1936), translations of Baudelaire. He served as editor of *Poetry* from 1937 to 1949. He thereafter lived in Richmond.

BOOKS: *Boy in the Wind*, 1927; *The Flowering Stone*, 1931; with Edna St. Vincent Millay, *Flowers of Evil* (translations from the French, with original texts of Charles Baudelaire, and preface by Edna St. Vincent Millay), 1936; trans., Racine, *Three Plays: Andromache, Britannicus, Phaedra*, 1961.

REFERENCES: *Who's Who in America*, Vol. 31, 1960-61; Kunitz and Haycraft, *Twentieth Century Authors*, 1942; Alfred Kreymborg, *Our Singing Strength*, 1929; Louis Untermeyer, ed., *Modern American Poetry*, 1930;

Nation, Feb. 10, 1932; *Poetry,* March, 1932, and Sept., 1935; *Virginia: A Guide to the Old Dominion,* 1942.

DODD, WILLIAM EDWARD (1869-1940), American historian, university professor, and United States Ambassador to Germany during the years of Hitler's rule (1933-38), was the author of distinguished biographies of President Wilson, Nathaniel Macon, and Jefferson Davis and wrote other equally distinguished books and articles.

He was born near Clayton, North Carolina, but later made his home in Round Hill, Virginia. He was a professor of history at Randolph-Macon College and the University of Chicago. After his death his papers from 1900 to 1940 were given to the Manuscript Division of the Library of Congress. (M.M.C.)

BOOKS: *Jefferson's Rückkehr zur Politik,* 1796, 1899; *Life of Nathaniel Macon,* 1903; *Life of Jefferson Davis,* 1907; *Statesmen of the Old South,* 1911; *Expansion and Conflict,* 1915; *The Cotton Kingdom,* 1919; *Woodrow Wilson and His Work,* 1920; ed., with Ray Stannard Baker, *The Public Papers of Woodrow Wilson,* 1925-27; *Lincoln or Lee,* 1928; *The Old South Struggles for Democracy,* 1937; *Ambassador Dodd's Dairy,* 1941.

REFERENCES: *North Carolina Authors: A Selective Handbook,* 1952; *Who's Who in America,* Vol. 20, 1938-39; Wendell Holmes Stephenson, *The South Lives in History,* 1955. See also Swem's *Virginia Historical Index,* Vol. 1, 1934.

DOS PASSOS, JOHN (1896-1970), poet and writer of both fiction and non-fiction, writes: "The fact that I'm an inhabitant of the Northern Neck is due to a series of incidents quite out of my control. My father, who was the self-made son of a Portuguese immigrant, had a love—perhaps inherited from his forebears—of the sea and sailing. He took a fancy to the sandy shores of the Chesapeake. He may have also inherited a taste for farming the land. Though he was a corporation lawyer born in Philadelphia, and in the latter part of his life practiced in New York and Washington, he long cherished the hope of retiring to the farm at the mouth of the Potomac where I now reside. He was a man of letters and had given himself a profound education in the classics in the old eighteenth century manner.

"As a child I probably picked up the habit of writing from him. Though he approved of my juvenile efforts, he used to tell me that if I was planning a career of authorship, I should take up some lucrative profession like the law to make a living by. It's taken me a good many painful years to discover how right he was. Of course at that time it never occurred to me that I was taking up a career as a writer. Each book was something I had to get off my chest before I could turn to the real business of life. Now at sixty it may be too late. Meanwhile, having spent most of my life away from them, I find myself taking some of the same pleasure that I took as a child in the pines and the beaches and the broad brackish waters of the tidewater country."

Mr. Dos Passos is a recognized authority on Jefferson. His historical work, *The Head and Heart of Thomas Jefferson,* was published in 1954. William Faulkner has ranked Mr. Dos Passos as the third greatest American author. French author and philosopher Jean Paul Sartre cited him as "the greatest living author." In 1957 Mr. Dos Passos was awarded the Gold Medal for Fiction of the National Institute of Arts and Letters. His books have generally gone through several editions, and many of them have been printed in foreign languages.

BOOKS: *One Man's Initiation,* 1917; *Three Soldiers,* 1921; *A Pushcart at the Curb,* 1922; *Rosinante to the Road Again,* 1922; *Streets of the Night,* 1923; *Manhattan Transfer,* 1925; *Orient Express,* 1927; *Three Plays,* 1934; *The 42nd Parallel, Nineteen Nineteen, The Big Money* were collected as *U. S. A.,* 1938; *In All Countries,* 1934; *Journey Between Wars,* 1938; *Adventures of a Young Man,* 1939; *The Living Thoughts of Tom Paine,* 1940; *Number One,* 1943; *The Grand Design,* 1949; *The Ground We Stand On,* 1941; *State of the Nation,* 1944; *First Encounter,* 1945; *Tour of Duty,* 1946; *The Prospect Before Us,* 1950; *Chosen Country,* 1951; *District of Columbia,* 1952; *Most Likely to Succeed,* 1945; *The Head and Heart of Thomas Jefferson,* 1954; *The Theme Is Freedom,* 1956; *The Men Who Made the Nation,* 1957; *The Great Days,* 1958; *Prospects of a Golden Age,* 1959.

REFERENCES: Geo. Dixon Snell, *Shapers of American Fiction, 1798-1947,* 1947; Robert Van Gelder, *Writers and Writing,* 1946; W. Taskee Witham, *Panorama of American Literature,* 1947; Frank N. Magill, ed., *Cyclopedia of World Authors,* 1958; Sinclair Lewis, *John Dos Passos' Manhattan Transfer,* 1926; John Chamberlain, *John Dos Passos: a Biographical and Critical Essay,* 1939; Max Eastman and others, *John Dos Passos: An Appreciation,* 1954. See also Robert E. Spiller, *et. al. Literary History of the United States,* 1965 (bibliography).

DOWDEY, CLIFFORD (1904-   ), writer of non-fiction and historical novels, states: "To begin at the beginning, I was born in Richmond in 1904 of very mixed heritage: one side was Galway County Spanish-Irish, and my name is Anglicized from Dowda; the other side was a direct line from the Blounts, who came to Jamestown in 1609, and were planters, first in Surry and then Chesterfield, until the Civil War, to which four of my grandmother's brothers went—one all the way to Appomattox. Since my grandmother remembered the war vividly, and lived in our house until her death when I was nineteen, my first impressions were of the Confederacy. I was eight years old before I realized we had lost, and I've been trying to recapture the first illusion ever since.

After attending Columbia University, he served as a reporter on the Richmond *News Leader* and reviewed books there under Dr. Freeman's (*q.v.*) tutelage. He then returned to New York, worked on the editorial staffs of various magazines, and wrote in his spare time. His first novel, *Bugles Blow No More,* started him on his career as a professional writer. He has since written for many magazines and done histories of various areas of Virginia's past, e.g. the Civil War in *Death of A Nation* (1958) and the eighteenth century in *The Golden* Age (1970).

BOOKS: *Bugles Blow No More*, 1937; *Gamble's Hundred*, 1939; *Sing for a Penny*, 1941; *Tidewater*, 1943; *Where My Love Sleeps*, 1945; *Experiment in Rebellion*, 1946; *Weep for My Brother*, 1950; *Jasmine Street*, 1952; *The Proud Retreat*, 1953; *The Land They Fought For*, 1955; *The Great Plantation*, 1957; *Death of a Nation*, 1958; *Lee's Last Campaign*, 1960; ed., *The Wartime Papers of Robert E. Lee*, 1961; *Last Night the Nightingale*, 1962; *The Seven Days: The Emergence of Lee*, 1964; *Lee*, 1965; *The Virginia Dynasties*, 1969; *The Golden Age*, 1970.

REFERENCES: H. R. Warfel, *American Novelists of Today*, 1951; Margaret H. Carpenter, *Virginia Authors' Yearbook*, 1956, 1957, 1958; *Contemporary Authors*, 11-12; *Who's Who in America; Who's Who in the South and Southwest;* Richmond *Times-Dispatch*, June 8, 1969. See also Swem's *Virginia Historical Index*, Vol. 1, 1934.

DREWRY, CARLETON (1901-   ), poet, was born in Culpepper County. After being educated in rural elementary schools (his only formal education), he went to work at seventeen, and published his first poem in the *Dial* four years later. He soon began to contribute work to *The Nation* and *The New Republic* and has since contributed to many of the nation's prestigious magazines. His collection *A Time for Turning* (1951) received the Poetry Awards prize for the best book of poetry of the year.

He has been poet in residence at Hollins, edited *The Lyric* (1929-49), and served as President of the Poetry Society of Virginia (1952-55).

BOOKS: *Proud Horne*, 1933; *The Sounding Summer*, 1948; *A Time of Turning*, 1951; *The Writhen Wood*, 1953; *Cloud Above Clocktime*, 1957.

REFERENCES: *Who's Who in America*, Vol. 31, 1960-61; *Who's Who in the South and Southwest*, Vol. 3, 1956; F. C. Rosenberger, *Virginia Reader*, 1948; Margaret H. Carpenter, *Virginia Authors' Yearbook*, 1956, 1957, 1958; Richmond *Times-Dispatch*, July 10, 1949.

EARLY, GEN. JUBAL ANDERSON (1816-1894), diarist, was born in Franklin County, Virginia. He was graduated from the United States Military Academy in 1837. The next year, when a lieutenant of artillery, he resigned from the army and returned to Franklin County to practice law. He was a member of the House of Delegates in 1841-42 and Commonwealth's Attorney of Franklin County from 1842 to 1852, except the period 1847-48, when he served in the Mexican War as Major of Volunteers. In the Confederate Army he was successively a colonel, brigadier-general, major general, and lieutenant-general. After the Civil War he made his home in Lynchburg.

He wrote a memoir of the last year of the war and two other books, both of which had lain in manuscript form for nearly fifty years before being edited and published by his niece, Miss Ruth Hairston Early *(q.v.)*. They are his autobiography and a book about slavery. (R.H.B.)

BOOKS: *A memoir of the Last Year of the War of Independence, in the Confederate States of America,* 1866; *Lieutenant General Jubal Anderson Early, C. S. A.: An Autobiographical Sketch and Narrative of the War between the States,* with notes by Ruth H. Early, 1912; *The Heritage of the South,* 1915.

REFERENCES: Manuscript Collection of Biographies of Lynchburg Writers at the Jones Memorial Library, Lynchburg, Virginia; M. K. Bushong, *Old Jube: A Biography of Jubal Early,* 1955. See also Swem's *Virginia Historical Index,* Vol. 1, 1934.

EARLY, RUTH HAIRSTON, (1849-1928), historical writer, was born in Charleston, West Virginia; but her parents moved to Lynchburg, Virginia, when she was a small child, and here she passed the remainder of her life. She was educated at Mrs. Brown's School in Lynchburg and finished at Patapsco Institute, Ellicott City, Maryland.

A niece of Confederate General Jubal A. Early *(q.v.),* she edited his war manuscripts and his book work on slavery, *The Heritage of the South.* Her abiding interest in the history of her own state was further reflected in her *By-ways of Virginia History,* which contained much valuable information crowded out of other writings. She spent many years working on a genealogical history of her family, *The Family of Early.* Her best work is considered to be *Campbell Chronicles and Family Sketches,* which appeared in her seventy-eighth year, just before her death. Her active participation in many civic and historical societies was well known, as was her association with the Swedenborgian Church, which was introduced into Virginia by her grandfather, Dr. John Jordan Cabell.

BOOKS: *By-ways of Virginia History,* 1907; *Campbell Chronicles and Family Sketches,* 1927; ed., *Lieutenant General Jubal Anderson Early, C.S.A.,* 1912; ed., *The Heritage of the South,* 1915.

REFERENCES: Manuscript Collection of Biographies of Lynchburg Writers at the Jones Memorial Library, Lynchburg, Virginia. See also Swem's *Virginia Historical Index,* Vol. 1, 1934.

EASTMAN, MARY HENDERSON ["MATILDA"] (1818-1880), romancer and short story and non-fiction writer, was born in Warrenton, Virginia. She was one of several Virginians of her time to live on the frontier in close contact with the Indians (her husband, Col. Seth Eastman, was stationed there). These experiences furnished her with background for a number of books on the American Indian which her husband illustrated (e.g. *Dahcotah* (1849) and *Romance of Indian Life* (1852)). She is perhaps best remembered, however, for *Aunt Phillis's Cabin: Or, Southern Life As It Is* (1852), one of several Southern replies to Harriet Beecher Stowe's *Uncle Tom's Cabin* (1851-52).

BOOKS: *Dahcotah: Or, Life and Legends of the Sioux Around Fort*

Snelling, 1849; *Aunt Phillis's Cabin: Or, Southern Life as it Is*, 1852; *The American Aboriginal Portfolio*, 1853; *Chicóra and Other Regions of the Conquers and the Conquered*, 1854; *The American Annual: Illustrative of the Early History of North America*, 1855; *Fashionable Life*, 1856; *Jenny Wade of Gettysburg*, 1864; *Easter Eyes*, 1879.

REFERENCES: Robert E. Spiller, *et. al., Literary History of the United States*, Vol. 1, 1960; *Library of Southern Literature*, Vol. 15.

ECKENRODE, HAMILTON JAMES (1881-1952), biographer, historian and fiction writer, was Virginia State Archivist (1907-14) and Historian of Virginia (1914-19). In the years 1920-30 he was the editor of *Southern Historical Papers*, Volumes 43-47. For a brief period (1914-16) he was Professor of Economics at the University of Richmond.

One of his articles points out the influence Sir Walter Scott's novels had on the Southern way of life between 1815 and 1860. In *Told in Story,* he takes excerpts from historical novels and uses them to tell the story of our country from its first settlement to the end of the Revolution. His novel *Bottom Rail on Top* is a portrayal of life in the South just before and immediately after the Civil War.

Dr. Eckenrode was born in Fredericksburg, Virginia. His parents were John and Mary Elizabeth (Myer) Hamilton Eckenrode. In 1905 he received his Ph.D. from Johns Hopkins University. (M.M.C.)

BOOKS: *The Political History of Virginia During the Reconstruction,* 1904; *The Revolution in Virginia*, 1916; *Life of Nathan B. Forest*, 1918; *Told in Story: American History*, 1922; *Jefferson Davis: President of the South*, 1923; *Rutherford B. Hayes: Statesman of Reunion*, 1930; *E. H. Harriman: the Little Giant of Wall Street* (with Pocahontas Wight Edmunds), 1933; *Bottom Rail on Top*, 1935; *James Longstreet: Lee's War Horse* (with Bryan Conrad), 1936; *George B. McClellan: the Man Who Saved the Union* (with Bryan Conrad), 1941; *This Government* (with De Witt S. Morgan and John J. Corson), 1938; *The Randolphs: the Story of a Virginia Family*, 1946.

REFERENCES: *Who's Who in America*, Vol. 26, 1950-51; Richmond *Times-Dispatch*, Oct. 2, 1949. See also Swem's *Virginia Historical Index*, Vol. 1, 1934.

EDMUNDS, CRADDOCK (1899-1959), poet, writes: "I was born at Halifax, Virginia, August 5, 1899; but grew up in Lynchburg. I received an A.B. degree from Randolph-Macon College, which, in 1956, elected me an honorary member of Phi Beta Kappa. I received an A.M. degree from the University of Virginia.

"I have devoted most of my serious effort to poetry and am the author of eleven books. All of the work that I care to save, with the exception of the revised, but yet unpublished *Five Men*, has been carefully worked over and included in *Thirty-Five Poems*, 1951; *The Renaissance*, 1954; *Thirty-Four New Poems*, 1956; and *Framed by a Cabin Window*, 1959.

"In addition to several feature articles, my work has been reviewed in the New York *Times*, The New York *Herald-Tribune*, *The Saturday Review of Literature*, *The Nation* and other leading papers and periodicals. Recently a special Craddock Edmunds Collection was started in the Rare Books and Manuscript Department of the Alderman Library at the University of Virginia."

Mr. Edmunds revised his autobiography in the summer of 1959. On November 4, 1959, he died. The cabin in the woods, which he built, and in which he lived for twenty years, will be maintained as a shrine. (M.M.C.)

BOOKS: *Ulysses: And Other Poems*, 1923; *Mass, and Other Poems*, 1927; *Geese Are Swan*, 1929; *Poems*, 1931; *The Renaissance*, 1932, 1933.

REFERENCES: Richmond *Times-Dispatch*, Sept. 4, 1949; Washington *Evening Star*, March 18, 1956; Charlottesville *Daily Progress*, Nov. 12, 1959; F. C. Rosenberger, *Virginia Reader*, 1948; Margaret H. Carpenter, Virginia *Authors' Yearbook*, 1956, 1957.

EDMUNDS, MURRELL (1898-   ), writer of short stories, novels, and verse, was born at Halifax, Virginia, on March 23, 1898, of a family which has long lived in Virginia. He grew up in Lynchburg, went to public school there and was graduated from high school as valedictorian of his class. He continued his education in the College and the Law School of the University of Virginia. Following his graduation, he was for a brief time a teacher of English and head coach of basketball at the Episcopal High School in Alexandria. In 1922 he began the practice of law in Lynchburg and at the same time became Assistant Commonwealth's Attorney for Campbell County. He found the law profitable, but uncongenial, however, and abandoned it for writing. He now lives in New Orleans and devotes most of his time to writing.

He has contributed many stories and poems to magazines, and his work has appeared in such anthologies as *The Virginia Reader, Lyric Virginia Today*, Vol. II, and *Anthology of Best Magazine Verse*. Several of his short stories have been on the Honor Roll of the American Short Story, and in the yearly anthologies. His later work shows an increasing concern with the theme of freedom and human brotherhood in the South.

BOOKS: *The Music Makers*, 1927; *Earthenware*, 1930; *Sojourn Among Shadows*, 1936; *Between the Devil*, 1939; *Red, White, and Black: Twelve Stories of the South*, 1945; *Time's Laughter in Their Ears*, 1946; *Behold, Thy Brother*, 1950; *Moon of My Delight*, 1960; *An Old Fashioned Garden*, 1961; *They Don't Cost You a Thin Dime: Or, Songs for Nothing*, 1961; *Passionate Journey to Winter*, 1962; *Laurel for the Un-Defeated*, 1964; *Beautiful Upon the Mountains*, 1966; *Shadow of a Great Rock*, 1969; *Dim Footprints Along A Hazardous Trail*, 1971.

REFERENCES: F. C. Rosenberger, *Virginia Reader*, 1948; Margaret H. Carpenter, *Virginia Authors' Yearbook*, 1956, 1957; Richmond *Times-Dispatch*, July 17, 1949.

EDMUNDS, POCAHONTAS WIGHT (1904-   ), biographer, short

46 VIRGINIA AUTHORS

story writer, and poet, writes: "I was born on November 8, 1904, in Richmond, Virginia, the daughter of Pocahontas Gay Wilson and Richard Cunningham Wight, Sr. My mother was named for her grandmother, Pocahontas Ferguson, whose parents were first cousins and both descendants of Pocahontas."

While attending St. Catherine's School in Richmond, she was inspired by the noted educator "Miss Jennie" Ellet and went on to a Bachelor's degree at Agnes Scott College, where she acquired methods of research and organization which later stood her in good stead in historical writing.

Her first article was "French and American Audiences—A Comparison," written while she was studying violin in Paris in 1926. She later collaborated with H. J. Eckenrode on biographies of Rutherford B. Hayes and E. H. Harriman. Since 1925 she has spent an average of four hours per day in research and writing, as well as many hours lecturing for schools, clubs, and historical associations.

BOOKS: *Rutherford B. Hayes: Statesman of Reunion*, with H. J. Eckenrode, 1930; *E. H. Harriman: Little Giant of Wall Street*, with Eckenrode, 1933; *Land of Sand—Legends of the North Carolina Coast*, 1941; *Tales of the Virginia Coast*, 1950; *Pocahontas-John Smith Story*, 1956; *Tar Heels Track the Century*, 1966.

REFERENCES: *Who's Who Among American Women Since 1935*; Stratford Company's *Poets of the Future*, 1925; *Who's Who Among North American Writers*, 1921-1940; Margaret H. Carpenter, *Virginia Authors' Yearbook*, 1958.

EGGLESTON, GEORGE CARY (1839-1911), editor and writer of fiction and non-fiction, began teaching at sixteen. His experiences were used in *The Hoosier Schoolmaster*, written by his older brother Edward.

Both Edward and George Cary were partially educated in Virginia, the latter at Richmond College. Access to some of the private libraries in rural Virginia gave George the opportunity to verse himself in the classics. *The First of the Hoosiers* gives a picture of the plantation library in the 50's.

When the Civil War brook out he left his law practice in Virginia to join the Confederate forces. In 1868 he married Marian Craggs. After the war he served for six years as literary editor of the New York *Evening Post*. Later he was editor-in-chief of *Hearth and Home*, a magazine of which his brother had been editor in the 70's. He was also editor of the *Commercial Advertiser*, and editorial writer of the *World*. (M.M.C.)

BOOKS: *The First of the Hoosiers*, 1903; *A Rebel's Recollections*, 1875; *Two Gentlemen of Virginia*, 1908; *A Man of Honour*, 1873; *Dorothy South*, 1902; *The Master of Warlock*, 1903; *Evelyn Byrd*, 1904.

REFERENCES: *Who Was Who in America*, Vol., 1, 1942; *Who's Who in America*, Vol. 6, 1910-11; *Dictionary of American Biography*, Vol. 6, 1931; *Library of Southern Literature*, Vol. 4.

FARRAR, ROWENA RUTHERFORD (1903-   ), novelist, short story writer, and biographer, writes: "My work began with short stories, articles and book reviews. My first historical novel, *Bend Your Heads All,* the story of the founding of my native city, Nashville, Tennessee, was published by Holt, Rinehart & Winston in 1965. My second, *A Wondrous Moment Then,* the story of the last dramatic chapter of the Woman's Suffrage Movement, followed in 1968. I am currently at work on a biography of the late Grace Moore, dynamic prima donna of the Metropolitan Opera Company."

BOOKS: *Bend Your Heads All,* 1965; *A Wondrous Moment Then,* 1968.
REFERENCES: *Who's Who of American Women,* 1970-71.

FAULKNER, NANCY (1906-   ), novelist, writes: "I was born in Lynchburg, Virginia, on January 8, 1906, and went to school there until I finished high school. Then, two years at the Baldwin School, Bryn Mawr, Pennsylvania, were followed by four years at Wellesley College where I took my B.A. in 1928. Later I went to Cornell University for graduate work in medieval and modern history and collected an M.A. The M.A. has gathered dust in a large way, but the research techniques I managed to acquire along the way have stood me in very good stead."

Though a voracious reader at an early age (with inspirations from the King James Bible, Scott, Dickens, and Thackeray), she held a variety of non-literary jobs between her college years and the publication of *Rebel Drums* (1952), the event which caused her to think of herself as a professional writer. Since then she has written numerous juvenile books—"junior historical novels," as she calls them—five of which have been set in Revolutionary Virginia. Three of her books—*Side Saddle for Dandy, Pirate Quest,* and *Undecided Heart*—have been Junior Literary Guild selections.

BOOKS: *Rebel Drums,* 1952; *The West Is on Your Left Hand,* 1953; *Side Saddle for Dandy,* 1954; *Pirate Quest,* 1955; *Undecided Heart,* 1957; *Sword of the Winds,* 1957; *The Yellow Hat,* 1958; *Daughter of the Narragansetts,* 1959; *Tomahawk Shadow,* 1959; *Mystery at Long Barrow House,* 1960; *Small Clown,* 1960; *A Stage for Rom,* 1962; *The Traitor Queen,* 1963; *Knights Besieged,* 1964; *The Secret of the Simple Code,* 1965; *Journey into Danger,* 1966; *The Limping Stranger,* 1967; *Small Clown and Tiger,* 1968; *Second Son,* 1970; *Great Reckoning,* 1970.

REFERENCES: *Current Biography,* 1956; Margaret H. Carpenter, *Virginia Authors' Yearbook,* 1956, 1957, 1958; *Contemporary Authors,* 4.

FISHWICK, MARSHALL W. (1923-   ), non-fiction writer and novelist, was born in Roanoke. He was educated in public schools in his native city and later at the University of Virginia, the University of Wisconsin (M.A.), and Yale (Ph.D.).

His first two publications were collections of poetry; he then began a career of writing on American culture—particular Southern—for which he has become well known. Among his most famous works in this genre are *Virginians on Olympus* (1950) and *American Heroes: Myth and Reality* (1954). In addition, he taught for many years at Washington and Lee University and served as faculty editor of *Shenandoah*, the University's literary magazine. He is currently affiliated with the Weymss Foundation of Wilmington, Delaware.

BOOKS: *The Face of Jang*, 1945; *Isle of Shoals*, 1946; *Virginians on Olympus*, 1950; *General Lee's Photographer* (the life and work of Michael Miley), 1954; *The Virginia Tradition*, 1955; *American Heroes: Myth and Reality*, 1954; *Virginia: A New Look at the Old Dominion*, 1959; *Lee After the War*, 1963; *Faust Revisited*, 1963; *Great Silver Crowns*, 1963; *Jamestown: First English Colony*, 1965; *Illustrious Americans: Clara Barton*, 1966; *Jane Addams*, 1968; *The Hero, American Style*, 1969.

REFERENCES: *Who's Who in the South and Southwest*, Vol. 6, 1959; Margaret H. Carpenter, *Virginia Authors' Yearbook*, 1956, 1957, 1958.

FITHIAN, PHILIP VICKERS (1747-1776), diarist, a native of New Jersey and a graduate of Princeton, became a tutor to the children of Robert Carter of "Nomini Hall" in Westmoreland County, Virginia, in 1773. The journal he kept during his year as tutor, and the letters he wrote, give an interesting first-hand account of plantation life just before the Revolution. Included in his account is a catalogue of Robert Carter's large library.

After he returned to New Jersey, he was licensed as a Presbyterian minister. Then followed a year in which he made two mission tours in Virginia and recounted his experiences in his journal. His marriage to Elizabeth Beatty took place the same year.

In 1776 he enlisted as a chaplain in the New Jersey militia and served in several battles with George Washington. He died in camp on October 8, 1776.

Three volumes of Fithian's writings have been published. The one most useful to Virginians is the third volume, in which the emphasis is placed on Virginia material. (M.M.C.)

BOOKS: *Philip Vickers Fithian: Journal and Letters, 1767-1774*, ed. by John Roger Williams, 1900, Princeton Historical Society; *Philip Vickers Fithian: Journal, 1775-1776, Written on the Pennsylvania Frontier and in the Army around New York*, edited by Robert Greenhalgh Albion and Leonides Dodson, 1934; *Journal and Letters of Philip Vickers Fithian, 1773-1774: A Plantation Tutor of the Old Dominion*, edited by Hunter Dickenson Farish, 1943.

REFERENCES: J. B. Hubbell, *The South in American Literature 1607-1900* (bibliography), 1954; Francis Coleman Rosenberger, *Virginia Reader*, 1948; *Philip Vickers Fithian, Journal and Letters, 1900*; Louis D. Rubin, Jr., ed., *A Bibliographical Guide to the Study of Southern Literature*, 1969. See also Swem's *Virginia Historical Index*, Vol. 1, 1934.

FLETCHER, LUCILLE (1912-   ), playwright and novelist, was born in

Brooklyn, New York and was graduated from Vassar College. In 1949 she married Douglass Wallop and in 1950 moved to Arlington, Virginia, where she keeps house and writes in her spare time.

Miss Fletcher is the author of numerous radio and television plays, most notably *Sorry, Wrong Number*, which she adapted into a motion picture for Hall Wallis Productions in 1948. Burt Lancaster and Barbara Stanwyck were the stars of the production. Miss Fletcher has also written two novels. In addition, *Sorry, Wrong Number* was novelized in 1948 and *Night Man* in 1951, both by Allan Ullman. (M.M.C.)

BOOKS: *Sorry, Wrong Number* and *The Hitch-Hiker (plays in one act)*, 1952; *The Daughters of Jasper Clay*, 1958; *Blindfold*, 1960; *And Presumed Dead*, 1963; *The Strange Blue Yawl*, 1964; *The Girl in Cabin B 54*, 1968.

REFERENCES: Washington *Post* and *Times Herald*, June 19, 1955; M. Dolbier, "Right Number," New York *Herald Tribune*, Mar. 9, 1958; *Contemporary Authors*, 13-14.

FLOURNOY, MARY H. BOYD (1872-1970), essayist, was born in Charlotte County, Virginia. She was graduated from the State Normal School of Virginia (now Longwood College) and, after teaching for several years, married the Reverend William Cabell Flournoy.

Mrs. Flournoy made Southern history her interest, all three of her books dealing with personalities and phases of the South. She was also widely known as a speaker and lecturer, and for other literary activities throughout Virginia.

BOOKS: *Twin Patriots: Washington and Lee*, 1929; *Side Lights on Southern History*, 1939; *Essays on American History*, 1949.

REFERENCES: Margaret H. Carpenter, *Virginia Authors' Yearbook*, 1957, 1958.

FLOYD, NICHOLAS JACKSON (1828-1919), novelist and biographer, was born at Brookfield, Campbell County, near Lynchburg. He was a member of the pioneer Floyd family of Virginia and Kentucky which gave Virginia two governors and the United States a Secretary of War, several Congressmen, and a galaxy of capable military officers.

Captain Floyd obtained a liberal education in the local schools, the Abingdon, Virginia, Academy, and Emory and Henry College. Upon completion of his education he joined the "gold rush" and became one of the forty-niners. Along with one of his brothers he succeeded as a gold miner, but owing to ill health had to leave California after about a year's residence.

When physically able, he took over one of his father's cotton plantations near Athens, Alabama, and edited a local newspaper until the outbreak of the Civil War, in which he was to rise to a captaincy.

Though his first novel, *Thorns in the Flesh* (1884), was an overwhelming success, he refused to allow a much-demanded second edition because some of his friends had objected to the book's portrayal of a Southern gentleman employing a mulatto housekeeper. He did, however, publish another story of antebellum life: "The Last Cavalier." His *Biographical Genealogies of the Virginia-Kentucky Floyd Families* is much respected by genealogists. He spent his last years in Baltimore, where he died in 1919. (M.M.C.)

BOOKS: *Thorns in the Flesh*, 1884; *Biographical Genealogies of the Virginia-Kentucky Floyd Families*, 1912.

REFERENCES: Manuscript Collection of Biographies of Lynchburg Writers, Jones Memorial Library, Lynchburg, Virginia.

FONTAINE, JOHN (1693-17?), diarist, after serving in Spain as an ensign of the British army, came to Virginia in 1714 when he was twenty-one. He is best known for his journal, which recounts the events of his trip of exploration in 1716 to the Shenandoah Valley with Governor Alexander Spottswood. This account has furnished material for later writers, among whom was William Alexander Caruthers (*q.v.*), who used it in *The Knights of the Horse-Shoe: A Traditionary Tale of the Cocked Hat Gentry in the Old Dominion*.

The "Journal" is only a part of the book named below. (M.M.C.)

BOOK: *Memoirs of a Huguenot Family: Translated and Compiled from the Original Autobiography of the Rev. James Fontaine*, 1852.

REFERENCES: Francis Coleman Rosenberger, *Virginia Reader*, 1948. See also Swem's *Virginia Historical Index*, Vol. 1, 1934.

FOX, JOHN [WILLIAM], JR. (1863-1919), short story writer and novelist, was born in Paris, Kentucky. As a youth he was trained under the tutelage of James Lane Allen. Later he studied at Transylvania University and at Harvard, where he was prominent in female dramatic roles and a member of the glee club.

After 1887 Fox settled at Big Stone Gap, Virginia, establishing himself in the mining business. Through his work of visiting the mines he became interested in the life of the mountaineers. In the early nineties he began writing stories of the mountain people, his first being "A Mountain Europa." This initial effort furnished the title for his first book (1894). In rapid succession appeared two more volumes, *A Cumberland Vendetta* and *Hell-Fer-Sartain*. The latter work described a locality high among the Cumberlands where there were fights, murders, moonshining, lovemaking, and revivals. The title story, which made his reputation, he sold for six dollars. This story contained the germ of much that he wrote later in his novels, and its motif of passion and courage runs through much of his work.

The Little Shepard of Kingdom Come, the most widely known of Fox's books, appeared in 1903. This is a romance of the Civil War. The scene is laid in the mountains of eastern Kentucky, in the Bluegrass region of the Piedmont and Lowland—the debatable land of the war. In the book Fox traces the social development of a nation from its birth in a log cabin to its highest point of culture.

The Trail of the Lonesome Pine, published in 1908, was highly successful. Subsequently it was dramatized and made into a motion picture. Many of Fox's novels went through several editions. (C.H.H.)

BOOKS: *A Cumberland Vendetta, and Other Stories,* 1896; *Hell Fer Sartain, and Other Stories,* 1897; *The Kentuckians: A Knight of the Cumberland,* 1898; *Crittenden: A Kentucky Story of Love and War,* 1900; *Blue-Grass and Rhododendron: Outdoors in Old Kentucky,* 1901; *The Little Shepherd of Kingdom Come,* 1903; *Following the Sun Flag,* 1905; *The Trail of the Lonesome Pine,* 1908; *The Heart of the Hills,* 1913; *In Happy Valley,* 1917; *Erskine Dale, Pioneer,* 1920.

REFERENCES: Kunitz, *Authors Today and Yesterday,* 1933; Burke and Howe, *American Authors and Books, 1640-1940,* 1943; James D. Hart, *Oxford Companion to American Literature,* 1965; E. F. Harkins, *Little Pilgrimages, Second Series,* 1903; *Who's Who in America,* Vol. 10, 1918-19; Warren I. Titus, *John Fox, Jr.,* Twayne Publishers, Inc., 1971; Louis D. Rubin, Jr., ed., *A Bibliographical Guide to the Study of Southern Literature,* 1969.

FREEMAN, DOUGLAS SOUTHALL (1886-1953), editor and biographer, wrote "I was born in Lynchburg, May 16, 1886, and left there at the end of March, 1892. My father then moved his general agency of the New York Life Insurance Company from Lynchburg to Richmond. You thus will see that my direct associations with the blessed old Hill City all precede my sixth birthday, though I have been back many times since 1892."

His journalistic career began in 1909 soon after he had received his Ph.D. from Johns Hopkins University. He was employed by the Richmond *Times-Dispatch* to write a series of editorial articles on the reform of the tax-system of Virginia. The articles led to his appointment as Secretary of the Virginia Tax Commission from 1910 to 1912.

In 1913 he became an editorial writer on the jointly owned *Times-Dispatch* and *News Leader;* and when the *Times-Dispatch* was sold, he remained with the *News Leader,* becoming its editor in 1915. Dr. Freeman resigned from his editorship in 1949, but his life remained as busy as ever.

Well remembered though these accomplishments may be, Dr. Freeman's lasting fame and memory derive mainly from his books, best known of which are his four-volume *R. E. Lee* (1934) for which he won the Pulitzer Prize; *Lee's Lieutenants* (1942-44), a study of the commanding officers who served under Lee; and *George Washington,* which has come to be considered the definitive work on its subject, as has his *R. E. Lee.*

In addition to his authorial and editorial achievements (*Life* called him "probably the sanest and soundest observer of the European War [W.W. II] in the United States), Dr. Freeman lectured on journalism at Columbia, made daily radio news broadcasts, and held high office in numerous educational and governmental organizations.

He attributed his success in so many areas to self-discipline, a virtue he practised religiously by rising at 2:30 A.M., reaching his desk by 3:00 and his newspaper office by 5:40. Then, after his daily radio broadcast he spent the afternoon writing and ended his day by 8:45. He said it should be a part of every man's daily discipline to attempt "the performance of something new, difficult, and awkward to him."

BOOKS: Ed., *A Calendar of Confederate Papers*, 1908; *Lee's Dispatches*, 1915; *Reports on Virginia Taxation*, 1912; *The Last Parade*, 1932; *R. E. Lee* (4 vols.), 1934-5; *The South to Posterity*, 1939; *Lee's Lieutenants* (3 vols.), 1942-44; *George Washington* (6 vols.), 1948-54. (The seventh volume of this work was written and published by J. A. Carroll and M. W. Ashworth in 1957.)

REFERENCES: Francis Rosenberger, *Virginia Reader*, 1948; *Webster's Biographical Dictionary; Who's Who in America*, Vol. 26, 1951 and later; Kunitz and Haycraft, *Twentieth Century Authors, First Supplement*, 1955; "Freeman Letters on George Washington" *American Heritage*, Feb., 1956.

FRIDELL, GUY (1921-   ), columnist, editor, and writer of non-fiction, was born in Atlanta, but educated at the University of Richmond (B.A., 1946) and at the Columbia School of Journalism (M.S., 1948). He has served as reporter on both the Lynchburg *News* and the Richmond *News Leader*. On the latter paper he wrote a column called "Off the Record." *Jack Straws* (1961) is a collection of columns. *What Is There About Virginia?* (1967) and *We Began at Jamestown* (1968) are intimate commentaries by a perceptive contemporary on his adopted state. Mr. Fridell currently edits the editorial page of the Norfolk *Virginian-Pilot*.

BOOKS: *Jack Straws*, 1961; *I Hate You, I Love You*, 1965; *What Is There About Virginia?*, 1967; *We Began at Jamestown*, 1968.

REFERENCES: Richmond *News Leader*, March 1, 1963.

GILMER, FRANCIS WALKER (1790-1826), lawyer, non-fiction writer, and educational diplomat, was the youngest of ten children and was born at "Pen Park," Albemarle County, Virginia. His early education was neglected, but he attempted to teach himself. During 1808-09 he attended school in Georgetown, D. C., and in 1810, after one year at the College of William and Mary, he took his degree. He was regarded as a child prodigy.

In 1811 he began to study law in Richmond under his brother-in-law, William Wirt (*q.v.*); but it was not until 1815 that he settled down to two years of practice at Winchester, Virginia. He was highly successful in his work, in addition to which he found time to publish, anonomously, in 1816, his *Sketches of American Orators*.

From Winchester he moved to Richmond, where he continued to be successful at the bar. While serving as reporter from 1820-21, he published *Reports of Cases Decided in the Court of Appeals of Virginia*.

Upon Jefferson's request he went to England in 1824 to procure professors, books, and equipment for the University of Virginia. Although his mission was highly successful, his health was damaged on the long and arduous journey. After returning to America, he continued to aid Jefferson in academic negotiations and then accepted the Professorship of Law at the University. His early death, however, prevented him from undertaking his duties. (M.M.C.)

BOOKS: *Sketches of American Orators*, 1816, 1822; *Reports of Cases Decided in the Court of Appeals of Virginia*, 1821; *Sketches, Essays and Translations*, 1828.

REFERENCES: Richard Beale Davis, *Francis Walker Gilmer: Life and Learning in Jefferson's Virginia*, 1939; Francis Coleman Rosenberger, *Virginia Reader*, 1948; *Dictionary of American Biography*, Vol. 7, 1931; J. B. Hubbell, *The South in American Literature 1607-1900* (bibliography), 1954; William P. Trent, *English Culture in Virginia: A Study of the Gilmer Letters and an Account of the English Professors Obtained by Jefferson for the University of Virginia*, 1889. See also Swem's *Virginia Historical Index*, Vol. 1, 1934.

GLASGOW, ELLEN ANDERSON GHOLSON (1874-1945), novelist, essayist, and short story writer, sprang from two distinguished Virginia traditions: on the maternal side the tidewater Anglican aristocracy; on the paternal the "Scotch-Irish" of the Valley of Virginia. Both lines furnished her with much Virginia history at an early age, and both figured in her work.

Though she never attended public school, Miss Glasgow received a liberal education from her father's library. Here she read Darwin, Lecky, James and Hardy. By the turn of the century, after having lived through the sentimentality of *fin de siecle* fiction, she boldly realized that what the South needed was more "blood and irony." In the nineteen novels which constitute the bulk of her fiction, she was a firm practitioner of this point of view. Only one of her novels, *The Battle-Ground* (1902), was given a Civil-War setting, and thus she attempted to reconstruct the past. She was concerned with the living present, and though she first chose New York as a setting (namely for her first two books, *The Descendant* (1897) and *Phases of an Inferior Planet* (1898)), she soon turned to the Old Dominion, of which she by now had a deep and intimate knowledge, as the place upon which to base her fourteen novelistic treatments of the modern South.

It is generally agreed that the most successful and mature of these novels are the last four: *Barren Ground* (1925), *The Sheltered Life* (1934), *Vein of Iron* (1935), and *In This Our Life* (1941). These concern modern Southerners (usually women) who, faced with difficulties which often threaten their destruction, realistically face up to their vicissitudes with courage and fortitude. Such characters are sometimes seen in contrast to others whose view of life is based upon sentimental mores of the Victorian past.

Her final major effort, *In This Our Life*, was awarded the Pulitzer Prize as the best piece of fiction for 1941.

BOOKS: *The Descendant*, 1897; *Phases of an Inferior Planet*, 1898; *The Voice of the People*, 1900; *The Freeman and Other Poems*, 1902; *The Battle-Ground*, 1902; *The Deliverance*, 1904; *The Wheel of Life*, 1906; *The Ancient Law*, 1908; *The Romance of a Plain Man*, 1909; *The Miller of Old Church*, 1911; *Virginia*, 1913; *Life and Gabriella*, 1916; *The Builders*, 1919; *One Man in His Time*, 1922; *The Shadowy Third and Other Stories*, 1923; *Barren Ground*, 1925; *The Romantic Comedians*, 1926; *They Stooped to Folly*, 1929; *The Sheltered Life*, 1932; *Vein of Iron*, 1935; *In This Our Life*, 1941; *A Certain Measure*, 1943; *The Woman Within*, 1954; *Letters of Ellen Glasgow*, 1958.

REFERENCES: Ellen Glasgow, *A Certain Measure* (bibliography), 1943; *The Woman Within*, 1954; James Donald Adams, *Shape of Books to Come*, 1944; James Branch Cabell, *Let Me Lie*, 1947; Edgar E. MacDonald, "The Glasgow-Cabell Entente," *American Literature*, Vol. 41, No. 1 (March 1969); Frederick P. W. McDowell, *Ellen Glasgow and the Ironic Art of Fiction*, 1960; Louis D. Rubin, Jr., ed., *A Bibliographical Guide to the Study of Southern Literature*, 1969.

GORDON, ARMISTEAD CHURCHILL (1855-1931), lawyer and author, was born in Albemarle County. He attended the University of Virginia from 1873 to 1875. In 1879 he was admitted to the bar. In 1883 he married Maria Breckenridge Catlett.

Interested in civic work, Mr. Gordon was mayor of Staunton from 1884 to 1886. Later he became City Attorney and then Commonwealth's Attorney. He served as Visitor of various colleges, including the University of Virginia and the College of William and Mary. He was Rector of the University of Virginia, and for a time served as Chairman of the State Library Board. He received honorary degrees from both the College of William and Mary and Washington and Lee University. (M.M.C.)

BOOKS: *Befo' de War: Echoes in Negro Dialect* (with Thomas Nelson Page), 1888; *Maje: A Love Story*, 1914; *Ommirandy—Plantation Life at Kingsmille*, 1917; *Jefferson Davis*, 1918; *Gordons in Virginia*, 1918; *Robin Aroon*, 1908; *Men and Events: Chapters in Virginia History*, 1923; *In the Picturesque Shenandoah Valley*, 1930.

REFERENCES: Armistead C. Gordon, Jr., *Virginian Writers of Fugitive Verse*, 1923; Armistead C. Gordon, Jr., *A Bibliography of Published Writings of Armistead Churchill Gordon*, 1923; *Webster's Biographical Dictionary*. See also Swem's *Virginia Historical Index*, Vol. 1, 1934.

GOULD, WALLACE (1882-1940), poet, was born in Maine in 1882 and died in Farmville in 1940, after residing in Virginia for twenty years. He is known chiefly for his two volumes of poetry, *Children in the Sun* and *Aphrodite*, and for contributions to "little magazines" and anthologies of verse published during the 1920's.

His poetry has been celebrated in critical essays by Alfred Kreymborg,

William Carlos Williams, Paul Rosenfeld, Marsden Hartley, and others. (M.M.C.)

BOOKS: *Children of the Sun*, 1917; *Aphrodite and Other Poems*, 1928.

REFERENCES: Pollyanna Martin Foard, "Wallace Gould: A Critical Study" (unpublished master's thesis, Longwood College).

GREEN, JULIAN (1900-   ), novelist, dramatist, and short story writer, was born in Paris of American parents (his father a Virginian). His native language thus became French, though he learned English well enough to speak it fluently but he preferred not to write it. After serving as an ambulance driver during World War I, he attended the University of Virginia (1919-22). His first novel, *Mont-Cinere* translated as *Avarice House* (1926), featured as its setting Kinloch, his aunt's house near The Plains, Virginia. The novel was written in only six months and won him instant success. One of his most famous works was *Adrienne Mesurat* translated as *The Closed Garden* (1928), which was chosen by the French Book-of-the-Month Club. Though most of his writing has been done in Paris, he returned to Virginia for a stay after the fall of France in World War II. In 1966 he published *Distant Land*, his third book of memoirs. On May 3, 1971, Green was elected to the French Academy, the only foreigner to have been so honored.

BOOKS: *Monte-Cinere*, 1926; *Adrienne Mesurat*, 1928; *Distant Land*, 1966.

REFERENCES: Haley F. Thomas, "Southerner Makes French First," Richmond *Times-Dispatch*, June 13, 1971; *Contemporary Authors*, 21-22.

GRIFFITH, RICHARD EDWARD (1912-1969), historian and critic of the motion picture industry, was born in Winchester, Virginia, and received his education at Haverford (B.A., 1935). His career began as a newspaper reporter, leading to the position of curator of motion pictures at the Museum of Modern Art in New York, and membership on the New York Film Council. His several books concern various aspects of the film industry (e.g., *The Movies* (1957) and *Samuel Goldwyn: The Producer and His Film* (1956).

BOOKS: *The World of Robert Flaherty*, 1953; *Samuel Goldwyn: The Producer and His Film*, 1956; *The Movies*, 1957; *The Anatomy of a Motion Picture*, 1959.

REFERENCES: *Contemporary Authors*, 1.

GWATHMEY, JOHN HASTINGS (1886-1956), writer of non-fiction, was born in Richmond and educated in the public schools and at the University of Richmond. He served in the Atlantic Fleet in World War I. Later he made a trip around the world as a Merchant Marine officer. Early in his career he worked on newspapers in North Carolina, Alabama, and Virginia. For many years he wrote an outdoors column for the Richmond *Times-Dispatch*. In 1933 he gave up newspaper work to write books about

Virginia. He wanted particularly to preserve some of the anecdotes of his boyhood. (M.M.C.)

BOOKS: *Legends of Virginia Courthouses*, 1933; *Legends of Virginia Lawyers*, 1934; *Justice John* (the celebrated police court justice, John Jeter Crutchfield), 1934; *The Love Affairs of Captain John Smith*, 1935; *Twelve Virginia Counties—Where the Western Migration Began*, 1937; *Historical Register of Virginians in the Revolution*, 1938; *Fly Fishing in the South*, 1942.

REFERENCES: Richmond *Times-Dispatch*, Nov. 6, 1949; Margaret H. Carpenter, *Virginia Authors' Yearbook*, 1957.

HALE, NANCY (1908-   ), novelist and short story writer, was born in Boston, Massachusetts, the only child of Philip L. and Lilian Westcott Hale, both artists. She was brought up in Dedham, Massachusetts, and went to the Winsor School in Boston. After her "coming out" in Boston, she attended the School of the Boston Museum of Fine Arts and studied in her father's studio as well. Her writing career began after she was married at twenty and went to New York to live. She became an assistant editor of *Vogue*, an assistant editor of *Vanity Fair*, and the first woman reporter on the New York *Times*.

In 1937 Miss Hale came to Virginia. With the exception of the war years, which she spent in Washington, D. C., and summers on Cape Ann, Massachusetts, she has lived in Charlottesville ever since.

In the early 1950's Miss Hale became interested in writing for the theater. She found a good laboratory in the Virginia Players at the University of Virginia, who produced her comedies *The Best of Everything* and *Somewhere She Dances*.

Miss Hale's short stories have appeared in more than thirty anthologies and many magazines. In 1932 she won the O. Henry Short Story Prize. Some of her books and stories have been reprinted in England, France, Germany, Argentina, and the Scandinavian countries. *The Prodigal Women* appeared in a French translation with an introduction by Andre Maurois. There was also a Swedish translation.

Nancy Hale is married to Professor Fredson Bowers, Linden Kent Memorial Professor of English at the University of Virginia. He is a leading authority in the field of bibliography, textual studies, and editing.

BOOKS: *The Young Die Good*, 1932; *Never Any More*, 1934; *The Earliest Dreams*, 1936; *The Prodigal Women*, 1942; *Between the Dark and the Daylight*, 1943; *The Sign of Jonah*, 1950; *The Empress's Ring*, 1955; *Heaven and Hardpan Farm*, 1957; *A New England Girlhood*, 1958; *Dear Beast*, 1959; *The Pattern of Perfection*, 1960; *Black Summer*, 1963; *New England Discovery*, 1963; *The Realities of Fiction*, 1963; *The Life in the Studio*, 1969; *Secrets*, 1971.

REFERENCES: J. Gray, *On Second Thought*, 1946; R. Van Gelder, *Writers and Writing*, 1946; Kunitz and Haycraft, *Twentieth Century Authors*,

First Supplement, 1955; *Wilson Library Bulletin,* Jan., 1943; Richmond *Times-Dispatch,* Jan. 2, 1949; J. K. Hutchins, New York *Herald Tribune Book Review,* Nov. 19, 1950; Margaret H. Carpenter, *Virginia Authors' Yearbook,* 1956, 1957, 1958.

HAMMOND, JOHN (fl. 1635-1656), native of England, published *Leah and Rachel, or Two Fruitful Sisters of Virginia and Maryland* in London in 1656. He lived in Maryland two years and in Virginia nineteen. His book was written primarily to inform the needy in the mother country that the New World offered them better living conditions than they had at home. (M.M.C.)

BOOK: *Leah and Rachel: Or Two Fruitful Sisters of Virginia and Maryland,* 1656, 1871.

REFERENCES: J. B. Hubbell, *The South in American Literature 1607-1900,* 1954; James D. Hart, *The Oxford Companion to American Literature,* 1965; Louis D. Rubin, Jr., ed., *A Bibliographical Guide to the Study of Southern Literature,* 1969.

HAMNER, EARL [HENRY], JR. (1920-   ), novelist and script writer, was born in Schuyler, Virginia, and educated at the University of Richmond (B.A., 1944). He did graduate study at the University of Kentucky, Northwestern University, and the Sorbonne. He wrote radio and television scripts for several years and received four "Dr. Christian" awards for his efforts. His novels reflect his first-hand knowledge of the Blue Ridge Mountains. The most famous of these is *Spencer's Mountain* (1961), which is the story of a mountain boy's efforts to attend the University of Richmond. Here the worlds of academia and the untutored mountain community stand in vivid relief to each other.

BOOKS: *Fifty Roads to Town,* 1953; *Spencer's Mountain,* 1961; *You Can't Get There From Here,* 1965.

REFERENCES: *Library Journal,* Oct. 1, 1953; *University of Richmond Alumni Bulletin,* April 1949, Oct. 1953, Jan. 1962.

HANES, LEIGH (1893-1967), poet, was born in Montvale, a few miles east of Roanoke. He was educated in a private school run by a lady who "seemed to know intuitively what sort of punishment would be most memorable for such a little boy." The punishment consisted of having him sit quietly in a corner and "cool off" after a misdemeanor and then be read to from "The Song of Hiawatha" or "Evangeline."

A teacher at Roanoke High School inspired him to write poetry, to teach it, and to edit it (for *The Lyric*). His verse has been widely anthologized and collected in *Song of the New Hercules, Green Girdle, The Star That I See,* and *Wide the Gate.* This verse conforms to traditional lines of prosody, which has not made it popular with the "new" critics, a situation to which Mr. Hanes replies: "I wish my first grade teacher could come back and make these new critics sit quietly for a few minutes, and then read a little of 'Evangeline' to them."

BOOKS: *Song of the New Hercules,* 1930; *Green Girdle,* 1939; *The Star That I See,* 1950; *Wide the Gate,* 1957.

REFERENCES: *Who's Who in America,* Vol. 17, 1932 and later; *Who's Who in the South and Southwest,* Vol. 3, 1956; Richmond *Times-Dispatch,* May 29, 1949; Margaret H. Carpenter, *Virginia Authors' Yearbook,* 1956, 1957, 1958.

HARIOT, THOMAS (1560-1621), writer of non-fiction, born and educated at Oxford, became a brilliant scientist, whom Sir Walter Raleigh appointed geographer to the second expedition to Virginia in 1585. He took back many samples of strange plants he found in Virginia, among them the uppowoc or tobacco. From his careful observation he wrote "A brief and true report of the new found land of Virginia," first published in 1588, in which he gave an account of what he had seen in the New World. The 1590 edition of the book, published by Hakluyt, was accompanied by imaginative drawings by another voyager, John White. (M.M.C.)

BOOK: *Narrative of the First English Plantation in Virginia,* London, 1588; de Bry's illustrated edition was printed at Frankfort, 1590. An edition was printed in London, 1893 by B. Quaritch.

REFERENCES: Henry Stevens, *Thomas Hariot,* 1900; Randolph Greenfield Adams, *A Census of the Copies of Hariot's Virginia, 1588 Quarto,* Ann Arbor, 1931, Edwards Bros.; Louis D. Rubin, Jr., ed., *A Bibliographical Guide to the Study of Southern Literature,* 1969. See also Swem's *Virginia Historical Index,* Vol. 1, 1934.

HARRISON, CONSTANCE CARY (1843-1920), novelist, a native of Fairfax County, was educated by private governesses. During the Civil War she lived in Richmond. After the death of her father, her mother took her abroad to continue her study of music and languages. Later she married Burton Harrison, a lawyer, and lived in New York.

Her first writing, under the name of "Refugitta," was published in the *Weekly Magnolia* and *Southern Illustrated News,* two Richmond magazines. She became well known for her essays, stories, and novels, in which she represented social life in the late nineteenth century. *The Anglomaniacs,* (1890) one of her most popular novels, portrays American social climbers in Europe. The book was published anonymously. (M.M.C.)

BOOKS: *Old Fashioned Fairy Book,* 1884; *Bar Harbor Days,* 1887; *The Anglomaniacs,* 1890; *Bellhaven Tales,* 1892; *A Daughter of the South,* 1892; *A Bachelor Maid,* 1894; *History of the City of New York,* 1896; *Good Americans,* 1898; *A Princess of the Hills,* 1901; *The Unwelcome Mrs. Hatch,* 1901; *Latter Day Sweethearts,* 1906; *Recollections, Grave and Gay,* 1911.

REFERENCES: *Who Was Who in America,* Vol. I, 1943; Burke and Howe, *American Authors and Books 1640-1940,* 1943; J. B. Hubbell, *The South in American Literature 1607-1900,* 1954; James D. Hart, *The Oxford*

Companion to American Literature, 1965; C. C. Harrison, *Recollections, Grave and Gay,* 1911, 1912.

HARRISON, HENRY SYDNOR (1880-1930), novelist, was a member of the staff of the Richmond *Times-Dispatch* from 1900 to 1910. He spent much of the next twenty years in writing novels, the best of which are *Queed* and *V. V.'s Eyes.* The former, dramatized by Gilbert Emery in 1921, is particularly successful in its characterization of an unworldly young hero who has to learn to meet reality. *V. V.'s Eyes* tells of a young doctor's attempts to reform a selfish young woman, the daughter of a factory owner. Though mildly reforming, its main purpose was the telling of the story. (M.M.C.)

BOOKS: *Captivating Mary Carstairs,* 1910; *Queed,* 1911; *V. V.'s Eyes,* 1913; *Angela's Business,* 1915; *When I Come Back,* 1919; *Saint Teresa,* 1922; *Andrew Bridee of Paris,* 1925; *The Good Hope,* 1931.

REFERENCES: James D. Hart, *Oxford Companion to American Literature,* 1965; Notes by Elizabeth Shepardson Curtis for the school text of *Queed,* 1928; Louis D. Rubin, Jr., *A Bibliographical Guide to the Study of Southern Literature,* 1969. See also Swem's *Virginia Historical Index,* Vol. 1, 1934.

HARRISON, MARION CLIFFORD (1893-1967), writer of non-fiction and verse, was born in Petersburg. After graduating from Petersburg High School (1910), he attended Randolph-Macon College (A.B., 1910) and the University of Virginia (M.A., 1914; Ph.D., 1921). His teaching career was spent at Virginia Polytechnic Institute.

An early interest in rhyming bore fruition in winning the poetry medal of the *Randolph-Macon Monthly* (1913) for writing the class poem. He wrote the University of Virginia class poem in 1914 and won the *University of Virginia Magazine* poetry prize in 1921.

Later awards include the Sidney Lanier Poetry Award (1939) and the South Carolina Poetry Society's humorous verse award (1951). His poetry has appeared in various periodicals. He also edited a school version of Scott's *Ivanhoe* (1925) and published *Home to the Cockade City* (1942) and *Old Dominion Echoes* (1960) (poems). (M.M.C.)

BOOKS: *Home to the Cockade City,* 1942; *Practical English Grammar,* 1959; *Old Dominion Echoes,* 1960; *From Sayler's Creek to Appomattox,* 1965.

REFERENCES: *Directory of American Scholars,* 1942; Richmond *Times-Dispatch,* July 31, 1949.

HART, SCOTT (1902-   ), novelist, writes: "I was born on November 10, 1902, in Farmville, then a delightful town of autumn tobacco smells, evening street corner singing, transient medicine shows, and a college full of girls. So distracting an environment, along with a congenital abhorrence of arithmetic, wrecked my formal education after some three attempts at the sixth and seventh grades."

He was saved, he says, be a "a magnificent lady . . . [who] spiced the teaching of reading and grammar with gratuitous doses of poetry and folk-lore. . . ." This interest in books led him to jobs on the Richmond *News-Leader* and *Times-Dispatch*, the Roanoke *Times* and *World News* and the Washington *Post;* such magazines as *Time, Coronet, Esquire,* and *Changing Times;* and finally to a stint as speech writer for the Democratic National Committee. Many of his free-lance pieces were done in collaboration with his wife, Val Hart, formerly of West Point, Virginia, and the author of *The Story of American Roads.*

Unsure as to whether or not the newspaper is a good apprentice field for would-be writers, he adds, "This is certain: something better than a seventh-grade education is a big help. I'll never forget sitting in my first news room, ignorant of where to put a comma, not to speak of the complexities of the semicolon."

BOOKS: *The Moon is Waning,* 1939; *Eight April Days,* 1949; *Stony Lonesome,* 1954; One chapter in *Dateline: Washington,* 1949; *Route Obscure and Lovely,* 1967; *Washington at War, 1941-1945,* 1965.

REFERENCES: Richmond *Times-Dispatch,* May 8, 1949, and Sept. 11, 1949.

HATCH, CHARLES E. (1913-   ), historical writer, was born at Cobbs Creek, Virginia. After attending the College of William and Mary and the University of Virginia, he was employed by the National Park Service of the Department of the Interior and has held posts at George Washington's Birthplace National Monument and since at the Colonial National Historical Park (Yorktown). He has written various historical pamphlets, contributed to historical journals, and written numerous book reviews and feature articles.

BOOKS AND PAMPHLETS: *Yorktown: Climax of the Revolution,* Washington, 1941, U. S. Department of Interior, National Park Service, Source Book Series, No. 1; *The Oldest Assembly in America and Its First Statehouse,* Wash., 1943, National Park Service, Popular Study Series, No. 15, and in Interpretive Series, 1947 and 1956, No. 2; *Yorktown and the Siege of 1781,* Wash., 1952, U. S. Gov't. Printing Office; ed. with Edward M. Riley, *James Towne in the Words of Contemporaries,* Wash., 1955, National Park Service, Source Book Series, No. 5; *Jamestown, Virginia: The Town Site and Its Story,* Richmond, 1950, National Park Service, cooperating with the Association for the Preservation of Virginia Antiquities, U. S. Park Service Historical Handbook Series, No. 2, also U. S. Gov't. Printing Office, 1957; *The First Seventeen Years: Virginia, 1607-1624* (one of the booklets published by the Virginia 350th Anniversary Celebration Corporation), Richmond, 1957, Garrett and Massie.

REFERENCE: Margaret H. Carpenter, *Virginia Authors' Yearbook,* 1958.

HAY, JAMES, JR. (1881-1936), novelist and non-fiction writer, was born in Harrisonburg, Virginia, the son of James and Constance (Tatum) Hay.

He was a student at the University of Virginia from 1899 to 1903. After graduation he worked for the Washington *Post* (1903-4), and for the Washington *Times* (1904-9). He then began to contribute fiction and special articles to magazines. His most famous novel was *The Bellamy Case*. In 1922 he married Millicent Larrick. He directed the nation-wide magazine publicity campaign for the George Washington Bicentennial Commemoration in 1931-32. (M.M.C.)

BOOKS: *The Man Who Forgot*, 1915; *Mrs. Marsden's Ordeal*, 1918; *The Melwood Mystery*, 1920; *No Clue*, 1920; *The Unlighted House*, 1921; *The Bellamy Case*, 1925; *That Washington Affair*, 1926; *The Hidden Woman*, 1928; with John L. Martin, *The Wayside Inn for Birds*, 1929.

REFERENCES: *Who Was Who in America*, Vol. I, 1943; Burke and Howe, *American Authors and Books 1640-1940*, 1943.

HEATH, JAMES EWELL (1792-1862), novelist and dramatist, was probably born in Northumberland County, the son of John Heath, the first president of Phi Beta Kappa. Though most of his professional life was spent as State Auditor, his two contributions to fiction were highly regarded. The first was *Edge-Hill: or, the Family of the Fitzroyals* (1828), a romance cast in the mold of Scott which was praised both by Poe (*q.v.*) and St. George Tucker (*q.v.*). *Whigs and Democrats: or, Love of No Politics,* anonymously published in Richmond in 1839, was written to show that the United States contained fitting subjects for drama. Heath was also important as a silent literary influence. He helped Thomas Willis White advance *The Southern Literary Messenger* through its first year (1834) by editing the first nine issues and giving helpful advice. Poe, who became editor the next year, referred to Heath as "almost the only person of any literary distinction" then in Richmond.

BOOKS: *Edge-Hill: Or, The Family of the Fitzroyals*, 1828; *Whigs and Democrats: or, Love of No Politics*, 1839.

REFERENCES: *Dictionary of American Biography*, Vol. 8; J. B. Hubbell, *The South in American Literature, 1607-1900*, 1954.

HENRY, ROBERT SELPH (1889-   ), writer of non-fiction, has lived in Alexandria since 1945. Born in Clifton, Tennessee, he did his undergraduate work at Vanderbilt University, from which he received his A.B. and LL.B. degrees. He did his post graduate work at Queens College, Cambridge, England.

Before World War I, in which he was a captain, he worked variously as a newspaper reporter, a private secretary to the governor of Tennessee, and as a lawyer in private practice. After the war he became assistant to a railway official. In 1934 he began working with the Association of American Railroads, in time becoming Vice-President.

His earliest work to attract attention is *The Story of the Confederacy*, which has gone through several editions. The late Douglas Southall Freeman, who furnished the foreword of the 1936 edition, wrote that it was "the

book with which to begin the study of the period and the book to which
to return when everything else on the period has been read."

In addition to history and biography, Mr. Henry has written much about
trains and railroading. His books are considered authoritative as well as
interesting. (M.M.C.)

BOOKS: *The Story of the Confederacy,* 1931; *Trains,* 1934; *On the
Railroad,* 1936; *Portraits of the Iron Horse,* 1937; *The Story of Reconstruc-
tion,* 1938; *"First with the Most" Forrest,* 1944; *This Fascinating Railroad
Business,* 1942; co-editor with F. P. Donovan, *Headlights and Markers,* 1946;
Story of the Mexican War, 1950.

REFERENCES: Richmond *Times-Dispatch,* June 11, 1950; *Contemporary Authors,* 1.

HENRY, WILLIAM WIRT (1831-1900), attorney and historian, was
born at "Red Hill," Charlotte County. A grandson of Patrick Henry, he
was named for the latter gentleman's most famous biographer. Though
formally educated at the University of Virginia (M.A., 1850), he is often
called a self-trained historian who wrote with a Virginia slant and who
tended toward its worship. He is noted for two works in particular: *Patrick
Henry: Life, Correspondence and Speeches,* 3. vols. (1891) and "A Concise
Historical Sketch of Virginia," which appeared in his *Eminent Representative Men of Virginia and the District of Columbia of the Nineteenth Century*
(1893).

BOOKS: *Patrick Henry: Life, Correspondence and Speeches* (3 vols.)
1891; *Eminent Representative Men of Virginia and the District of Columbia
of the Nineteenth Century,* 1893; *The Presbyterian Church and Religious
Liberty in Virginia,* 1900.

REFERENCES: *Dictionary of American Biography,* Vol. 8; *Virginia
Magazine,* Jan., 1901.

HERNDON, BOOTON (1916-   ), fiction and non-fiction writer, began
his writing career in his home-town of Charlottesville, by reporting on a
football game in which he was a player. Then, after being schooled at Wood
berry Forest and the University of Virginia, he worked for the New Orleans
Item. His short stories began appearing in 1949 in the *Saturday Evening Post*
and *Collier's.* Later he added a long list of articles to these.

"I've written hundreds of articles, some fiction, and two books," he
wrote several years ago. "I am completely without specialty. I wrote dozen
of articles for *Sports Illustrated* when it was just getting started, for example
and at the same time I was delving into the world of *haute couture* for my
book, *Bergdorf's on the Plaza.* Last week, in connection with an article, I
had to learn to skin dive, grubbing around, a tank on my back and a nozzle
in my mouth, on the bottom of a murky brackish bay with a bunch o
loathsome creatures of the deep. . . ."

BOOKS: *Praised and Damned: The Story of Fulton Lewis, Jr.,* 1954
*Bergdorf's on the Plaza: The Story of Bergdorf Goodman and a Half Century
of American Fashion,* 1956; *Young Men Can Change the World,* 1960; *The*

Sweetest Music this Side of Heaven, 1964; ed., *The Humor of J.F.K.,* 1964; *The Unlikeliest Hero,* 1967; *Ford,* 1969.

REFERENCE: Margaret H. Carpenter, *Virginia Authors' Yearbook,* 1958; *Contemporary Authors,* 9-10.

HILL, LESLIE PINCKNEY (1880-   ), writer of verse and plays, was born in Lynchburg, Virginia, where he attended grade school. He was graduated from high school in East Orange, New Jersey, and continued his education at Harvard University, from which he received both his B.A. and M.A. degrees.

He was principal of the Industrial School at Manassas, Virginia, and subsequently taught at Tuskegee Institute and later became principal of the Cheyney Training School for teachers at Cheyney, Pennsylvania.

In 1921 he published *The Wings of Oppression,* a book of poetry with a philosophical rather than a lyrical quality. In 1928 he published *Toussaint L'Ouverture—A Dramatic History,* a play in five parts. (M.M.C.)

BOOKS: *The Wings of Oppression,* 1921; *Toussaint L'Ouverture,* 1928.

REFERENCES: James Weldon Johnson, *The Book of American Negro Poetry,* 1922, 1931, 1959; Robert Thomas Kerlin, *Negro Poets and Their Poems,* 1935.

HOFFMAN, WILLIAM (1925-   ), novelist, was born in Charleston, West Virginia. He attended Kentucky Military Institute and later graduated from Hampden-Sydney College.

He began to write while a law student at Washington and Lee. His early fruitful period of writing was followed by two "dry" years. Then, in 1950 he attended the Writers' Workshop at the University of Iowa, went on to work for a newspaper in Washington, D.C., and then for the Chase National Bank in New York. Finally, in 1952, he was given an instructorship at Hampden-Sydney and the following summer finished his first novel. While it was making the rounds of publishers, he wrote a second, "to keep my mind off the first." The first, *The Trumpet Unblown,* was published by Doubleday in 1955. He still teaches at Hampden-Sydney and continues to write novels.

BOOKS: *The Trumpet Unblown,* 1955; *The Days in the Yellow Leaf,* 1958; *A Place for My Head,* 1960; *A Walk to the River,* 1970.

REFERENCE: Margaret H. Carpenter, *Virginia Authors' Yearbook,* 1956; *Contemporary Authors,* 21-22.

HOPE, JAMES BARRON (1829-1887), poet and non-fiction writer, was born in Norfolk and educated at the College of William and Mary. He studied law and entered practice at Hampton, where he became a Commonwealth's Attorney in 1856.

His literary interests became obvious in early youth, and took several directions: first poetry and later journalism. His early poems were published in the *Southern Literary Messenger,* but ultimately he became best known as a commemorative poet, delivering dedicatory verses (e.g. at the unveiling of

Crawford's equestrian statue of Washington in Richmond (1858)). After the Civil War, in which he served as a major under Joseph E. Johnston, he gave up law for journalism and in 1883 established the Norfolk *Landmark*. In 1881 he was named the official poet of Congress in being chosen to write a poem for the Yorktown Centennial. His final honor came in 1887, when he became Superintendent of the Norfolk Public Schools.

BOOKS: *Leoni di Monota and Other Poems*, 1857; *A Collection of Poems*, 1859; *Under the Empire*, 1878; *Arms and the Man: A Metrical Address*, 1882; *A Wreath of Virginia Bay Leaves* (poems edited by his daughter, Janey Hope Marr), 1895.

REFERENCES: Kunitz and Haycraft, *American Authors, 1600-1900* 1938; Charles William Hubner, *Representative Southern Poets*, 1906; Francis Coleman Rosenberger, *Virginia Reader*, 1948. See also Swem's *Virginia Historical Index*, Vol. 1, 1934.

HUBBELL, JAY B[ROADDUS] (1885-), professor, critic, biographer, historian and editor, was born in Smyth County, Virginia. He received his education at the University of Richmond (B.A., 1905), Harvard (M.A., 1908) and Columbia (Ph.D., 1922). Though he has taught at many Southern colleges and universities and as a visiting lecturer abroad (at Vienna and Athens), the majority of his career has been spent at Duke University. Here he became founding editor (1929) of *American Literature* and wrote *The South in American Literature* (1954), which has become the standard work in its field. In addition, he has published many other book and article-length studies on English and American literature. He is best known, however, for his leadership in developing the study of Southern literature into a separate discipline and is considered the dean of scholars in this area.

BOOKS: *Lives of Franklin Plato Eller and John Carlton Eller*, 1910; *Virginia Life in Fiction*, 1922; *An Introduction to Drama*, 1927; *The Enjoyment of Literature*, 1929; ed., *American Life in Fiction*, 1936; *The Last Years of Henry Timord, 1864-1867*, 1941; *The South in American Literature, 1607-1900*, 1954; *Southern Life in Fiction*, 1960; *South and Southwest*, 1965.

REFERENCE: *Directory of American Scholars*, 2

JACOB, CARY F. (1885-), novelist and poet, was born in Richmond and influenced from an early age by such then-standard authors as Cooke, Dickens, and Cooper. A teen-age interest in music merged into a mature interest in literature, and he went on to obtain the bachelor's, master's and doctor's degrees in English from the University of Virginia and to pursue post-graduate studies in a number of European universities.

In addition to his scholarly writing, he has published a collection of poems, *Driftwood and Foam* (1914), six novels (the latter under pseudonyms) and nine plays.

BOOKS: *Driftwood and Foam*, 1914; *The Foundations and Nature of Verse*, 1918.

REFERENCES: Margaret H. Carpenter, *Virginia Authors' Yearbook* 1956, 1957, 1958; *Virginia Lives*.

JANNEY, SAMUEL (1801-1880), poet, biographer, and essayist, was born in Loudoun County, Virginia. A Quaker, he soon developed the Friends' dislike for slavery and wrote a number of anti-slavery essays for the Alexandria *Gazette* (beginning in 1827). His concern for civil matters was also shown in his leadership of the movement to form a system of free public schools for Virginia (made law in 1846) and in his dedication to the cause of the American Indian. In 1839 he had written a collection of poems, *The Last of the Lenapé,* and in 1869-71 he was made Superintendent of Indian Affairs for the seven northern tribes and was headquartered in Omaha, Nebraska. This experience is recounted in his *Memoirs* (1881). Two final examples of his Quakerism are his biographies of William Penn (1851) and George Fox (1853).

BOOKS: *The Last of the Lenapé,* 1839; *The Life of William Penn,* 1851; *The Life of George Fox,* 1853; *Memoirs,* 1881.

REFERENCES: *Library of Southern Literature,* Vol. 6.

JEFFERSON, THOMAS (1743-1826), third president of the United States (1801-1809), was reared in the western part of the colony. At the Reverend James Maury's school he studied Greek and Latin for two years, and at the age of fifteen, the year after his father's death, entered the College of William and Mary.

Much of Jefferson's education resulted from frequent meetings with Dr. William Small, George Wythe, and Governor Francis Fauquier, around the Governor's table. Jefferson had an eager curiosity that directed his interests into literature, language, music, architecture, education, agriculture, science, economics, law, and political science.

His first published work of importance, *A Summary View of the Rights of British America* (Williamsburg, 1774), was written as a pamphlet he hoped would be used by the Virginia Convention of 1774 as instructions to the delegates elected to the Continental Congress. The document seemed too radical for the Convention, but some members gave it the title which it bears and published it anonymously.

Notes on the State of Virginia (1784), his only book, was written to answer questions put to him by the Marquis of Barbe-Marbois, Secretary of the French Legation in Philadelphia, rather than for publication. In 1809, the year he retired from the presidency, he would not allow a collected edition of his works. He said he saw no merit in their publication.

Thomas Jefferson founded the University of Virginia, which he planned as architect, and organized as a modern liberal institution of higher learning. His talents as an architect are also manifest in his home, "Monticello," and in the Virginia State Capitol.

No American of his time exerted a greater cultural influence on the country by scholarship in languages and sciences, and as a connoisseur and patron of the arts. (C.C.C.)

BOOKS: *Notes on the State of Virginia,* published in Paris in 1784, is

Jefferson's only full length book. The total body of Virginia's most productive writer was enormous. A selection of the 18,000 letters still in existence may be found in a twenty-volume edition, *The Writings of Thomas Jefferson*, 1905, by A. A. Lipscomb and A. E. Bergh. Selections of Jefferson's writings have been published in many one-volume editions. Notable among these are: *The Living Thoughts of Thomas Jefferson*, edited by John Dewey, 1940; *Jefferson Himself*, edited by Bernard Mayo, 1942; *The Complete Jefferson*, edited by Saul K. Padover, 1943; and *The Selected Writings of Thomas Jefferson*, edited by Adrienne Koch and William Peden, 1944. Thomas Jefferson has been the subject of innumerable biographies.

REFERENCES: Jay B. Hubbell, *The South in American Literature, 1607-1900* (bibliography), 1954; Earl Gregg Swem, *Virginia Historical Index*, Vol. 1, 1934; Louis D. Rubin, Jr., ed., *A Bibliographical Guide to the Study of Southern Literature*, 1969.

JENKINS, WILLIAM FITZGERALD ["MURRAY LEINSTER"] (1896-   ), was born in Norfolk. His first writing was a school-room exercise honoring General Lee, for which a Confederate veteran sent him five dollars, his first earnings from writing.

Convinced he wanted to be a professional writer, he sold twelve epigrams to the *Smart Set* in 1915. Editor George Jean Nathan asked him to reserve use of his name exclusively for that magazine in the future, and this caused him to write for lesser magazines under the pseudonym Murray Leinster. He estimates the number of stories he has written since 1915 at 1,300. In addition, he has produced "something over forty books . . . and a number of motion pictures, radio and television broadcasts, and other reproductions of [his] work." His stories have been translated into fifteen languages and widely published.

BOOKS: *City on the Moon*, 1957; *Gamblin' Kid*, 1933; *Fighting Horse Valley*, 1934; *Murder of the U.S.A.*, 1946; *Sidewise in Time*, 1953; *Guns for Achin*, 1943; *The Brain Stealers*, 1954; *Colonial Survey*, 1957; *The Forgotten Planet*, 1954; *Gateway to Elsewhere*, 1954; *Operation Outer Space*, 1954; *Space Platform*, 1953; *Space Tug*, 1953; *Operation Terror*, 1962; *The Monster from Earth's End*, 1959; *The Other Side of Nowhere*, 1964; *A Murray Leinster Omnibus*, 1968.

REFERENCES: *Who's Who in America*, Vol. 31, 1960-61; *Who's Who in the South and Southwest*, Vol. 3, 1956; Margaret H. Carpenter, *Virginia Authors' Yearbook*, 1957, 1958.

JOHNSTON, MARY (1870-1936), novelist, was born in Buchanan County, and spent fifteen years there in a house opposite the old Botetourt Hotel. Then the family moved to Birmingham, Alabama. The early death of her mother left Mary Johnston responsible for much of the care of her younger brothers and sisters. Books were her recreation, and her father's library furnished them in abundance, paticularly books of history. Here was the background for the twenty-two novels she was later to write.

After her father's death Miss Johnston came to Richmond where she lived until she built "Three Hills" near Warm Springs, Virginia, in 1913. In spite of the ill health that plagued her, she left "Three Hills" for occasional trips to New York and abroad.

She began writing early and sent her stories to publishers, but if a story was rejected once, it was destroyed. *Prisoners of Hope,* her first historical novel, was published in 1898; her second, *To Have and To Hold* (1900), was a "phenomenal best-seller." Most of her novels were popular.

She spent much time in research, and all of her novels were thoroughly documented. William Allen White wrote that she "made historical novels out of wax portraits of the early aristocrats of the Atlantic Coast," but that "her facts were sound and her story-making instincts true." The shy, retiring Southern lady with a firm jaw "did not know how to be uninteresting," he added.

Commonweal called her romantic novels about history "rosy-hued, swashbuckling novels, skimming the surface of thought and reveling in action." Although compelling in historic atmosphere," they were "minor in the authentic tradition of the great Sir Walter Scott." (M.M.C.)

BOOKS: *Prisoners of Hope,* 1898; *To Have and to Hold,* 1900; *Audrey,* 1902; *Sir Mortimer,* 1904; *The Goddess of Reason,* 1907; *Lewis Rand,* 1908; *The Long Roll,* 1911; *Cease Firing,* 1912; *Hagar,* 1913; *The Witch,* 1914; *The Fortunes of Garin,* 1915; *The Wanderers,* 1917; *Pioneers of the Old South,* 1918; *Michael Forth,* 1919; *Sweet Rocket,* 1920; *Silver Cross,* 1921; *Croatan,* 1923; *The Slave Ship,* 1924; *The Great Valley,* 1926; *The Exile,* 1927; *Hunting Shirt,* 1931; *Miss Delicia Allen,* 1932; *Drury Randall,* 1934.

REFERENCES: Burke and Howe, *American Authors and Books 1640-1940,* 1943; Kunitz and Haycraft, *Twentieth Century Authors,* 1942; James D. Hart, *Oxford Companion to American Literature,* 1965; *Commonweal,* May 22, 1936; *Saturday Review,* May 23, 1936; Louis D. Rubin, Jr., ed., *A Bibliographical Guide to the Study of Southern Literature,* 1969.

JONES, HUGH (c. 1670-1760), a clergyman and a graduate of the University of Cambridge, came to Virginia in 1716. He became a teacher of mathematics at the College of William and Mary, a chaplain to the House of Burgesses, and at the same time rector in the parishes of Jamestown and Williamsburg. Later he was rector of St. Stephen's Parish in Maryland.

His book, *An Accidence to the English Tongue,* published in 1724, is the first English grammar written in America. During a time spent in England from 1721 to 1724, he wrote and published *The Present State of Virginia,* in which, like his contemporary Robert Beverley, he aimed to inform his native country about Virginia and to correct, among other misconceptions, those about the nature of the people and the treatment of slaves and indentured servants. A portion of the book relating to habits, life, customs, computations, etc., is included in the *Virginia Reader* by Francis Coleman Rosenberger. (M.M.C.)

BOOKS: *An Accidence to the English Tongue*, 1724; *The Present State of Virginia: Giving a Particular and Short Account of the Indian, English, and Negroe Inhabitants of that Colony*, etc., 1865, 1924.

REFERENCES: James D. Hart, *The Oxford Companion to American Literature*, 1965; Francis Coleman Rosenberger, *Virginia Reader*, 1948; J. B. Hubbell, *The South in American Literature 1607-1900*, 1954; Louis D. Rubin, Jr., ed., *A Bibliographical Guide to the Study of Southern Literature*, 1969. See also Swem's *Virginia Historical Index*, Vol. 1, 1934.

JONES, VIRGIL CARRINGTON ["PAT JONES"] (1906-   ), writer of non-fiction, was born in Charlottesville and grew up on a farm encompassed by the Trevilians battlefield. Though he started out to be educated as an engineer, he soon followed his mother's advice and chose writing as his profession. This led him to study journalism at Washington and Lee University. Early in the Depression (1931) he became city editor of the Huntsville [Ala.] *Times*. In 1937 he became a feature writer and political reporter for the Richmond *Times-Dispatch*. Here he began work on his first book, *Ranger Mosby* (1944).

Continuing with his journalistic career in Washington, he shortly moved to the Washington public relations office of the Curtis Publishing Company, of which he was to become manager. Later books are *The Hatfields and McCoys* (1948); *Gray Ghosts and Rebel Raiders* (1956) (source of the television series "The Gray Ghost"); and *Eight Hours Before Richmond* (a narrative of the Kilpatrick-Dahlgren raid on the Confederate capital in the winter of 1864).

BOOKS: *Ranger Mosby*, 1944; *The Hatfields and the McCoys*, 1948; *Gray Ghosts and Rebel Raiders*, 1956; *Eight Hours Before Richmond*, 1957; *The Civil War at Sea*, 1960.

REFERENCES: Margaret H. Carpenter, *Virginia Authors' Yearbook*, 1958; *Contemporary Authors*, 2.

JORDAN, CORNELIA JANE MATTHEWS (1830-1898), prolific writer of prose and verse, was the daughter of Edwin Matthews, a former mayor of Lynchburg. One volume of her poetry, *Corinth and Other Poems* (1865), was burned by order of the Federal government on the court house steps in Lynchburg. It was said to be too incendiary for Reconstruction days.

Under the pseudonym "Hope Dare," Mrs. Jordan wrote of local society events for the Lynchburg *Gazette*. She was largely responsible for getting subscriptions for the Confederate Memorial Association's monument to Confederate dead in the Old Methodist Cemetery in Lynchburg. (R.H.B.)

BOOKS: *Echoes from the Cannon*, 1899; *Flowers of Hope and Memory*, 1861; *Corinth and other Poems*, 1865.

REFERENCES: Manuscript Collection of Biographies of Lynchburg Writers at the Jones Memorial Library, Lynchburg, Virginia.

KARIG, WALTER (1898-1956), non-fiction writer and novelist, though born in New York City's Greenwich Village, lived most of his adult life in Virginia. Educated at home until he was eleven, he won first prize in a newspaper literary contest when he was only ten. And though he studied art at Parson's and the Ecole Julien de Paris, his major interest remained writing. After a stint in the Canadian Army, he came to Portsmouth, Virginia, and married Eleanor Freye, art supervisor in the public schools.

His writing career began with journalism and led into writing juvenile stories under pseudonyms and a book of travel experiences called *Asia's Good Neighbor* (1937). During World War II, in which he worked as an organizer of writing and publishing facilities in the Department of the Navy, Karig was given special permission to write the six-volume *Battle Report*, which became the basis for the television serial *Victory at Sea*. Karig served the serial as technical director. His first novel was *Lower than the Angels* (1945). It was followed in 1947 by *Zotz!*, selected by the Book-of-the-Month Club in 1947. His post-war work continued the military theme.

BOOKS: *Hungry Crawford: Legionnaire*, 1929; *Asia's Good Neighbor*, 1937; *Lower Than the Angels*, 1945; *War in the Atomic Age*, 1946; *Zotz!*, 1947; *The Fortunate Islands*, 1948; *Caroline Hicks*, 1951; *Battle Report* (co-author and ed.) (6 vols.), 1944-1952; *Neely*, 1953; *Don't Tread on Me*, 1954; *Battle Submerged: Submarine Fighters of World War II* (co-author), 1951.

REFERENCES: Warfel, *American Novelists of Today*, 1951; Kunitz and Haycraft, *Twentieth Century Authors, First Supplement*, 1955; New York *Herald Tribune* Jan. 8, 1950; *Saturday Review*, Feb. 16, 1946; Richmond *Times-Dispatch*, Jan. 22, 1950; Margaret H. Carpenter, *Virginia Authors' Yearbook*, 1956, 1957. Obituaries: *Britannica Book of the Year*, 1957; New York *Times*, Oct. 1, 1956; *Newsweek*, Oct. 8, 1956; *Publishers' Weekly*, Oct. 22, 1956; *Time*, Oct. 8, 1956.

KERCHEVAL, SAMUEL (1767-1845), historian, was collecting information for his *History of the Valley of Virginia* at a time when there were residents still living who could remember the earliest settlers and the Valley Indians. Although Kercheval used public documents as a source of some of his information, his main source was the "word of mouth accounts" of the elderly Valley residents. He was careful to identify his information with the name of the person who gave it. His method of using recollections, though subject to error, resulted in a colorful account, particularly good as background reading to give an interpretation of the early settlements.

The book has gone through four editions, the last supplemented by the Reverend Dr. Joseph Doddridge's notes on the early settlement and the Indian wars in the western part of the state, and on the state of society and manners of the people. (M.M.C.)

BOOK: *History of the Valley of Virginia*, 1833, 1850, 1902, 1925.

REFERENCES: William Couper, *History of the Shenandoah Valley*, Vol. 2, 1952; John W. Wayland, *History of Shenandoah County, Virginia*,

1927; John W. Wayland, *Twenty-five Chapters on the Shenandoah Valley,* 1957. See also Swem's *Virginia Historical Index,* Vol. 1, 1934.

KEYES, FRANCES PARKINSON (1885-1970), non-fiction writer and novelist, though born at the University of Virginia, where her father, John Henry Wheeler, was chairman of the Greek Department, lived but a few years in the Commonwealth. She was educated in private schools in Boston, Switzerland, and Berlin and when only eighteen married Henry Wilder Keyes. Her married years took her to residences at "Pine Grove Farm," to the Governor's mansion in New Hampshire, and to Washington, when her husband became a Senator in 1919. Then finally, in 1938, she purchased an old mansion in Alexandria, Virginia, which she named "Tradition." She spent intermittent periods here for many years thereafter.

Her prolific career produced dozens of novels and also took her into such literary by-paths as editing and writing a syndicated newspaper column. She was always true to her self-made promise of visiting the scene of whatever story she was writing and actually working there.

BOOKS: *The Old Gray Homestead,* 1919; *The Career of David Noble,* 1921; *Letters from a Senator's Wife,* 1924; *Queen Anne's Lace,* 1930; *Silver Seas and Golden Cities,* 1931; *Lady Blanche Farm,* 1931; *The Safe Bridge,* 1934; *Senator Marlowe's Daughter,* 1935; *The Happy Wanderer,* 1935; *Honor Bright,* 1936; *Written in Heaven,* 1937; *Capital Kaleidoscope,* 1937; *Parts Unknown,* 1938; *The Great Tradition,* 1939; *Along a Little Way,* 1940; *The Sublime Shepherdess,* 1940—reissued in 1953 as *Bernadette of Lourdes; Fielding's Folly,* 1940; *The Grace of Guadalupe,* 1941; *All that Glitters,* 1941; *Crescent Carnival,* 1942; *Also the Hills,* 1943; *The River Road,* 1945; *Once an Esplanade,* 1947; *Came a Cavalier,* 1947; *Dinner at Antoine's,* 1948; *Therese: Saint of a Little Way,* 1950; *All This is Louisiana,* 1950; *The Cost of a Best Seller,* 1950; *Joy Street,* 1950; *Steamboat Gothic,* 1952; *The Royal Box,* 1954; *The Frances Parkinson Keyes Cookbook,* 1955; *St. Anne: Grandmother of our Saviour,* 1955; *Blue Camellia,* 1957; *The Land of Stones and Saints,* 1959; *Roses in December,* 1960; *The Rose and the Lily,* 1961; *Madame Castle's Lodger,* 1962; *The Restless Lady,* 1963; *Three Ways of Love,* 1963; *The Explorer,* 1964; *Silver Seas and Golden Cities,* 1964; *Tongues of Fire,* 1966.

REFERENCES: Warfel, *American Novelists of Today,* 1951; Kunitz and Haycraft, *Twentieth Century Authors, First Supplement,* 1955; Walter Romig, ed., *Book of Catholic Authors,* 1957; *Frances Parkinson Keyes: A Biographical Sketch,* 1958; F. P. Keyes, *Cost of a Best Seller,* 1950 (same abridged, *Atlantic Monthly,* Sept. 1950); John Anthony O'Brien, ed., *Road to Damascus,* 1949; *The New York Times Book Review,* Dec. 10, 1950; *World,* 1956; *Life,* April 6, 1959.

KIEFFER, ALDINE S. (1840-1904), poet, was born in Missouri of native Virginian parents. After his father's death, his mother returned with her family in 1847 to Rockingham County. There the printing house of his grandfather, Joseph Funk, at Singer's Glen (then Mountain Valley), was familiar to the boy from the time he was seven. There, too, in 1869 he was the co-founder of *Musical Million,* a musical journal in which many of his poems, frequently set to music, were published.

In 1878 when he and his partner, Ephraim Ruebush, took over the printing business from the Funk brothers, they removed it to Dayton where it became a part of the Ruebush-Kieffer press. The partners continued to publish *Musical Million* in Dayton.

Kieffer compiled and edited fifteen or more music books, among them *Christian Harp* and *Temple Star.* The latter sold over 500,000 copies in thirty years' time. The book contained some of his best poetry and is considered his greatest achievement. His most popular song is "Twilight is Falling." (M.M.C.)

BOOKS: *Hours of Fancy: Or Vigil and Vision,* 1881; ed., *Christian Harp, Temple Star.*

REFERENCES: Lyon G. Tyler, ed., *Men of Mark,* first series, 1906-09; John W. Wayland, *History of Rockingham County, Virginia,* 1915; William Couper, *History of the Shenandoah Valley;* F. V. N. Painter, *Poets of Virginia,* 1903.

KILMER, ALINE MURRAY (1888-1941), poet and essayist, was born in Norfolk. She was educated at Rutgers Preparatory School in New Jersey and shortly thereafter (1908) married poet Joyce Kilmer, who was killed in World War I (1918). She subsequently became active in poetry circles as both a practising poetess (e.g. *Candles That Burn* (1919)) and a lecturer on poetic subjects. She was also known as an essayist (e.g. *Hunting A Hair Shirt and Other Spiritual Adventures* (1925)).

BOOKS: *Candles that Burn,* 1919; *Hunting a Hair Shirt and Other Spiritual Adventures,* 1923; *The Poor King's Daughter and Other Poems,* 1925; *A Buttonwood Summer,* 1929.

REFERENCES: *Who Was Who,* Vol. 1, 1897-1942.

KILPATRICK, JAMES JACKSON (1920-   ), columnist, was born in Oklahoma City and educated at the University of Missouri, where he received his degree in journalism in 1941. The same year he began work on the Richmond *News Leader* as a reporter; was made chief editorial writer in 1949; and editor in 1951. He resigned from this position in 1967 to write a syndicated column, which still appears in the *News Leader.* Professing the conservative side in American politics, he characteristically writes with this bent, both in his columns and in *The Sovereign States* (1957).

BOOKS: Ed., with Louis D. Rubin, Jr., *The Lasting South,* 1957; *The Sovereign States,* 1957; *The Smut Peddlers,* 1960; *The Southern Case for School Segregation,* 1962; *The Doors Hang Awry,* 1963.

REFERENCE: *Who's Who in the South and Southwest,* Vol. 6.

LANE, SIR RALPH (c. 1530-1603), one of the company sent by Sir

Walter Raleigh, who determined to establish a colony in Virginia, dispatched seven vessels from Plymouth on April 9, 1585, under the command of his cousin, Sir Richard Grenville. Sir Ralph Lane became the first governor of the little colony established on Roanoke Island. After ten months of precarious living, the colonists agreed to return to England with Sir Francis Drake.

Lane's contribution to literature is "An account of the particularities of the imployments of the English men left in Virginia by Richard Greeneville under the charge of Master Ralph Lane Generall of the same, from the 17. of August 1585. until the 18. of June 1586. at which time they departed the Countrey; sent and directed to Sir Walter Raleigh." (M.M.C.)

WRITING: "An account," etc., (see above) was published in Boston, 1902, in *Old South Leaflets,* by the Directors of Old South Work; also in the *Virginia Reader* by Francis Coleman Rosenberger, N. Y., 1948, E. P. Dutton and Co.

REFERENCES: James D. Hart, *The Oxford Companion to American Literature,* 1965; Francis Coleman Rosenberger, *Virginia Reader,* 1948.

LANGHORNE, ORRA (Mrs. Thomas N.) (1841-1904), columnist, essayist, and fiction writer, was born at *Collicello,* near Harrisonburg, Virginia. Her family were Union sympathizers, and it is perhaps from them that she first received the liberal ideas which informed the frequent columns she wrote for *The Southern Workman and Hampton School Record* and later collected as *Southern Sketches from Virginia, 1881-1901.* Though frankly admitting that she had been a slave-owner, she made numerous gestures of compensation during Reconstruction. She sent a number of the former slaves owned by her family to Hampton Institute a few years after its founding in 1868; she was an avid Republican at a time when it was quite daring; and she was known for many acts of kindness, especially in Lynchburg, where she settled following her marriage in 1871. Though known to have written one volume of poetry, *A Southern Girl's Resolve and Other Poems,* nothing is known of its date or place of publication, and no copy is known to exist. She is thus chiefly remembered for her *Sketches,* which show an advanced and compassionate attitude toward the emerging black race.

BOOKS: *A Southern Girl's Resolve and Other Poems; Aunt Pokey's Son,* 1890; Charles E. Wynes, ed., *Southern Sketches from Virginia, 1881-1901,* 1964.

REFERENCES: Charles E. Wynes, "Introduction" to *Southern Sketches from Virginia, 1881-1901.*

LATOUCHE, JOHN TREVILLE (1917-1956), lyricist-poet, dramatist, composer, and writer of non-fiction, was born in Richmond. He received his preparatory education at Riverdale-on-the-Hudson School and at the Richmond Academy of Arts and Sciences. He died August 7, 1956, at his summer home in Calais, Vermont. Mr. Latouche had just finished the revisions on the American folk opera, *Ballad of the Baby Doe,* which had its premiere in Central City, Colorado, in July, 1956.

The lyricist-poet began writing for the theater while he was still a student at Columbia University and quit school to devote his time to writing. He was almost constantly at work with various composers from then until his death. The National Broadcasting Company set up "The Listeners' Playhouse" for him, and one of his plays, *Icarus,* won a radio award. The variety of his work ranged from lyrics for popular tunes to the experimental *Ballet Ballads* that were produced on Broadway.

Among his best known works are *The Golden Apple,* a musical in two acts; "Banjo Eyes," for Eddie Cantor; "Cabin in the Sky," 1940; and "Ballad for Americans," sung in 1939, when Latouche was twenty-two, by Paul Robeson. The song originally appeared in the WPA theater production, *Sing for Your Supper.*

Mr. Latouche also wrote one book of non-fiction: *Congo,* based upon his two years in Africa, for the Belgian Government. (M.M.C.)

BOOKS: *Congo,* 1945; *The Golden Apple* (a musical in two acts with music by Jerome Morass), 1954; *Candide* (a comic operetta based on Voltaire's satire; book by Lillian Hellman, lyrics by Richard Wilbur, others by John Latouche and Dorothy Parker), 1957.

REFERENCES: Richmond *Times-Dispatch,* Feb. 6, 1949; Washington *Evening Star,* Aug. 8, 1956; *Theater Arts,* Mar., 1957. Obituaries: *Current Biography,* Oct., 1956; *Current Biography Yearbook,* 1957; *Publishers' Weekly,* Aug. 20, 1956; *Theater Arts,* Oct., 1956; *Time,* Aug. 20, 1956.

LeCATO, NATHANIEL JAMES WALTER (1835-1911), novelist, wrote *Mahalinda: or, The Two Cousins,* published at Locust Mount, Virginia, in 1858. It may be the first novel published on the Eastern Shore of Virginia and the first novel written by a Virginia schoolteacher. LeCato was born in Accomac County, and it was during the time he was teaching school at Bradford's Neck that he wrote *Mahalinda.* (R.C.S.)

BOOKS: *Mahalinda: Or, The Two Cousins,* 1858; *Theodora and Other Poems,* 1871; *Aunt Sally's Boy Jack,* 1888; *Tom Burton: Or, The Days of '61,* 1888; *The Curse of Caste,* 1903.

LEE, RICHARD HENRY (1732-1794), writer of political pamphlets, was born in Westmoreland County, Virginia, educated at home, and then at the Wakefield Academy in Yorkshire, England. Upon his return to Virginia, he continued his studies in law, literature, and rhetoric.

He was said to be second only to Patrick Henry as an orator, and that he actually outshone him in voice quality, diction, and grace of gesture. In literature, he is best known for two pamphlets supporting a bill of rights in the new Constitution and arguing against hasty adoption of the document. After the Constitution had been ratified, he was elected to the Senate, where he helped pass the Bill of Rights and authored the Tenth Amendment.

74 VIRGINIA AUTHORS

BOOKS AND PAMPHLETS: *Observations Leading to a Fair Examination of the System of Government, etc.*, 1787; *An Additional Number of Letters from the Federal Farmer to the Republican*, 1788; *The Letters of Richard Henry Lee*, ed. by James Curtis Ballagh, 1911-14; *Memoir of the Life of Richard Henry Lee and His Correspondence*, ed. by his grandson, Richard Henry Lee (2 vols.), 1825.

REFERENCES: James D. Hart, *The Oxford Companion to American Literature*, 1965; J. B. Hubbell, *The South in American Literature 1607-1900* (bibliography), 1954; *Memoir of the Life of Richard Henry Lee. . .* (see above); Louis B. Wright, *The First Gentlemen of Virginia*, 1940; Louis D. Rubin, Jr., ed., *A Bibliographical Guide to the Study of Southern Literature*, 1969. See also Swem's *Virginia Historical Index*, Vol. 2, 1936.

LEITCH, MARY SINTON (1876-1954), poet, was born in New York City, the daughter of Charleton T. and Nancy Lewis Sinton. She was educated in private schools, Smith College, and Columbia University. She studied also in France and Germany.

Before settling in Virginia, she traveled about the world on tramp steamers and sailing vessels. Many of her experiences are recounted in *Himself and I: Our Sea Saga*, written in collaboration with "Himself," her husband, John David Leitch.

In her varied life she was an inspector of women's prisons in New York state, and a contributing editor to *Harper's Monthly*, the New York *Herald*, and the New York *Evening Post*. After she came to Virginia, she once served as chairman of a committee for securing a juvenile court in Norfolk.

She was president of the Poetry Society of Virginia, associate editor of *The Lyric* for one year, and editor of the 1932 edition of *Lyric Virginia Today* (Vol. I).

Her wanderlust lasted throughout her life. With the advent of the trailer she took up what she called "gypsying" as a recreation. Other recreations besides writing were swimming and gardening. (M.M.C.)

BOOKS: Three dramatic pieces, produced locally, but unpublished: *The Coming of the Cross*, 1927; *The Black Moon*, 1929; *Two Mile Tree*, 1931; *The Wagon and the Star*, 1922; *The Unrisen Morrow*, 1926; *Spider Architect*, 1937; *From Invisible Mountains*, 1943; *Nightingales on the Moon*, 1952; *Himself and I: Our Sea Saga*, 1950.

REFERENCES: *Who's Who in America*, Vol. 28, 1954-55; *Biographical Dictionary of Contemporary Poets*, 1938; Richmond *Times-Dispatch*, Jan. 30, 1949; Norfolk *Virginian-Pilot*, Aug. 21, 1954.

LOGAN, JOHN (c.1725-1780), Chief of the Cayuga Indians, is noted for an address of protest sent to Lord Dunmore. Thomas Jefferson, in his *Notes on the State of Virginia*, included this message by John (or James) Logan. The message protested the killing of John's family and other Indians by a band of frontiersmen. The raid precipitated "Lord Dunmore's War" in 1774, which culminated in the battle of Point Pleasant, a bloody conflict won by General Andrew Lewis. Logan refused to help negotiate the peace after the battle; instead he sent his eloquent address to protest to Lord Dunmore. (M.M.C.)

REFERENCES: Francis Coleman Rosenberger, *The Virginia Reader,* 1948; James D. Hart *The Oxford Companion to American Literature,* 1965; John D. Hicks, *The Federal Union,* 1948.

LOWNSBERRY, ELOISE (1888-   ), author of juveniles, came to live in Virginia in 1932, after her marriage to Carl Stearns Clancy. Before this, she had been educated at Wellesley and had lived in New York City and in Hollywood, California. But it was her service during World War I working in France with the Quakers that was most influential in shaping her career. The Quakers had instilled into her the love of peace, and she saw that the best place to spread this message was through children, who could profit from "ideas of peace, of right relationships, of a philosophy of life which could withstand shocks."

The first production of this resolve was *This Boy Knight of Reims* (1927), based upon the fierce warrior Clovis, who had accepted Christian baptism at Reims Cathedral in 496. This was followed by *Out of the Flame* (1931), a story of Francois I and his sister Marguerite d'Angouleme. Then came *Lighting the Torch* (1934), the story of Erasmus and the liberation of ideas through the printing press. *Saints and Rebels* (1937) is a collection of biographies of those who fought for freedom of expression from the Middle Ages to modern times. Later works concern liberation of the spirit and Miss Lownsberry's extensive travels.

BOOKS: *Boy Knight of Reims,* 1927; *Out of the Flame,* 1931; *Lighting the Torch,* 1934; *Saints and Rebels,* 1937; *A Camel for a Throne,* 1941; with R. Lal Singh, *The Gift of the Forest,* 1942; *Marta the Doll,* 1948.

REFERENCES: Kunitz and Haycraft, *The Junior Book of Authors,* 1951.

MADISON, JAMES (1751-1836), political essayist and third president of the United States, had an early interest in literature. At Princeton he joined Philip Freneau and Hugh Henry Brackenridge in forming the American Whig Society, whose purpose it was to cultivate friendship, morality, and literature. The young men wrote essays and debated questions of government, fostering in Madison an interest that later surpassed his interest in literature.

During the Federal Constitutional Convention of 1787, Madison's knowledge of governments, ancient and modern, made his influence valuable in the forming of the American Constitution. He was a member of the committee appointed to polish the important document.

The Federalist is Madison's chief claim to literary fame. According to his record he wrote numbers 10, 14, 18-20, 37-58, and 62-63—twenty-nine of the eighty-five papers. This listing has been disputed in widely circulated editions of *The Federalist,* but disinterested research tends to suggest its truth. (M.M.C.)

BOOKS: *The Federalist*, 10, 14, 18-20, 37-58, 62, 63.

REFERENCES: J. B. Hubbell, *The South in American Literature 1607-1900*, 1954; William T. Hutchinson, and others. *The Papers of James Madison* (3 Vols.), 1962-69; Edward M. Burns, *James Madison: Philosopher of the Constitution*, 1938; William C. Rives, *History of the Life and Times of James Madison* (3 Vols.), 1859-1868; Ralph Ketcham, *James Madison*, 1971.

MAGILL, MARY TUCKER (1830-1899), novelist and historian, was born in Jefferson County, West Virginia, but spent her formative years in Charlottesville and Richmond. In 1848, she moved to Winchester to live with the family of her grandfather, Henry St. George Tucker. Left destitute by the Civil War (she was a loyal Confederate), she opened a girls' school early in the Reconstruction era with the aid of her daughters. She soon abandoned this enterprise for writing. Beginning with articles and stories, she graduated to booklength narratives (e.g. *The Holcombes; a Story of Virginia Life*, 1871) and to book-length historical studies (e.g. *History of Virginia*, 1873), written for use in the public schools.

BOOKS: *Women: Or, Chronicles of the Late War*, 1871; *The Holcombes: A Story of Virginia Life*, 1871; *History of Virginia*, 1873; *Pantomimes*, 1882; *Under the Pruning Knife: A Story of Southern Life*, 1888; *Stories from Virginia History*, 1897.

REFERENCE: *Library of Southern Literature*, Vol. 8.

MAGRUDER, JULIA (1854?-1907), novelist, was born in Charlottesville. At eighteen she published her first novel and won a prize of three hundred dollars awarded by the Baltimore *Sun*. Altogether she wrote about twenty novels. Chief among these were *Princess Sonia* and *Manifest Destiny*. *Princess Sonia*, like several of her other novels, was illustrated by Charles Dana Gibson. Her fiction, often serialized, was directed toward women. Her heroine's problem was usually a deterrent to marriage or an unwise marriage that threatened to ruin her life.

In non-fiction Miss Magruder voiced her interest in the changing social status of women and her concern about child labor questions. She wrote some children's books also, and many short stories. (M.M.C.)

BOOKS: *Across the Chasm*, 1885; *At Anchor*, 1887; *Honored in the Breach*, 1888; *A Magnificent Plebeian*, 1888; *The Child Amy*, 1894; *Princess Sonia*, 1895; *The Violet*, 1896; *Dead Selves*, 1897; *Labor of Love*, 1898; *Miss Ayr of Virginia and Other Stories*, 1898; *A Realized Ideal*, 1898; *A Heaven-Kissing Hill*, 1899; *Struan*, 1899; *Manifest Destiny*, 1900; *A Sunny Southerner*, 1901; *Her Husband: The Mystery of a Man*, 1911.

REFERENCES: Alice Archer Graham, "Julia Magruder," Monograph, Feb., 1934, George Washington U. Library; *Who's Who in America*, Vol. 4, 1906-07; *Library of Southern Literature*, Vol. 8; M. L. Rutherford, *The South in History and Literature*, 1907. See also Swem's *Virginia Historical Index*, Vol. 2, 1936.

MANDELKORN, EUGENIA ["EUGENIA MILLER"] (1916-), author of juveniles, has lived for several years in both France and Italy, two countries which have furnished her materials for achieving one of her primary aims in fiction: presenting "historical unknown facts" in such a way as to let her young readers "see" back into former ages. A good example of this aim is *The Sign of the Salamander* (1965), a story of da Vinci's last three years in Amboise, France. Though she enjoys searching out the little known revealing fact, she has stated that her main object is "to tell a story."

BOOKS: *Deadline at Spook Cabin*, 1958; *Rocking Hill Road*, 1959; *The Golden Spur*, 1964; *The Sign of the Salamander*, 1965.

REFERENCES: *Contemporary Authors*, 11-12.

MARSHALL, JOHN (1755-1835), biographer and juridical writer, was born near Germantown (now Midland), Virginia. His early education was under the tuteledge of his father and local clergymen. He then went on to study law at the College of William and Mary. His political career consisted of roles as Burgess, foreign emissary, Congressman, Secretary of State, and Chief Justice of the Supreme Court (1801-1835).

Marshall's literary accomplishments consist of his *Life of George Washington* (1804-07) (famous, though not much honored by historians), a *History of the Colonies* (1824), and numerous decisions concerning Constitutional law (usually considered his most valuable contribution).

BOOKS: *The Life of George Washington*, 1804-07; *A History of the Colonies Planted by the English on the Continent of North America*, etc., 1824; *The Writings of John Marshall*, 1839; *The Constitutional Decisions of John Marshall*, ed. with introductory essay, by Joseph P. Cotton, Jr., 1905; *An Autobiographical Sketch by John Marshall: Written at the Request of Joseph Story*, etc., ed. by John Stokes Adams, 1937.

REFERENCES: Kunitz and Haycraft, *American Authors 1600-1900*, 1938; J. B. Hubbell, *The South in American Literature 1607-1900*, 1954; James B. Thayer, *John Marshall*, 1901; John F. Dillon, ed., *Complete Constitutional Decisions of John Marshall*, 1903; Henry Flanders, *The Life of John Marshall*, 1904; Joseph P. Cotton, ed., *The Constitutional Decisions of John Marshall* (2 Vols.), 1905; John E. Oster, *The Political and Economic Doctrines of John Marshall*, 1914; Irwin S. Rhodes, *The Papers of John Marshall: A Descriptive Calendar* (2 Vols.), 1969.

MARTIN, MRS. FRED E. ["FRAN MARTIN"] (1906-), writer of children's fiction and poet, though born and reared in New Jersey, has spent much of her adult life in Norfolk. Using her own three children as models, she began her career of writing juvenile fiction with *Knuckles Down!* (1942), the story of a marble contest. Later she wrote two more books based upon her Norfolk experiences—*No School Friday* and *Sea Room*—which were illustrated by his sister, Dorothy McEntee. *Nine Tales of Coyote* and *Nine Tales of Raven* are retellings of Indian legends which contain popular folk motifs found in many literatures and mythologies.

78 VIRGINIA AUTHORS

Mrs. Martin has also written several children's plays, most of them
dramatizations of popular juvenile stories (e.g. *Puss in Boots, The Traveling
Musicians, The Nutcracker Prince, The Sleeping Beauty,* and *Snow White
and the Seven Dwarfs*).

BOOKS: *Knuckles Down,* 1942; *No School on Friday,* 1945; *Sea Room,*
1947; *Nine Tales of Coyote,* 1950; *Nine Tales of Raven,* 1951; *Pirate Island,*
1955.

REFERENCES: Margaret H. Carpenter, *Virginia Authors' Yearbook,*
1956, 1957, 1958; *Virginia Lives; Who's Who of American Women,* 2nd. ed.,
Vol. 2.

MASON, EMILY VIRGINIA (1815-1909), biographer and poet, was born
in Lexington, Kentucky, but came to live in Fairfax County, Virginia, fifteen
years before the Civil War. During the War she served as a hospital volun-
teer and as matron in several hospitals. Her close association with the conflict inspired two of her works: *A Popular Life of General Lee* (1871) and
Southern Poems of the War (1867). For over a decade after the War she
served as assistant principal of a girls' school in Paris.

BOOKS: Ed., *Southern Poems of the War,* 1867; *Journal of a Young
Lady of Virginia in 1798,* 1871; *Popular Life of General Robert E. Lee,* 1871.

REFERENCE: *Who Was Who,* 1897-1942.

MAURY, MATTHEW FONTAINE (1806-1873), distinguished ocean-
ographer, was born near Fredericksburg, Virginia. He became a midshipman
in 1825 and spent the next ten years at sea. In 1841, when he became lame
as the result of an accident and could no longer qualify for active duty, he
was appointed Superintendent of the Depot of Charts and Instruments of
the Navy Department. Here he began his research on winds and currents
and in 1847 issued his "Wind and Current Chart." This was followed in
1848 by explanatory sailing directions which were finally called, in 1851,
*Explanations and Sailing Directions to Accompany the Wind and Current
Charts.* His suggestions were accepted widely, and the sailing time saved by
their use brought him world fame. At the outbreak of the Civil War, the
Russian admiralty offered him the hospitality of Russia in which to continue
his studies. He refused their offer to join the cause of Virginia. He spent the
first few years after the war out of the country, but returned in 1868 to
become professor of meteorology at the Virginia Military Institute and died
there February 1, 1873. He was the author of many scientific publications.
His *Physical Geography of the Sea* (1855) is now recognized as the first text
book of modern oceanography. (M.M.C.)

BOOKS: *Explanations and Sailing Directions to Accompany the Wind
and Current Charts,* 1851; *Physical Geography of the Sea,* 1855.

REFERENCES: *Dictionary of American Biography,* Vol. 17; Francis C.
Rosenberger, the *Virginia Reader,* 1948; Frances Leigh Williams, *Matthew
Fontaine Maury: Scientist of the Sea,* 1963. See also Swem's *Virginia Historical
Index,* Vol. 2, 1936.

MAYS, DAVID J[OHN] (1896-1970), historian, was born in Richmond, where he spent the majority of his life. He was educated at Randolph-Macon College (B.A., 1920) and the University of Richmond (L.L.B., 1924). In addition to his law practice and his active participation in many civic affairs, he was a historian of note. His finest contribution was a two-volume biography of Edmund Pendleton (1952), which won him the Pulitzer Prize in 1953. At the time of his death he was preparing an edition of the letters of Pendleton's ward, John Taylor of Caroline (*q.v.*).

BOOKS: *Edmund Pendleton, 1721-1803*, 1952; *The Letters and Papers of Edmund Pendleton*, 1967.

REFERENCES: *Who's Who in the South and Southwest*, Vol. 6; *Virginia Lives.*

McCLELLAND, MARY GREENWAY (1853-1895), poet and romancer, was born in Nelson County, Virginia, and educated privately by her mother, who read Scott to her at an early age. Quite naturally, her later prose writings took the form of the then-popular romance. However, her interests were rigorous enough to embrace such topics as social castes in the South (e.g. *A Self-Made Man*, 1877), as well as divorce and heredity. She was also noted for her treatment of plain country folk and her use of Negro dialect (e.g. *Old Ike's Memories*, 1884).

BOOKS: *Manitou Island*, 1892; *The Old Post Road*, 1894; *St. John's Wooing*, 1895; *Princess*, 1866; *Jean Monteith*, 1887; *Madame Silva*, 1888; *Burkett's Lock*, 1889; *Eleanor Gwynn*, 1890; *Broadoaks*, 1893; *Mammy Mystic*, 1895.

REFERENCES: *Library of Southern Literature*, Vol. 8.

McCORMICK, VIRGINIA TAYLOR (1873-1957), critic, lecturer, poet, and editor, was born in Berryville, Virginia, but lived in Norfolk for many years. Always active in the Norfolk and the Virginia Poetry groups, she was one of the founders of *The Lyric,* and its second editor. She published five books of poetry. (M.M.C.)

BOOKS: *Star Dust and Gardens*, 1920; *Voices in the Wind*, 1924; *Charcoal and Chalk*, 1931; *Radio to Daedalus*, 1931; *Winter Apples*, 1942.

REFERENCES: Armistead Churchill Gordon, Jr., *Virginian Writers of Fugitive Verse*, 1923; *University of North Carolina Extension Bulletin*, Vol. 8, Oct. 16, 1928, pp. 13-14; Margaret Haley Carpenter, *Virginia Authors' Yearbook*, 1958.

McCOY, JOHN PLEASANT (1906-   ), novelist, was born in Grundy, Virginia, and was graduated from the University of Richmond (B.A., 1927). Before becoming a writer he played semi-professional baseball, farmed, and taught in the public schools. His first novel, *Swing the Big-eyed Rabbit* (1944), was written in a hospital room, where McCoy was recuperating from a wound which left him partially paralyzed. It was a story based upon his teaching experiences in a mountain school. In addition to the novel's local color interest its humor is outstanding—a clear descendant of the school of the Old Southwestern humorists. The same is true of *Big As Life* (1950). His third novel, *The Secret Doorways* (1971), is set in the mythical town of Montcliff, Virginia and features a Richmond banker and his family as main characters.

BOOKS: *Swing the Big-eyed Rabbit*, 1944; *Big As Life*, 1950; *The Secret Doorways*, 1971.

REFERENCE: Lewis F. Ball, "The Real McCoy," University of Richmond *Alumni Bulletin*, April, 1950.

McDOWELL, CHARLES R., SR. (1895-1968), novelist, writes: "I was born in Danville, Kentucky, on August 26, 1895, attended a local prep school and was graduated from Centre College in Danville; later I was graduated from the Yale Law School and took a Master's degree at Columbia University.

"Before finishing law school, I had spent two years coaching athletic teams and two years in the Naval Air Service.

"After three years of the practice of law, I came to Washington and Lee University as a law teacher and have been here ever since except for the four years of World War II, which I spent in the Naval Air Service.

"My only published book is *The Iron Baby Angel*, based upon memories of my early boyhood in Danville, Kentucky.

"I did write a serial or novelette called 'The Ringer' several years ago, which was published in the *Argosy Magazine*. It was based almost entirely upon my experiences in connection with athletics in Southern colleges."

BOOKS: *The Iron Baby Angel*, 1954.

REFERENCES: *Library Journal*, April 1, 1954; *New York Herald Tribune Book Review*, April 11, 1954; *Booklist*, April 15, 1954; Chicago *Sunday Tribune*, May 2, 1954; New York *Times*, Aug. 1, 1954.

McDOWELL, CHARLES R., JR. (1926-   ), columnist, was born in Danville, Kentucky, and reared in Lexington, Virginia, where his father, Charles R. McDowell, Sr. (*q.v.*) was a law professor and avocational writer. He was graduated from Washington and Lee University and the Columbia School of Journalism. Since 1949 he has written for the Richmond *Times-Dispatch*. His regular column has a large following, especially when the fictional "Aunt Gertrude" is featured. His tone is slightly wry, though always gentle and engaging. *What Did You Have in Mind?* (1963) and *One Thing After Another* (1960) are collections of columns.

BOOKS: *One Thing After Another*, 1960; *What Did You Have in Mind?*, 1963; *Campaign Fever: The National Folk Festival from New Hampshire to November, 1964*, 1965.

REFERENCE: *Arts in Virginia*, II, 2 (Winter, 1962).

McGUFFEY, WILLIAM HOLMES (1800-1873), compiler of text books rather than an imaginative writer, had a distinguished career as an educator and preacher in Ohio, after which he became Professor of Moral Philosophy at the University of Virginia and spent the last twenty-eight years of his life in Charlottesville.

"McGuffey Readers," with their discriminating choice of the world's literature, didactic though some of the selections were, set the tone for reading in the nation. Many a boy and girl became articulate through the assimilation of their fare.

The famous series began in 1836 with the *First* and *Second Readers*. The next year the *Primer, Third,* and *Fourth Readers* were published; in 1836, the *Speller*. The *Fifth Reader* was published in 1844 and the *Sixth* in 1857.

Alexander McGuffey, a young brother, worked with William McGuffey and is thought to have been the sole compiler of the *Speller* and the *Fifth Reader*. Many revisions of the texts were made as well as supplementary units, elocution texts, and high school readers. More than 122,000,000 copies were sold. As late as 1920 new editions were printed for class room use. In the 1940's a complete set of the readers (a collector's item) could be found in many book stores.

There is a collection of the "McGuffey Readers" in the McGuffey Museum at Miami University in Ohio. (M.M.C.)

BOOKS: *The Eclectic First Reader*, 1838; *The Eclectic Third Reader*, 1839. Later editions were published in Cincinnati and New York by Wilson, Hinkle and Co.; W. B. Smith and Co.; Van Antwerp, Bragg and Co.; Clark and Maynard Co. and the American Book Co. Facsimile Reprints were issued by Van Nostrand, Reinhold Co., 1969.

REFERENCES: *Dictionary of American Biography*, Vol. 12, 1933; Kunitz and Haycraft, *American Authors 1600-1900*, 1938; Henry Hobart Vail, *A History of the McGuffey Readers*, 1910, 1911; Harvey C. Minnich, *William Holmes McGuffey and the Peerless Pioneer McGuffey Readers*, 1928, reprinted in 1936 as *William Holmes McGuffey and His Readers;* Melancthon Tope, *Biography of William Holmes McGuffey*, 1929.

McNAMARA, LENA BROOKE ["EVALINA MACK"] (1891-), mystery and juvenile writer, has spent a substantial part of her life as a professional portrait painter, illustrator, and teacher of art. Most of her mysteries (e.g. *Death of A Portrait* (1952) and *Murder in Miniature* (1959), were written under her pseudonym. Her abilities as a juvenile writer and illustrator are both seen in *Deux Enfants en France* (1957) and *Deux Enfants à la Mère* (1957). Her art has been exhibited nationally, and she has taught both at the Hermitage Foundation in Norfolk and in her own studio.

BOOKS: *Death of a Portrait*, 1952; *The Corpse in the Cove*, 1955; *Deux Enfants en France*, 1957; *Deux Enfants à la Mère*, 1957; *Death Among the Sands*, 1957; *Murder in Miniature*, 1959; *The Penance Was Death*, 1964.

REFERENCE: *Contemporary Authors*, 11-12.

MEACHAM, HARRY MONROE (1901-), poet, writes: "I was born in Petersburg, Virginia, July 19, 1901, the son of B. T. (Tom) and Julia

Webb Meacham. My father was a poet *(Rhymes of a Crossroads Man)* and a scholar who would recite Shakespeare, Burns, or the Psalms at the first pause in conversation. I was strongly influenced by my literary environment. I am largely self-educated with the help of special courses. At St. Johns I studied the Greek language and literature; at Richmond Professional Institute, philosophy. My first poem was published in a newspaper when I was thirteen; the next one, thirty years later."

He has held many notable positions in learned societies in Virginia and is currently a contributor to the Richmond *News-Leader* and to *Commonwealth* magazine.

BOOK: *The Caged Panther: Ezra Pound at St. Elizabeths,* 1967.

REFERENCES: *Who's Who in America,* Vol. 30, 1958-1959; *Who's Who in the South and Southwest,* Vol. 6, 1959.

MEADE, JULIAN RUTHERFORD (1909-1940), novelist and non-fiction writer, was born in Danville, Virginia. He attended the University of Virginia and later followed various occupations. His first book, *I Live in Virginia* (1935), gives an account of his experiences as teacher, reporter, student, secretary, and mill-worker in different parts of Virginia, as well as his impressions of strikes, bosses, laborers, society life, and his literary friends. Here is keen observation of life in Virginia in the 1930's.

Although his gardening books contain some practical information, their inherent charm lies in the author's gift for painting portraits and reporting conversations. *Adam's Profession and Its Conquest of Eve* gives pictures of his father and mother, the servants, and the neighbors. *Bouquets and Bitters: a Gardener's Medley* covers his visits to gardens of distinguished persons from Maine to Hollywood during the period of a year.

The Back Door, his first novel, tells the story of a young Negro girl, who does kitchen work for a Southern white family, and her handsome husband, who works in a tobacco factory.

Three books for children complete his literary output from 1935 through 1940. These are characterized by wit and humor and are charmingly illustrated by Grace Paull. (M.M.C.)

BOOKS: *I Live in Virginia,* 1935; *Adam's Profession and Its Conquest of Eve,* 1936; *Teeny and the Tall Man,* 1936; *The Back Door,* 1938; *Miss Couch and the Scamps,* 1938; *Bouquets and Bitters,* 1938; *Peter by the Sea,* 1940.

REFERENCES: *Dictionary of American Authors,* 1951; Francis C. Rosenberger, *Virginia Reader,* 1948.

MEADE, WILLIAM (1789-1862), writer of non-fiction, was born in Frederick County, Virginia, the son of Col. Richard Kidder Meade, aide on Washington's staff during the Revolution, and Mary Fitzhugh (Grymes). He was sent to a private school in New Jersey. In 1806 he entered the junior class in the College of New Jersey (Princeton) and was graduated two years later as valedictorian. He prepared for the ministry under the Reverend

Walter Addison of the Episcopal Church of Maryland. He was ordained a priest by Bishop Claggett of Maryland in 1814.

Bishop Meade is noted for his influence in reviving the Episcopal Church in Virginia. As a strong and notable preacher, he was a power for good in the State. His interest in the spiritual condition of Negroes led him to free his own slaves at an early date, but later he believed this to be a mistaken kindness. Although strongly opposed to secession, he sided with his State, and at a convention in Columbia, South Carolina, October 16, 1862, he became the presiding bishop of the Confederacy.

Bishop Meade is buried in Alexandria, Virginia, at the Theological Seminary, which he helped to establish in 1823. (M.M.C.)

BOOKS and Other Writing: Many tracts, addresses, charges to the clergy, and sermons on special occasions. The best known of his writings is *Old Churches, Ministers, and Families of Virginia* (2 vols.), 1857, which contains extensive information about the colonial period.

REFERENCES: *Dictionary of American Biography*, Vol. 8; Richmond *Times-Dispatch*, May 8, 1949. See also Swem's *Virginia Historical Index*, Vol. 2, 1936.

MITCHELL, JOSEPH B. (1915-   ), military historian, was born in Fort Leavenworth, Kansas, the son of famed aviation pioneer William A. Mitchell. He says that except for two years at Episcopal High School in Alexandria, his entire life has been spent "in the West Point atmosphere."

It was during the sixteen years that he spent as an Army officer following his graduation from West Point in 1937 that he served as Chief of the Historical Division of the American Battle Monuments Commission, a position he held after his retirement from the Army. Here he began to write his histories of battles and battle heroes, beginning with *Decisive Battles of the Civil War* (1955). His most recent work is *The Badge of Gallantry* (1968), containing recollections of Civil War soldiers who won the Congressional Medal of Honor.

BOOKS: *Decisive Battles of the Civil War*, 1955; *Twenty Decisive Battles of the World*, 1964; *Discipline and Bayonets*, 1967; *The Badge of Gallantry*, 1968.

REFERENCES: *Library Journal*, May 15, 1955; Chicago *Sunday Tribune*, July 17, 1955; *Christian Science Monitor*, Aug. 4, 1955; New York *Times*, Aug. 14, 1955; *Booklist*, Sept. 15, 1955; *New Yorker*, Oct. 29, 1955; San Francisco *Chronicle*, Nov. 6, 1955; *Contemporary Authors*, 11-12.

MONSELL, HELEN ALBEE (1895-1971), author of novels, short stories, plays, and juveniles, was born in the shadow of Lee's Monument in Richmond, on February 24, 1895. After being educated in Richmond public schools, The University of Richmond (B.A.), and Columbia (M.A.), she worked as a high school teacher, as Secretary for the State Department of Public Instruction, and as an editor. In 1922, she became Registrar of

Richmond College, a post which she held until retirement in 1961. Just before her retirement, the University awarded her an honorary LL.D.

Both during her career at Richmond and after her retirement, she was a popular professor of children's literature at both the University of Richmond and Virginia Commonwealth University.

Her writing career, which she said began at eight with the writing of a sequel to *Alice in Wonderland*, started with the publication of several poems in children's magazines. "Since then," she wrote, "I've tried my hand, in turn or all at once, on short stories, novels, children's stories, stories for religious publications, plays for amateur production, mystery stories for girls, and principally on juvenile biographical fiction." One title in the last genre, *Boy of Old Virginia: Robert E. Lee,* has become a classic.

BOOKS: *Secret of the Chestnut Tree,* 1936; *Secret of the Gold Earring,* 1938; *Lucy Fights for Her Rights,* 1940; *Paddy's Christmas,* 1942; *In Her Own Hands,* 1943; *The Mystery of Grandfather's Coat,* 1948; *Boy of Old Virginia: Robert E. Lee,* 1937; *Thomas Jefferson,* 1939; *Young Stonewall: Thomas Jackson,* 1942; *Dolly Madison,* 1944; *Henry Clay,* 1947; *John Marshall,* 1949; *Woodrow Wilson,* 1940; *Susan B. Anthony,* 1954; *Her Own Way: The Story of Lottie Moon,* 1958; *The Story of Cousin George,* 1961; *Woodrow Wilson: Boy President,* 1962; *With Patrick Henry's Help,* 1966.

REFERENCES: Richmond *Times-Dispatch,* July 23, 1950; Margaret H. Carpenter, *Virginia Authors' Yearbook,* 1956, 1957, 1958.

MOORE, VIRGINIA (Mrs. John Jefferson Hudgins) (1903-   ), poet, novelist, and non-fiction writer, was born to parents whose roots extend far back into Virginia's history. She was educated at the Brenau School in Georgia, at Hollins College (B.A., 1923), and at Columbia (M.A., 1924; Ph.D., 1952). Her writing career embraces many genres: poetry (e.g. *Homer's Golden Chain* (1936)); biography (e.g. *The Life and Eager Death of Emily Brontë* (1936)); novel (e.g. *Rising Wind* (1928)); criticsm (e.g. *The Unicorn: William Butler Yeats' Search for Reality* (1954)); and history (e.g. *Scottsville on the James* (1969)). One of her most famous works for Virginia readers is *Virginia Is A State of Mind* (1943). This book, which presents the composite character of the Commonwealth by discussing many of its well-known personalities and places, has been called a "State biography." Her interest in religion and philosophy (in which she took her doctorate) is reflected in *The Whole World, Stranger* (1957), the theme of which is the common bonds shared by all peoples of the world.

BOOKS: *Not Poppy,* 1926; *Sweet Water and Bitter,* 1928; *Rising Wind,* 1928; *Distinguished Women Writers,* 1934; *Homer's Golden Chain,* 1936; *The Life and Eager Death of Emily Brontë,* 1936; *Virginia is a State of Mind,* 1943; *Ho For Heaven,* 1946; *The Unicorn: William Butler Yeats' Search for Reality,* 1954.

REFERENCES: *Who's Who of American Women,* 1968-1969; *Virginia Lives;* Richmond *Times-Dispatch,* June 16, 1946.

VIRGINIA AUTHORS 85

MORDECAI, SAMUEL (1786-1865), historian, was born in New York, but came to Richmond in 1802, went into business there, and stayed until 1821, when he transferred his tobacco and cotton operation to Petersburg. These years in Richmond, plus a later residence there (1849-64), furnished him with much first hand information for his *Richmond in By-Gone Days* (1856; rev. ed., 1860). This volume has become one of the most important sources for the history of Virginia's capital and one of the best known works of local history ever written in Virginia. Mordecai died in Raleigh, North Carolina.

BOOK: *Richmond in By-Gone Days*, 1856, rev. 1860, reprinted 1946.

REFERENCES: Ruth K. Nuernberger, "Some Notes on the Mordecai Family," *Virginia Magazine of History and Biography*, 49 (Oct., 1941); and Alexander Wilbourne Weddell, "Samuel Mordecai, Chronicler of Richmond, 1786-1865," *Virginia Magazine of History and Biography*, 53 (Oct., 1945).

MORELAND, JOHN RICHARD (1879-1947), poet and editor, was born in Norfolk, Virginia, where he spent most of his life. In 1920 he helped found *The Lyric*, a magazine of poetry, and served as its first editor. His poems appeared in many periodicals and anthologies. He published at least ten collections of poetry. (B.P.D.)

BOOKS: *Red Poppies in the Wheat*, 1921; *The Sea and April*, 1928; *Newry*, 1930; *The Moon Mender*, 1933; *From Dingle to Derry*, 1936; *A Blue Wave Breaking*, 1938; *A World Turning*, 1940; *What of the Night*, 1942; *Bridle for a Unicorn*, 1944; *Shadow at My Heel*, 1946.

REFERENCES: Armistead Churchill Gordon, Jr., *Virginian Writers of Fugitive Verse*, 1923; *University of North Carolina Extension Bulletin*, Oct. 16, 1928, Vol. 8; Clipping File, Norfolk Public Library.

MORTON, OREN FREDERICK (1857-1926), writer of non-fiction, was born in Freyburg, Maine. He received his B.L. degree from the University of Nebraska in 1879. Until 1907 he was a teacher and a general newspaper writer in Winchester, Virginia. He also wrote histories of the following counties: Pendleton, W. Va. (1910); Highland, Va. (1911); Preston, W. Va. (1913); Monroe, W. Va. (1916); Bath, Va. (1917); Rockbridge, Va. (1919); Allegheny, Va. (1922); Winchester, Va. (1924). (M.M.C.)

BOOKS: *Under the Cottonwoods*, 1900; *Winning or Losing*, 1901; *Land of the Laurel*, 1903; *Story of Daniel Boone;* 1913.

REFERENCES: *Who Was Who in America*, Vol. 1, 1942.

MUNFORD, ROBERT (*c.*1730-1783), playwright and poet, the third of that name, was born at "Wakefield" in Prince George County. He was educated in the Wakefield School of Yorkshire, England, with his cousin, William Beverley, and the Lee brothers of Virginia; but unlike them, he did not go on to an English university. His father had left an estate heavily mortgaged, and the condition of the family finances probably precluded further schooling in England.

In 1782 he became proprietor of "Richland," and held ninety-one slaves, more than any other planter in the county. He had served as county-lieutenant and sheriff and represented his county in the House of Burgesses and its successor, the House of Delegates.

His wife was his first cousin Anne (or Anna) Beverley, daughter of William Beverley of "Blandfield." It was their son William (*q.v.*), himself a poet and playwright, who fourteen years after his father's death, had published in Petersburg, *A Collection of Plays and Poems, by the Late Colonel Robert Munford, of Mecklenburg, in the State of Virginia.* In the book were two plays, *The Candidates* and *The Patriots,* along with a translation of the first book of Ovid's *Metamorphoses,* and several poems. It is for the two comedies that Colonel Munford is to be remembered.

The Candidates gives us firsthand information about elections in eighteenth century Virginia, and *The Patriots,* in which a Negro comedian makes his first appearance, shows us real and pretended patriotism in an amusing satire.

Whether or not the plays were produced in Colonel Munford's time is not known, but it is quite possible that they were. It is known, however, that they were written ten years or more before Royal Tyler's *The Contrast,* generally considered the first American comedy of importance, was produced in New York in 1787. The first line of *The Candidates* indicates that the writing of the play followed closely upon the death of Governor Botetourt on October 15, 1770.

Both *The Patriots* and *The Candidates* were subsequently published in the *William and Mary Quarterly. The Candidates* proved to be good theater when the Williamsburg players produced it in 1949. (M.M.C.)

BOOK: *A Collection of Plays and Poems,* 1798.

REFERENCES: James D. Hart, *Oxford Companion to American Literature,* 1965; J. B. Hubbell, *The South in American Literature, 1607-1900* (bibliography), 1954; Louis D. Rubin, Jr., ed., *A Bibliographical Guide to the Study of Southern Literature,* 1969. See also Swem's *Virginia Historical Index,* Vol. 2, 1936.

MUNFORD, WILLIAM (1775-1825), poet, translator, and critic, the only son of Colonel Robert Munford (*q.v.*), was nine when his father died. George Wythe took an interest in the youth and supervised his studies in Greek, Spanish, and Italian, and later in law. The young man showed much literary promise, but the premature publication of some of his immature work brought adverse criticism and proved a deterrent to his development as a writer. He continued to write occasional poems for the papers, but mainly his publications were law reports.

In his free time he translated the *Iliad.* Pope's translation, which was the standard English version, he said, was unfaithful to the original Greek poem. Cowper's translation also erred, he thought.

At the time of his death, William Munford had been making preparations for the publication of his translation. Twenty years later his sons, John and William, had the book appraised by the classical scholar, Cornelius C. Felton, and after receiving his approval had it published in Boston.

The book met with varying criticism. It was praised for its faithfulness to the original, but some critics found his versifying less skillful than Homer's poem merited.

In spite of his own literary efforts, William Munford is noted chiefly for having his father's plays published. (M.M.C.)

BOOKS: *A General Index to the Virginia Law Authorities, 1790-1819, etc.*, 1819; *Poems, and Compositions in Prose on Several Occasions*, 1798; Translation of the *Iliad*, 1846.

REFERENCES: James D. Hart, *Oxford Companion to American Literature*, 1965; J. B. Hubbell, *The South in American Literature 1607-1900* (bibliography), 1954. See also Swem's *Virginia Historical Index*, Vol. 2, 1936.

MYERS, ROBERT MANSON (1921-   ), critic, dramatist, and satirist, was born in Charlottesville, Virginia. He was educated at Vanderbilt (B.A., 1941) and Columbia (M.A., 1942; Ph.D., 1948) Universities and taught at the College of William and Mary and Newcomb College before assuming his present position as professor of English at the University of Maryland. Though he has written several scholarly books (e.g. *Handel, Dryden, and Milton*, 1956), he is best known to the general reading public as the author of *From Beowulf to Virginia Woolf, An Astounding and Wholly Unauthorized History of English Literature* (1952). This satiric romp through the sacred halls of English literature displays a humorous and satiric tone seldom seen since Oscar Wilde. In 1969 his dramatization of Henry James' *The Spoils of Poynton* was featured on the stage in London.

BOOKS: *Handel's Messiah*, 1946?; *Anna Seward*, 1947; *Handel's Messiah: A Touchstone of Taste*, 1948; *Handel, Dryden and Milton*, 1956; *Restoration Comedy*, 1961. Also see above sketch.

REFERENCES: *Dictionary of American Scholars*, 2.

NELSON, ELLEN DOUGLAS KABLER (1874-1958), poet and resident of Lynchburg for many years, was born at New London, Virginia, where her family had lived for several generations. She was educated at the New London Academy.

For outstanding work as a writer of poetry for children, Mrs. Nelson was made an honorary member in the Eugene Field Society, National Association of Authors and Journalists in 1945. She was a member of the Virginia Poetry Society and several other organizations.

Her poems have been included in *The Lantern, The Circle, Fantasy*, and *Selected Magazine Verse* (Paebar Co.). She published five volumes of poems. (R.H.B.)

BOOKS: *Poems*, 1924; *With the Little People Fairies and Flowers*, 1925;

Poems and Stories for the Children's Hour, 1931; *Winged Fancies,* 1932; *Wings of Songs,* 1951.

REFERENCES: Manuscript Collection of Biographies of Lynchburg Writers at the Jones Memorial Library, Lynchburg, Virginia; The Collection of Writings by Virginia Women at Lipscomb Library, Randolph-Macon Woman's College, Lynchburg, Virginia.

NILES, BLAIR (1888-1959), writer of fiction and non-fiction, was born at Coles Ferry, Virginia. Her first husband was the naturalist William Beebe, whom she accompanied on expeditions to Central and South America and the Orient. After being divorced from Beebe, she married architect Robert Niles, with whom she likewise made extensive travels. *Casual Wanderings in Eucador* (1923), *Colombia: Land of Miracles* (1924), and *Black Haiti* (1926) all reflect these travels and contain photographs taken by Niles.

Much of her fiction has to do with such social issues as prison life, homosexuality, slavery, and miscegenation. Of special interest to Virginians is her book *The James,* written for a series on great rivers of the world. Among her honors was the Gold Medal of the Society of Women Geographers.

BOOKS: *Casual Wanderings in Eucador,* 1923; *Colombia: Land of Miracles,* 1924; *Black Haiti,* 1926; *Condemned to Devil's Island,* 1928; *Free,* 1930; *Strange Brother,* 1931; *Light Again,* 1933; *Maria Paluna,* 1934; *Day of Immense Sun,* 1936; *A Journey in Time: Peruvian Pageant,* 1937; *The James,* 1939; *East by Day,* 1941; *Passengers to Mexico,* 1943; *The James from Iron Gate to Sea,* 1945; *Journeys in Time,* 1946; *Martha's Husband: An Informal Portrait of George Washington,* 1951.

REFERENCE: Kunitz and Haycraft, *Twentieth Century Authors,* 1942, also *First Supplement,* 1955; H. R. Warfel, *American Novelists of Today,* 1951; Washington, D. C., *Evening Star,* April 15, 1959.

NOEL-HUME, IVOR (1927-   ), archaeologist, was born in London. After being educated at Framlingham and St. Lawrence Colleges in England, he worked in two London museums before coming to Colonial Williamsburg in 1957 as chief archaeologist. In 1965 he was named director of Williamsburg's Department of Archaeology. Author of numerous papers on archaeology and antiques, he is perhaps best known for *Here Lies Virginia* (1963), a study of archaeological sites and discoveries in the Old Dominion.

BOOKS: *Treasure in the Thames,* 1956; *Great Moments in Archaeology,* 1958; *Excavations at Rosewell in Gloucester County, Virginia, 1957-1959,* 1962; *Here Lies Virginia,* 1963; *Excavations at Clay Bank in Gloucester County, Virginia, 1962-1963,* 1966; *Excavations at Tutter's Neck in James City County, Virginia, 1960-1961,* 1966.

REFERENCE: *Virginia Lives.*

NORWOOD, HENRY (1615-1689), writer of non-fiction, with two friends, set sail for Virginia, in mid-September, 1649, on the ship *The Virginia*

Merchant. A vivid account of the voyage is given in *A Voyage to Virginia,* written in 1649. The piece was published in London in 1732 in Awnsham Churchill's *A Collection of Voyages and Travels.* From 1661 to 1673 Henry Norwood was Treasurer of Virginia. (M.M.C.)

BOOKS: "A Voyage to Virginia," printed in *A Collection of Voyages and Travels,* Vol. 6, London, 1732, by Awnsham Churchill; "A Voyage to Virginia in 1649," reprinted in *Tracts,* by Peter Force, Washington, 1836-46, Vol. 3, 1844, No. 10; "Colonel Norwood's voyage to Virginia in 1648," in *The Virginia Historical Register,* Richmond, 1849.

REFERENCES: Francis Coleman Rosenberger, *Virginia Reader,* 1948; *The Virginia Magazine of History and Biography,* Vol. 33, 1925; Louis D. Rubin, Jr., ed., *A Bibliographical Guide to the Study of Southern Literature,* 1969. See also Swem's *Virginia Historical Index,* Vol. 2, 1936.

NELSON, JAMES POYNTZ (1849-   ), short story writer and poet, born in Richmond, was by profession a Valuation Engineer of the Chesapeake and Ohio Railway Company. Much of his writing was professional. He published one book of short stories and did a number of translations in verse—from the Greek lyric poet Anacreon, from the German of Uhland, and from others, including Italian poets. He also wrote love songs, sonnets, occasional poems, and a few children's poems and nonsense rhymes. Many of these remain unpublished. (C.H.H.)

BOOK: *Balla, and Other Stories,* 1914.

REFERENCES: Swem's *Virginia Historical Index,* Vol. 2, 1936.

PAGE, THOMAS NELSON (1853-1922), short story writer, novelist, and essayist, was born in Hanover County, Virginia, at "Oakland." After graduation from Washington and Lee and the University of Virginia, he began to practice law in Richmond. Subsequent to publishing a series of dialect verses in *Scribner's Monthly,* he published "Marse Chan," the story which made his literary reputation, in 1884. A decade later, he had left law for writing. After spending twenty years in Washington, D.C. (1893-1913), he was named by President Wilson as ambassador to Italy.

Though quite successful as a diplomat, his fame rests in literature, and in a few stories (e.g. "Marse Chan," "Meh Lady," and "Polly"). Though these are romantic tales written in a realistic age, they have become classics of this particular genre.

BOOKS: *In Ole Virginia,* 1887; *Two Little Confederates,* 1888; *The Old South,* 1892; *The Burial of the Guns,* 1894; *Unc' Edinburg: A Plantation Echo,* 1895; *Red Rock,* 1898; *Gordon Keith,* 1903, 1909; *John Marvel: Assistant,* 1909, 1919; *The Red Riders,* 1924, 1927; *Italy and the World War,* 1920; *The Novels, Stories, Sketches and Poems of Thomas Nelson Page,* 1906-18.

REFERENCES: Kunitz and Haycraft, *American Authors 1600-1900,* 1938; *American Fiction,* 1936; Edwin Mims, "Thomas Nelson Page," *South-*

ern Writers, Vol. 2; J. B. Hubbell, *The South in American Literature 1607-1900* (bibliography), 1954; Louis D. Rubin, Jr., ed., *A Bibliographical Guide to the Study of Southern Literature,* 1969. See also Swem's *Virginia Historical Index,* Vol. 2, 1936.

PEEL, ALFREDA MARION (1890-1953), ballad collector, attended Radford State Teachers' College and Virginia College in Roanoke. She taught in the Salem public schools for thirty-five years.

Since 1911, when Miss Peel began collecting folklore, she has contributed many of the English and Scottish ballads to the collection of more than 2500 assembled by the Folklore Society at the University of Virginia. In addition to studying the American versions of the ballads, she studied the originals of the Virginia ballads, which she found at Balliol College, Oxford.

Miss Peel wrote *Witch in the Mill* and assisted C. Alphonso Smith and Arthur Kyle Davis with *Traditional Ballads of Virginia.* (M.M.C.)

BOOK: *Witch in the Mill,* 1947.

REFERENCE: Richmond *Times-Dispatch,* Feb. 26, 1950.

PENDLETON, JAMES D. (1930-   ), playwright, was born at Fort Bragg, North Carolina. He was graduated from Davidson College (B.S., 1952) and the University of North Carolina (M.A., 1958). Since 1958, he has been on the English faculty of Virginia Commonwealth University. The author of five plays, he has won numerous awards for playwriting. (e.g. *The Oaks of Mamre* won the TRAV-TV writing award in 1962). Both his published and unpublished dramas have been presented in many American cities.

PUBLISHED DRAMAS: *The Oaks of Mamre,* 1963. *The Brief and Violent Reign of Absalom,* 1969.

PRODUCED DRAMAS: *The Defender,* 1961; *Nightsong,* 1964; *The Trial of Judas,* 1968.

REFERENCES: Richmond *Times-Dispatch,* Feb. 14, 1968, July 14, 1969, and Feb. 20, 1972; Richmond *News Leader,* Jan. 19, 1963; *Fayetteville* (N.C.) *Observer,* Feb. 14, 1968; *Scottsbluff* (Neb.) *Daily Star Herald,* Jan. 26, 1968.

PEPLE, EDWARD HENRY (1869-1924), author of plays, novels, short stories, and light verse, was born in Richmond and received his education in the John P. McGuire Academy and other schools there. In 1895, he went to New York where he worked as an accountant in various institutions, notably the American Bridge Company. He held membership in the Southern Society and The Virginians.

One of Shirley Temple's most successful movies was his *The Littlest Rebel.* Many of his books went through several editions, and some of them were translated into foreign languages. He was honored with the Litt. D. by the University of the South. (M.M.C.)

BOOKS: *A Broken Rosary,* 1904; *The Prince Chap,* 1904; With C. T. Brady, *Richard the Brazen,* 1906; *Semiramis,* 1907; *The Mallet's Masterpiece,* 1908; *The Spitfire,* 1908; *A Night Out,* 1909; *The Littlest Rebel,* 1911; *The Cur and the Coyote,* 1913; *A Pair of Sixes,* 1914; *An Auto-Biography,* 1915; *The War Dog,* 1918; *The Jury of Our Peers,* 1925.

REFERENCES: *Who Was Who in America,* Vol. 1, 1943; Dr. Edward C. Peple (author's nephew), of the University of Richmond, letters to the editors, dated May 4, 1955, and Nov. 15, 1960.

PERCY, ALFRED (1898-   ), writer of various modes of non-fiction, was born in Lynchburg and educated for the law at the University of Virginia. After a brief practice, he turned to writing. He bought his own press and in 1949 published *Piedmont Apocalypse,* which is representative of several titles on central Virginia. His *Old Place Names* (1950) is a valuable contribution to American etymology. He has published many monographs on Virginia historical subjects.

BOOKS: *Piedmont Apocalypse,* 1949; *Old Place Names,* 1950; *The Central Virginia Blue Ridge,* 1952; *The Devil in the Old Dominion,* 1952; *The Origin of the Lynch Law—1780,* 1959; *The Amherst County Story: a Virginia Saga,* 1961; *Unsung Victory in the Revolution,* 1964.

REFERENCES: *Virginia Magazine of History and Biography,* April, 1960; Margaret H. Carpenter, *Virginia Authors' Yearbook,* 1956, 1957, 1958; *Who's Who in the South and Southwest,* 1963-64.

PERCY, GEORGE (*c.*1580-1632), writer of non-fiction, at twenty-six was a member of the expedition that sailed for Virginia on December 19, 1606. He succeeded John Smith as president of the colony and served during the fateful winter of 1609-1610 when 440 of the 500 colonists died. Later he returned to England. *Observations Gathered out of a Discourse of the Southern Colonie in Virginia by the English* is his account of exploration in the New World. The time parallels that of John Smith's *True Relation,* but the piece was not published until 1625, seventeen years after Smith's account. (M.M.C.)

BOOKS: *Observations Gathered out of a Discourse of the Southern Colonie in Virginia by the English, 1606,* Written by the Honourable gentleman, Master George Percy. Reprint from *Purchas, his Pilgrimes,* London, 1625. Also in *The Founding of Jamestown,* edited by Albert B. Hart, 1907, "American History Leaflets," No. 36.

REFERENCES: James D. Hart, *The Oxford Companion to American Literature,* 1956; Francis Coleman Rosenberger, *Virginia Reader,* 1948; Louis D. Rubin, Jr., ed., *A Bibliographical Guide to the Study of Southern Literature,* 1969. See also Swem's *Virginia Historical Index,* Vol. 2, 1936.

PEYTON, JOHN LEWIS (1824-1896), writer of non-fiction, was born at "Montgomery Hall" near Staunton, Virginia. Ready for college at fifteen, he entered V. M. I. but withdrew because of ill health. He was graduated from the University of Virginia in 1844 with a degree in law, and practiced in Staunton until 1852, when he was sent on a secret mission abroad by President Fillmore.

Although Peyton opposed the secession of Virginia in 1861, he helped to organize and outfit a Virginia regiment. After he was physically incapacitated in the field, he served the Confederacy abroad. He is credited with influencing England to maintain its neutrality in the struggle. For ten years after the war he lived on the Island of Guernsey and then returned to "Steephill" near Staunton to write and to farm.

He held membership in many learned societies at home and abroad. He contributed articles to several of the periodicals of his time and was the author of many books, most of which are historical. (C.H.H.)

BOOKS: *The American Crisis: Or, Pages from the Note Book of a State Agent during the Civil War in America* (2 vols.), 1867; *Over the Alleghenies and Across the Prairies*, 1869; *Memoir of William Madison Peyton*, 1873; *History of Augusta County, Virginia*, 1882; *Rambling Reminiscences of a Residence Abroad*, 1888; *The Adventures of My Grandfather*, 1867; *Tom Swindel: Or, The Adventures of a Boomer*, 1893; *Memoir of John Howe Peyton*, 1894.

REFERENCES: *Dictionary of American Biography*, Vol. 14. See also Swem's *Virginia Historical Index*, Vol. 2, 1936.

PHARR, ROBERT DEANE (1916-   ), novelist and non-fiction writer, was born in Richmond, attended public schools there, and was graduated from Virginia Union University in 1939. His varied career has included stints as waiter and bell-hop while serving his writing apprenticeship. His first novel, *The Book of Numbers* (1969), was a solid success and was consistently praised in national magazines and reviews. The novel reflects his knowledge of Negro life in the South as he was growing up and his interest in "the economy of numbers" (i.e. the numbers game). Though his protagonists Dave Green and Blueboy Harris form a successful numbers operation and become leaders of their race, they can be seen as universal characters involved in the game of life. Mr. Pharr is presently at work on a second novel, *S.R.O.*

BOOKS: *The Book of Numbers*, 1969.

REFERENCES: Richmond *News Leader*, May 15, 1969; *The New York Times Book Review*, April 27, 1969; *Newsweek*, June 16, 1969.

PICKETT, LASALLE CORBELL (Mrs. George Edward Pickett) (1848-1931), historian, editorialist, and poet, was born in Nansemond County. She began writing during the Civil War, in which her husband served as a Confederate general. Her first articles were for the *Illustrated News*. Later she published numerous poems and feature articles and after the war lectured widely on Southern history and folklore. One of her most valuable contributions to history is *Pickett and His Men* (1899); and to literature, *Literary Hearthstones of Dixie* (1912). She died in Washington, D.C.

BOOKS: *Pickett and His Men,* 1899; *Literary Hearthstones of Dixie,* 1912; *The Bugles of Gettysburg,* 1913.
REFERENCE: *Who Was Who,* 1897-1942.

POE, EDGAR ALLAN (1809-1849), short story writer, poet, and critic, was born in Boston, the son of impoverished actors. Upon the death of his mother, he was taken as a young child into the family of John Allan, a rich tobacco merchant of Richmond. He was not, however, legally adopted. He was educated in England and at the University of Virginia, which he left after one year because of circumstances related to his debts. His departure from the University occasioned a violent quarrel with his foster father. Thereupon Poe enlisted in the army, and afterwards entered West Point. Here his career was cut short by expulsion for insubordination. Mr. Allan now completely severed his connection with him, and Poe's life continued to be unhappy, poor, and frustrated. Prior to the break with Mr. Allan, he had, however, already published three slender volumes of poetry: *Tamerlane and Other Poems* (1827), *Al Aaraaf, Tamerlane, and Minor Poems* (1829), and *Poems by Edgar A. Poe* (1831).

Unable to support himself by poetry, Poe went to Baltimore to live in the household of his distant cousin, Mrs. Clemm, whose thirteen-year-old daughter, Virginia, he married in 1836. He had previously turned to journalism and fiction, because they were more lucrative than poetry. He made an analysis of the most successful fiction then being published in the popular magazines, and concluded that there was a market for the tale of terror with a single effect. Having discovered the formula, he put it to good use in all of his best-known stories, now classics of American literature, such as "The Masque of the Red Death," "Ligeia," "The Fall of the House of Usher," etc. The careful structure of Poe's stories did much to advance American fiction.

Poe supported himself and his wife by a career as editor or staff member of *The Southern Literary Messenger, Burton's Gentleman's Magazine,* and the New York *Evening Mirror.* Cursed by poverty—for all his literary work was poorly rewarded—he could not properly provide for his family's needs. In 1847, his wife died amid distressing conditions. During his remaining two years, he lectured and wrote some of his best poetry, including "Ulalume" (1847), written on the death of his wife; "Anabel Lee" (1849); and "Eldorado" (1849). He died in Baltimore in 1849. (L.G.L.)

BOOKS: *The Narrative of Arthur Gordon Pym,* 1839; *Tales of the Grotesque and Arabesque,* 1940; *The Prose Romances of Edgar Allan Poe,* 1843; *Tales,* 1845; *The Raven and Other Poems,* 1845; *Eureka: A Prose Poem,* 1848; James A. Harrison, ed., *The Complete Works of Edgar Allan Poe* (17 vols.), 1903. A. H. Quinn and E. H. O'Neill, eds., *The Complete Poems and Stories of Edgar Allan Poe, with Selections from His Critical Writings,* 1946.

REFERENCES: J. B. Hubbell, *The South in American Literature 1607-1900* (bibliography), 1954; James D. Hart, *The Oxford Companion to Ameri-*

can Literature, 1965; Hervey Allen, *Israfel,* 1926; Arthur H. Quinn, *Edgar Allan Poe: A Critical Biography,* 1941; Louis D. Rubin, Jr., ed., *A Bibliographical Guide to the Study of Southern Literature,* 1969.

POLLARD, EDWARD ALFRED (1931-1872), journalist and historian, was born in Albemarle County. He supplemented his education in the liberal arts (at the University of Virginia) and in law (at the College of William and Mary) with travels in Central America and the Orient. His friend Bishop Meade (*q.v.*) insisted that he study for the Episcopal ministry, and he began to do so. Soon, however, journalism drew him away, and he became associated with the *Daily Richmond Examiner* in the year that the Civil War broke out. He staunchly supported the Confederate cause, though he consistently denounced Jefferson Davis. One biographer refers to him as "undoubtedly the ablest writer in behalf of the Confederacy." His writings enjoyed quite a large following, and he was on his way to England near the end of the War to promote sales of his work when he was captured and incarcerated in Fort Warren and Fortress Monroe. These episodes he recounted in the volume *Observations* (1865). Virtually all his work concerned the Confederacy and continued after the war (e.g. *A Southern History of the War* (1862-66) and *Lee and His Lieutenants* (1867). Pollard died in Lynchburg.

BOOKS: *The Southern Spy: Or, Curiosities of Negro Slavery in the South,* 1859; *The Southern Spy: Letters on the Policy and Inauguration of the Lincoln War,* 1861; *The Second Battle of Manassas,* 1862; *The First Year of the War,* 1862; *The First Year of the War in America,* 1863; *Southern History of the Great Civil War in the United States,* 1863; *The Second Year of the War,* 1863; *The Rival Administration: Richmond and Washington in December, 1863,* 1864; *Observations in the North: Eight Months in Prison and on Parole,* 1865; *The War in America, 1863-64,* 1865; *Echoes from the South,* 1866; *The Lost Cause Regained,* 1868; *Life of Jefferson Davis,* 1869; *Memoirs of the Assassination of Henry Rives Pollard,* 1869; *The Virginia Tourist,* 1870; *The Early Life, Campaigns, and Public Services of Robert E. Lee,* 1870; *A Southern Historian's Appeal for Horace Greeley,* 1872.

REFERENCES: *Library of Southern Literature,* Vol. 19; *National Cyclopaedia of American Biography,* Vol. 11; *Dictionary of American Biography,* Vol. 15.

PRESTON, MARGARET JUNKIN (1820-1897), poet, was born in Philadelphia, but came to Virginia as a young woman of twenty-eight, when her father, the Reverend George Junkin, D.D., became President of Washington College (now Washington and Lee University). She married Professor Preston of the Virginia Military Institute in 1857 and lived in Lexington the remainder of her life.

Mrs. Preston is considered the representative woman poet of the Confederacy. Her poem, "The Shade of the Trees," is founded on the last words of Stonewall Jackson; and "Gone Forward," on the last words of Robert E. Lee. (M.M.C.)

BOOKS: *Silverwood: A Book of Memories,* 1856; *Beechenbrook,* 1866; *Old Songs and New,* 1870; *Cartoons,* 1875; *For Love's Sake,* 1886; *Colonial Ballads, Sonnets, and Other Verse,* 1887.

REFERENCES: Elizabeth Preston Allan, *The Life and Letters of Margaret Junkin Preston,* 1903; Kunitz and Haycraft, *American Authors, 1600-1900,* 1938; *Dictionary of American Biography,* 1928–1937; *Southern Writers: Second Series,* 1903; F. V. N. Painter, *Poets of Virginia,* 1903; Charles W. Hubner, *Representative Southern Poets,* 1906; Marshall W. Fishwick, "Margaret Junkin Preston: Virginia Poetess," *Commonwealth,* July, 1951; Baltimore *Sun,* Mar. 29, 1897. See also Swem's *Virginia Historical Index,* Vol. 2, 1936.

PRYOR, SARA AGNES RICE (1830-1912), writer of non-fiction, was born in Halifax County, Virginia, and was educated privately. In 1848 she married Roger Atkins Pryor, a journalist, who later became a general in the War Between the States.

Her first book was published when she was over seventy. (M.M.C.)

BOOKS: *The Mother of Washington and Her Times,* 1903; *Reminiscences of Peace and War,* 1904; *The Birth of the Nation: Jamestown, 1607,* 1907; *My Day: Reminiscences of a Long Life,* 1909; *The Colonel's Story,* 1911.

REFERENCES: *Who Was Who in America,* Vol. 1, 1943. See also Swem's *Virginia Historical Index,* Vol. 2, 1936.

PUTNAM, SALLIE A. BROCK ["VIRGINIA MADISON"] (1828-1911), essayist, critic, editorialist, was born at Madison Court House, the area which later furnished her with her *nom de plume.* She was educated by governesses and tutors, and spent the years 1850-58 with her father at the University of Virginia. She was living in Richmond when Fort Sumter was fired upon, and after the War published a memoir, *In Richmond During the War* (1867). Its importance is reflected by its reprinting in 1961.

BOOKS: *In Richmond During the War,* 1867; *The Southern Amaranth,* 1869.

REFERENCE: *Living Female Writers of the South,* 1872.

RANDALL, RUTH PAINTER (1892-   ), writer of non-fiction, was born in Salem, Virginia, the daughter of Dr. F. V. N. Painter, a well known literary scholar at Roanoke College. The majority of her writing has centered on Lincoln and his family, an interest which began by helping her husband, the late James G. Randall, prepare the first two volumes of his *Lincoln the President* in the early 1940's.

BOOKS: *Mary Lincoln: Biography of a Marriage,* 1953; *Lincoln's Sons,* 1955; *The Courtship of Mr. Lincoln,* 1957; *Lincoln's Animal Friends,* 1958; *I Mary,* 1959; *I Varina,* 1962; *I Jessie,* 1963; *I Elizabeth,* 1966; *I Ruth,* 1968.

REFERENCES: *Who's Who in America,* Vol. 30, 1958-59; *Current Biography Yearbook,* 1958; *Wilson Library Bulletin,* Dec., 1957; *Chicago Tribune Magazine,* Feb. 12, 1956; *Christian Science Monitor,* Feb. 11, 1958; *Austin American,* Austin, Texas, April 13, 1960.

REDDING, JAY SAUNDERS (1906-   ), poet, novelist, and writer of non-fiction, was born in Wilmington, Delaware, of a Virginia mother and has spent a number of his mature years in the Old Dominion. After being educated at Brown and Columbia Universities, he became a college instructor and began writing to supplement his income, and has achieved marked success. *No Day of Triumph* (1942) was awarded the Mayflower Prize; *Stranger and Alone* (1950) was named "one of the ten outstanding first novels" of the year by the *Saturday Review of Literature.*

BOOKS: *To Make a Poet Black,* 1939; *No Day of Triumph,* 1942; *Stranger and Alone,* 1950; *They Came in Chains,* 1950; *On Being Negro in America,* 1951; with I. Taylor, *Reading for Writing,* 1952; *An American in India,* 1954; *The Lonesome Road,* 1958; *The Negro,* 1967.

REFERENCES: *Who's Who in America,* Vol. 36, 1970-71; *Who's Who in the South and Southwest,* Vol. 3, 1956; *Who's Who in Colored America,* 1950; *Twentieth Century Authors,* 1942, *Supplement,* 1955; *Directory of American Scholars,* 2, 1942 and later; *The New York Times Book Review,* Mar. 5, 1950; New York *Herald Tribune Book Review,* July 16, 1950; *Saturday Review of Literature,* Feb. 17, 1951.

REID H. (1925-   ), was born in Norfolk and educated at the College of William and Mary (B.A., 1946). He has served on the editorial staffs of a number of Virginia newspapers, and since 1951 has held various editorial positions on the Newport-News *Times-Herald.* In the realm of Virginia letters at large, his major contribution has been numerous articles and books on the history of Southern railroads, a subject of considerable interest to many Virginians (e.g., *Rails Through Dixie* (1965) and *The Virginian Railway* (1961)). He has also written music criticism. He is presently working on a new railroading history, to be called *Norfolk and Western.*

BOOKS: *The Virginian Railway,* 1961; *Extra South,* 1964; *Rails Through Dixie,* 1965.

REFERENCES: *Contemporary Authors,* 19-20.

RICH, RICHARD (fl. 1610), ballad writer, who signed himself "R. Rich, Gent. one of the Voyage," sailed for Virginia on the ship *Sea Adventure* when it left England with Somer's Fleet, June 2, 1609. His experiences, including the eleven months' trip, a ship wreck off Bermuda, the building of two ships, and an account of Virginia, are told in *Newes from Virginia,* written in verse and published when he returned to England in 1610. The ballad has been reprinted several times. (M.M.C.)

BOOKS: *Newes from Virginia,* 1610; also 1922, American Series, photostat reproductions by the Massachusetts Historical Society.

REFERENCES: James D. Hart, *The Oxford Companion to American Literature*, 1965; Francis Coleman Rosenberger, *Virginia Reader*, 1948; Louis D. Rubin, Jr., ed., *A Bibliographical Guide to the Study of Southern Literature*, 1969. See also Swem's *Virginia Historical Index*, Vol. 2, 1936.

RIVES, AMÉLIE [LOUISE] (1863-1945), novelist, poet, and playwright, spent most of her life at "Castle Hill," the Rives estate in Albemarle County, Virginia. The plantation escaped harm during the Civil War, and Amélie was able to grow up largely unaffected by the rigors of Reconstruction. In 1888, she published *The Quick or the Dead?* in *Lippincott's* which, to her surprise, became a scandalous success, selling over 300,000 copies.

Her life at "Castle Hill" figured prominently in most of her work, as did her marriages—first to John Armstrong Chanler and later to Prince Pierre Troubetzkoy, a famous portraitist.

BOOKS: *A Brother to Dragons, and Other Old Time Tales*, 1888; *The Quick or the Dead?*, 1888, 1916; *Virginia of Virginia*, 1888; *According to St. John*, 1891; *Tanis*, 1893; *Barbara Dering*, 1893; *A Damsel Errant*, 1898; *The Golden Rose*, 1898; *Trix and Over-the-Moon*, 1909; *Pan's Mountain*, 1910; *Hidden House*, 1912; *World's End*, 1914; *Shadows of Flames*, 1915; *The Ghost Garden*, 1918; *The Queerness of Celia*, 1926; *Firedamp*, 1930; *Herod and Mariamne*, 1889; *Athelwold*, 1893; *The Fear Market*, 1916; *Augustine the Man*, 1906; *Seléné*, 1905; *As the Wind Blew*, 1920.

REFERENCES: Kunitz and Haycraft, *Twentieth Century Authors*, 1942; James D. Hart, *Oxford Companion to American Literature*, 1965; *Who's Who in America*, Vol. 16, 1930-31; Welford Dunaway Taylor, "Amélie Rives: A Virginia Princess," *Virginia Cavalcade* (Spring 1963); Louis D. Rubin, Jr., ed., *A Bibliographical Guide to the Study of Southern Literature*, 1969. See also Swem's *Virginia Historical Index*, Vol. 2, 1936.

RIVES, HALLIE ERMINIE (Mrs. Post Wheeler) (1876-1956), was born in Christian County, Kentucky. She started writing after surreptitiously reading *The Quick or the Dead?* (1888), the supposed scandalous novel written by her father's first cousin, Amélie Rives (q.v.). *Hearts Courageous* (1902), her first published effort, was written in only six weeks. Like so many romances in Southern literature, this one featured a real historical personage: Patrick Henry. (*The Castaway* (1904) was to feature Lord Byron.) In 1906 she married Post Wheeler, a career diplomat whose position took them to many parts of Europe, South America, and the Orient. *Kingdom of the Slender Swords* (1910) reflects the author's Japanese experience, and its character Aloysius Thorn is a thinly disguised Lafcadio Hearn. The Wheelers retired to Amherst County, Virginia, and in 1955 published a joint memoir: *Dome of Many-Coloured Glass*.

BOOKS: *Hearts Courageous*, 1902; *The Castaway*, 1904; *Kingdom of the Slender Swords*, 1910; *The Valiants of Virginia*, 1912; *The Magic Man* (play title, *Two Worlds*), 1926; *The Golden Barrier*, 1934; *Dome of Many-Coloured Glass* (with her husband), 1955.

REFERENCES: *Current Biography*, 1956; *Who Was Who*, 1897-1942; New York *Times*, Aug. 18, 1956.

RIVES, WILLIAM CABELL (1792-1868), historian and biographer, was born in Amherst County. He was graduated from the College of William and Mary and studied law under Thomas Jefferson. After serving in the Virginia House of Delegates, he went on to serve in both houses of the United States Congress. On two occasions he was U.S. Minister to France. His chief contribution to Virginia letters is his *History of the Life and Times of James Madison* (3 vols.) (1859-68), which, though only complete through 1797, is highly regarded. He died in the year the third volume appeared.

BOOKS: *Discourses on the Uses and Importance of History*, 1847; *History of the Life and Times of James Madison* (3 vols.), 1859-1868.

REFERENCES: *Dictionary of American Biography*, Vol. 8.

ROBERTS, RUBY ALTIZER (1907-   ), poet and editor, is well known in Virginia poetry circles. She has published two collections of her own poems, has edited *The Lyric* and "The Poetry Corner" for the Newport News *Times Herald*. Her honors include the Bellmann Award (1959) and honorary life membership in the International Beta Sigma Phi Society. In 1950, she was named Poet Laureate of Virginia—to that date the only woman ever to hold the title.

BOOKS: *Forever Is Too Long*, 1946; *Command the Stars*, 1948; ed., *The Lyric*.

REFERENCES: *Who's Who in the South and Southwest*, 1956; *International Who's Who in Poetry*, Vol. 1, 1958; *Who's Who of American Women*, Vol. 1, 1958-59; Richmond *Times-Dispatch*, May 22, 1949 and Oct. 15, 1950.

ROPER, FLORENCE WILSON (1878-1958), poet, was born in Richmond. Though her first poetic effort (at age seven) was laughed at by her family, her second—coming over thirty-five years later—won excellent reviews. This was "The Shadow of Magnitude," a sonnet sequence. Two more collections and numerous awards have followed.

BOOKS: *A Kiss for Judas*, 1932; *Flame Against the Wind*, 1937; *Home to the Hills*, 1954.

REFERENCES: Margaret H. Carpenter, *Virginia Authors' Yearbook*, 1956.

ROSENBERGER, FRANCIS COLEMAN (1915-   ), poet and writer of non-fiction, was born in Manassas, Virginia. He was graduated from both the College and Law School of the University of Virginia, where he began writing both poetry and book reviews. Though he has published two collections of poems (*The Virginia Poems* (1943) and *XII Poems* (1946)), he is best known for having edited the anthology *The Virginia Reader: A Treasury of Writings from the First Voyages to the Present* (1953).

He has reviewed books for the Richmond *Times-Dispatch,* the Washington *Post,* the New York *Times,* the New York *Herald Tribune,* and the *Virginia Quarterly Review.* He has been a contributor to numerous historical publications and has served as an editor of the *Federal Bar Journal.* He has also served for some years on the legal and legislative staff of the U.S. Senate, and several times as adviser to American delegations in Geneva.

BOOKS: *The Virginia Poems,* 1943; *XII Poems,* 1946; ed., *The Virginia Reader: A Treasury of Writings from the First Voyages to the Present,* 1948; *Some Notes on the Rosenberger Family in Pennsylvania and Virginia, 1729-1950,* 1950; *American Sampler: A Selection of New Poetry,* 1951; ed., *Jefferson Reader: A Treasury of Writings About Thomas Jefferson,* 1953.

REFERENCES: *Francis Coleman Rosenberger: A List of Published Writings, 1938-1958,* intro. by Millicent Barton Rex, Washington, 1959; Pennsylvania Historical Junto: "Virginia Writers: Francis Coleman Rosenberger"; Richmond *Times-Dispatch,* June 12, 1949; *The New York Times Book Review,* Nov. 28, 1948 and Feb. 15, 1953; Margaret H. Carpenter, *Virginia Authors' Yearbook,* 1956, 1957, 1958; *Who's Who in the South and Southwest,* 1963-64.

ROTHERY, AGNES (Mrs. Harry Rogers Pratt) (1887-1954), writer of non-fiction, was born in Brookline, Massachusetts. Soon after she was graduated from Wellesley in 1909, she began her writing career in the editorial department of the *Ladies' Home Journal.* Later she became the editor of the woman's page of the *Boston Herald* and then the literary editor of the same paper. She was also contributing editor to *Youth's Companion* and *House Beautiful.*

She came to Virginia when her husband joined the staff of the Department of Music and Dramatic Art at the University of Virginia. *Fitting Habitation* (1944), an autobiographical essay, tells of their first Charlottesville house, "The Mews," which is on the University grounds.

She and her husband traveled widely, and many of her twenty books were about the places they visited—Norway, Denmark, Sweden, Finland, South and Central American Countries. She was awarded King Christian X's Medal of Liberation in recognition of her war-time writing in behalf of Denmark. (M.M.C.)

BOOKS: *A Fitting Habitation,* 1944; *Cape Cod: New and Old,* 1918; *The Coast Road from Boston to Plymouth,* 1920; *New Roads in Old Virginia,* 1929; *Virginia: The New Dominion,* 1940; *Maryland and Virginia Roundabout,* 1947; *Houses Virginians Have Loved,* 1954.

REFERENCES: *Who's Who in America,* Vol. 27, 1952-53; Richmond *Times-Dispatch,* Jan. 23, 1949.

ROUSE, PARKE SHEPHERD (1915-   ), historian, was born in Smithfield, Virginia, and was educated at Washington and Lee University (A.B.,

1937). He has worked as an editorial writer on the Richmond *Times-Dispatch* and as a public relations man in Richmond, Williamsburg and Jamestown. He is currently executive director of the Jamestown Festival Park. His many publications are primarily in the realm of Southern history, particularly Virginia history (e.g. *Jamestown, First English Colony* (1965); *The City That Turned Back Time* (1952)).

BOOKS: *They Gave Us Freedom*, 1951; *The City that Turned Back Time*, 1952; *Williamsburg in Color*, 1954; *The Printer in Eighteenth Century Williamsburg*, 1955; *Jamestown: First English Colony*, 1965; *Virginia: The English Heritage in America*, 1966; *Below the James Lies Dixie*, 1968; *Planters and Pioneers*, 1968; *Tidewater Virginia in Color*, 1968; *Endless Harbor: The Story of Newport News*, 1969; *James Blair of Virginia*, 1971.

REFERENCES: *Contemporary Authors*, 17-18; *Commonwealth*, Oct., 1951.

RUBIN, LOUIS D[ECIMUS], JR. (1923-), critic, novelist, and historian, was born in Charleston, South Carolina. He was educated at the University of Richmond (B.A., 1946) and at Johns Hopkins University (Ph.D., 1954). He has taught at the University of Pennsylvania, Hollins College, and (since 1967) at the University of North Carolina. For one year (1956-57) he was associate editor of the Richmond *News Leader*. He is well known as a critic (e.g. *The Curious Death of the Novel* (1967)) and as a novelist (e.g. *The Golden Weather* (1961)). As one of the leading scholars in the field of Southern literature, his name appears as author or editor on many articles and books. He is also a popular lecturer and has been a visiting professor in numerous American universities and a Fulbright lecturer in France.

BOOKS: ed. with Robert D. Jacobs, *Southern Renascence*, 1953; *Thomas Wolfe: The Weather of His Youth*, 1955; ed. with James Jackson Kilpatrick, *The Lasting South*, 1957; *No Place on Earth*, 1959; *The Golden Weather*, 1961; ed., *The Idea of an American Novel*, 1961; ed., *South: Modern Southern Literature in its Cultural Setting*, 1961; *The Faraway Country: Writers of the Modern South*, 1963; *The Curious Death of the Novel*, 1967; *The Teller in the Tale*, 1967; ed., *The Hollins Poets*, 1967; ed., *The Experience of America*, 1969; ed., *A Bibliographical Guide to the Study of Southern Literature*, 1969; *George Washington Cable*, 1969.

REFERENCES: *Who's Who in America*, Vol. 36, 1970-71; *Contemporary Authors*, 1-4; *Directory of American Scholars*, 5th ed., Vol. 2; *Who's Who in the South and Southwest*, 1967 and later.

RUSSELL, WALTER (1871-1963), scientist, theologian, and philosopher, was born in Boston and attended various schools there and in Philadelphia and Paris. Early in his career he wrote and illustrated for numerous magazines. In the early years of this century he painted a good deal, but after 1927 he gave most of his time to sculpture, one of his most famous works being the Mark Twain Memorial at Hannibal, Missouri. Propounder of numerous scientific theses and compiler of the Russell Chart of Elements, his scientific studies led him increasingly into the realm of philosophy and religion. In 1948 he founded the University of Science and Philosophy at Swananoa, near Afton, Virginia. *The Russell Cosmology: A New Concept of the Universe* (1953) and (with his wife, Lao) *Natural Law and Living Philosophy* (1950) exemplify the culminating interests of his last years.

BOOKS: *The Russell Cosmology: A New Concept of the Universe*, 1953; with his wife Lao, *Natural Law and Living Philosophy*, 1950.

REFERENCES: *Who Was Who*, Vol. 4, 1961-68; *Who's Who in the South and Southwest*, Vol. 6.

RYAN, ABRAM JOSEPH (1838 or 1839-1886), poet, was born in either Norfolk, Virginia, or Hagerstown, Maryland, but spent some time in Virginia. Educated for the Roman Catholic priesthood, he served as a chaplain in the Confederate Army and after the war lived in various Southern cities.

His poetry is intensely patriotic and profoundly religious. His lines are simple and musical. He is best remembered by two poems, "The Conquered Banner" and "The Sword of Robert E. Lee." He died in Louisville, Kentucky, in 1886. (M.M.C.)

BOOKS: *Father Ryan's Poems*, 1879; *Poems: Patriotic, Religious, Miscellaneous*, 1880; *A Crown for Our Queen*, 1882.

REFERENCES: Burke and Howe, *American Authors and Books 1640-1940*, 1943; Kunitz and Haycraft, *American Authors 1600-1900* (bibliography), 1938; J. B. Hubbell, *The South in American Literature 1607-1900* (bibliography), 1954. Louis D. Rubin, Jr., ed., *A Bibliographical Guide to the Study of Southern Literature*, 1969. See also Swem's *Virginia Historical Index*, Vol. 2, 1936.

SAMPSON, EMMA SPEED (1868-1947), author of humorous novels and juvenile fiction, was born near Louisville, Kentucky, of parents whose families had been on opposite sides during the Civil War. Her mother was a grandniece of John Keats. After studying art in New York and in Paris (under Charles Lazar), she taught for a time in Louisville. In 1896, she married Virginia-born Henry Aylett Sampson, an insurance executive, and eventually moved to Richmond, which she came to regard as her permanent home.

After serving for a time on the Virginia motion picture censorship board, she became a columnist for the Richmond *Times-Dispatch*. These activities, however, are secondary to her career as a novelist. Beginning in 1913, when she was forty-five, she began to write books in several girls' series—"Molly Brown"; the "Carter Girls"; the "Tucker Twins." In 1918 it was suggested that she write a sequel to *Miss Minerva and William Green Hill*, a Kentucky based novel written by Frances Boyd Calhoun in 1909. She complied with *Billy and the Major* (1918) and went on to contribute eleven books to the series, the last being *Miss Minerva's Vacation* (1939). It is upon this series that her reputation finally rests. Her characters' exploits represent fictional portrayals of life in the Reconstruction South.

BOOKS: *Mammy's White Folks*, 1919; *Miss Minerva's Baby*, 1920; *Miss Minerva's Neighbors*, 1921; *The Shorn Lamb*, 1922; *The Comings of Cousin Ann*, 1923; *Miss Minerva on the Old Plantation*, 1923; *Masquerading Mary*, 1924; *Miss Minerva Broadcasts Billy*, 1925; *Miss Minerva's Scallywags*, 1927; *The Spite Fence*, 1929; *Miss Minerva Goin' Places*, 1931; *Miss Minerva's Cook Book*, 1931; *Priscilla*, 1931; *Priscilla at Hunting Hill*, 1932; *Miss Minerva's Mystery*, 1933; *Miss Minerva's Problem*, 1936; *Miss Minerva's Vacation*, 1939.

REFERENCES: John Letcher Fugate, ed., *An Edition of 'Great Day':* *The Autobiography of Emma Speed Sampson* (unpublished M.A. thesis, University of Richmond, 1968). Guy Fridell, "I Remember Miss Minerva," *Commonwealth*, 31 (July 1964).

SANDBURG, HELGA (1918-   ), novelist, short story writer, and poet, was born in Maywood, Illinois, but moved to Falls Church, Virginia, in 1951 and took a position at the Library of Congress. She left in 1958 to write her first novel, *The Wheel of Earth*. Since that time, she has kept up a regular schedule of writing. In 1958 she won the *Virginia Quarterly Review*'s Emily Clark Balch Prize for her short story "Witch Chicken."

BOOKS: *The Wheel of Earth*, 1958; *Measure My Love*, 1959; *The Owl's Roost*, 1962; *Blueberry*, 1963; *Joel and the Wild Goose*, 1963; *Sweet Music*, 1963; *Gingerbread*, 1964; *Bo and the Old Donkey*, 1965; *The Unicorns*, 1965; *The Wizard's Child*, 1967; *Above and Below*, 1969; *Anna and the Baby Buzzard*, 1970; *To a New Husband*, 1970.

REFERENCES: *Library Journal*, Feb. 1, 1958; *Saturday Review*, April 26, 1958 and Nov. 29, 1958; Washington *Post* and *Times Herald*, April 6, 1958, April 20, 1958, and April 19, 1959; *Who's Who of American Women*, 1972-73.

SANDYS, GEORGE (1578-1644), traveler, scholar, prose writer, and poet, came to Virginia in 1621 as treasurer of the Virginia Company. He was the son of Edwin Sandys, Archbishop of York, and the brother of Sir Edwin Sandys. Besides taking an active part in the colony's administration and defense, he continued to work on his translation of Ovid's *Metamorphoses*, five books of which had already been published in England.

In 1624 he became a member of the Jamestown Council, by which time he had become a plantation owner as well. In spite of the extra duties these responsibilities entailed, he was able to publish in 1626 the remaining ten books of the *Metamorphoses*. The translation met with praise in the mother country, and like the first five books went quickly through several editions. With Sandys' translation the purely literary writing in the colony began.

In 1631, Sandys retired to Bexley Abbey in Kent, where he devoted himself to poetry and contemplation. He died in the spring of 1644. (M.M.C.)

BOOKS: Translation of Ovid's *Metamorphoses*, 1626.

REFERENCES: Richard Beale Davis, *George Sandys: Poet-Adventurer*, 1955; James Gilmer McManaway, "The First Five Bookes of Ovid's Metamorphosis, 1621, Englished by Master George Sandys," *Bibliographical Society Papers*, Vol. 1 (1948-49); Louis D. Rubin, Jr., ed., *A Bibliographical Guide to the Study of Southern Literature*, 1969.

SCRUGGS, PHILIP LIGHTFOOT (1898-   ), novelist and newspaper editor, was born in Lynchburg and attended the University of Virginia, where a number of his writings were published in the student literary magazine. After a period of editing and free-lance writing in New York, he published *Man Cannot Tell*, a novel about Bacon's Rebellion, in 1942. That same year he was asked to become editor of the Lynchburg *Daily Advance*, a post he long held. He says of this vocation: "This meant the end of free-lancing and slow progress in writing the second and third novels of the trilogy of which *Man Cannot Tell* was to be the first volume."

BOOKS: *Man Cannot Tell*, 1942; *The History of Lynchburg, Virginia, 1786-1946*, 1971.

REFERENCES: Richmond *Times-Dispatch*, Mar. 13, 1949; Margaret H. Carpenter, *Virginia Authors' Yearbook*, 1956, 1957; *Virginia Lives*.

SEAWELL, MOLLY ELLIOT (1860-1916), novelist and non-fiction writer, was born at her parents' plantation "The Shelter," in Gloucester County, Virginia, and learned storytelling from an uncle, Joseph Seawell, who told her of his adventures at sea. Also she learned much lore of the Tidewater region and of the Chesapeake Bay. One of her earliest stories, *Little Jarvis* (1890), won a prize from *Youth's Companion*, as did numerous later tales. Her subjects can be divided into five areas: naval subjects, Virginia before and after the Civil War, Parisian and provincial French life, English history, and Washington society. The latter three areas reflect experiences of her mature years.

BOOKS: *The Berkeleys and Their Neighbors*, 1888; *Throckmorton*, 1890; *Midshipman Paulding*, 1891; *Children of Destiny*, 1893; *A Virginia Cavalier*, 1896; *The History of Lady Betty Stair*, 1897; *The Lively Adventures of Gavin Hamilton*, 1899; *The House of Egremont*, 1900; *Papa Bouchard*, 1901; *Franceska*, 1902; *The Fortunes of Fifi*, 1903; *The Chateau of Montplaisir*, 1906; *The Victory*, 1906; *The Secret of Toni*, 1907; *The Last Duchess of Belgrade*, 1908; *The Imprisoned Midshipman*, 1908; *The Whirl: A Romance of Washington Society*, 1909; *Betty's First Christmas*, 1914; *The Diary of a Beauty*, 1915; *Betty at Fort Blizzard*, 1916; *Twelve Naval Captains*, 1897.

REFERENCES: *Library of Southern Literature*, Vol. 11; *Who's Who in America*, Vol. 9, 1916-17; *American Women*, 1935-36; *Dictionary of American Biography*, Vol. 16, 1935; *Who Was Who in America*, Vol. 1, 1942; New York *Herald*, Nov. 16, 1916. See also Swem's *Virginia Historical Index*, Vol. 2, 1936.

SEWARD, WILLIAM W., JR. (1913-   ), novelist and critic, was educated at the University of Richmond and has been a member of the English

Department of Old Dominion University for more than two decades. Though he has published a novel (*Skirts of the Night* (1950)), he is perhaps best known for his criticism (e.g. *Contrasts in Modern Writers* (1963)). His most recent effort is a slim autobiographical volume, *My Friend Ernest Hemingway* (1969), recounting his friendship with the late fiction writer.

BOOKS: *Skirts in the Night*, 1950; *Contrasts in Modern Writers*, 1963; *My Friend Ernest Hemingway*, 1969.

REFERENCES: *Who's Who in America*, Vol. 31, 1959-1960; *Directory of American Scholars*, 3rd ed., 1947; Richmond *Times-Dispatch*, May 7, 1950.

SILVETTE, HERBERT ["Barnaby Dogbolt"] (1906-   ), writer of whimsy in the manner of P. G. Wodehouse, was born in Richmond, into a family of portrait painters of the Commonwealth. He attended the University of Virginia, from which he received a bachelor's, master's and doctor's degree, and except for brief periods was on the faculty there from 1928 to 1947.

Dr. Silvette's career has been varied. On the one hand he has been a successful teacher and publishing scholar in the field of pharmacology, on the other a writer of numerous novels. His books often center on improbable humorous situations in which the medical or academic world serves as backdrop. His *Never Say Die* (1961) contains an incisive satire of James Branch Cabell, who appears as Campbell Twigg.

BOOKS: *Eve's Second Apple*, 1946; *The Goose's Tale*, 1947; *Maiden Voyage*, 1950; *Grave Example*, 1953; *My Orange Has Bitter Rind; The Medlars*, 1957; *Come Unto Me*, 1958; *Never Say Die*, 1961.   ·

REFERENCES: *Saturday Review*, July 29, 1950; New York *Herald Tribune Book Review*, July 23, 1950; *Kirkus Review*, May 15, 1950; Chicago *Sun Book Week*, Aug. 3, 1947; New York *Times*, Aug. 14, 1947.

SMITH, JOHN (1580-1631), chronicler, was born at Willoughby in Lincolnshire, England, and educated in the free schools of the neighboring towns of Alford and Louth. His was a life of adventure and travel. He aspired to a military career and was very successful, attaining for himself the title of captain, and a coat of arms. He also received a worthy pension.

His interest in Virginia led him to join the expedition in 1606 of the London Company. Because of a rebellion during the crossing, he arrived in chains but later became the president of the colony and is referred to by some as its founder.

At the age of forty, with no prospect of employment, he settled down to write. He published nine books and pamphlets—some being only repetitions and enlargements of earlier ones. They are partly autobiographical, recording his achievements, adventures and travels; partly historical, giving the government, customs and habits of the people in the early settlement. He wrote two works on sea-faring, and he attempted some poetry. His complete works appeared in 1884; a later edition was published in 1910. The authenticity of his works is questioned by some historians. (C.H.H.)

BOOKS AND PAMPHLETS: *A True Relation of such Occurrences and*

Accidents of Noate as hath hapned in Virginia since the first planting of that Colony, 1608; *A Map of Virginia with a Description of the Country*, 2nd edition, 1612; *A Description of New England*, 1616; *New England's Trials*, 1620, 1622; *The General Historie of Virginia, New England, and the Summer Isles*, 1624; *Advertisements for the Unexperienced Planters of New England, or Anywhere: Or the Pathway to Erect a Plantation*, 1631; *An Accidence: Or the Pathway to Experience necessary for all young Seamen*, 1626, recast as *The Sea Man's Grammar*, 1627; *The True Travels, Adventures and Observations of Captain John Smith*, 1630.

REFERENCES: *Dictionary of American Biography*, Vol. 17; Howard Mumford Jones, *The Literature of Virginia in the Seventeenth Century*, 1946; James D. Hart, *Oxford Companion to American Literature*, 1965; Kunitz and Haycraft, *American Authors 1600-1900*, 1938; J. B. Hubbell, *The South in American Literature* (bibliography), 1954; John Gould Fletcher, *John Smith—Also Pocahontas*, 1928; J. B. Hubbell, *Virginia in Life and Fiction*, 1922. Louis D. Rubin, Jr., ed., *A Bibliographical Guide to the Study of Southern Literature*, 1969. See also Swem's *Virginia Historical Index*, Vol. 2, 1936.

SNEAD, GEORGIA TILLMAN (1863-1940), novelist and writer of verse, was born in Bedford County, the daughter of George and Martha Spinner Snead. She was educated in Lynchburg schools and taught school in and around Lynchburg. She lived in the city most of her life and called it her home. (R.H.B.)

BOOKS: *Beneath Virginia Skies*, 1904; *Agatha Ann*, 1913; *Lynchburg of Ye Olden Tymes*, 1931.

REFERENCE: Manuscript Collection of Biographies of Lynchburg Writers at the Jones Memorial Library, Lynchburg, Virginia; Collection of Writings by Virginia Women at Lipscomb Library, Randolph-Macon Woman's College.

SPENCER, ANNE (1882-   ), poet, was born on February 6, 1882, at Bramwell, West Virginia, and moved to Lynchburg, Virginia, when she was a child of eleven. She was educated at Virginia Seminary in Lynchburg, and served for many years as librarian of Dunbar High School there. Her verse was widely anthologized in such volumes as *The Book of American Negro Poetry*, by James Weldon Johnson; *Caroling Dusk*, by Countee Cullen; *The Negro Caravan*, by Sterling Brown, *et. al.*; *The Virginia Reader*, by Francis Coleman Rosenberger; *American Poetry Since 1900*, by Louis Untermeyer; and *Negro Poets and Their Poems*, by Robert T. Kerlin. (M.E.)

BOOKS: Anthologized in books listed above.

REFERENCES: James Weldon Johnson, *The Book of American Negro Poetry*, 1922, 1931; Robert T. Kerlin, *Negro Poets and Their Poems*, 1923, 1935; Francis Coleman Rosenberger, *Virginia Reader*, 1948; Louis Untermeyer, *American Poetry Since 1900*, 1923; Herman Dreer, *American Literature by Negro Authors*, 1950.

STANARD, MARY MANN PAGE NEWTON (1865-1929), historian, was born in Westmoreland County, Virginia, and attended the Leache-Wood School in Norfolk. A citizen of the Old Dominion for her entire life, her reputation rests upon the several volumes she wrote about its past (e.g. *The Story of Virginia's First Century* (1928); *Richmond: its People and Its Story* (1923)). Her work is now very scarce and is generally honored by historians of Virginia.

BOOKS: *The Story of Bacon's Rebellion*, 1907; *The Dreamer: A Romantic Rendering of the Life of Edgar Allan Poe*, 1909; *Colonial Virginia: Its People and Customs*, 1917; *Richmond: Its People and its Story*, 1923; *John Brockenbrough Newton*, 1924; *The Story of Virginia's First Century*, 1928.

REFERENCES: *Who Was Who*, Vol. 1, 1889-1942; Richmond *Times-Dispatch*, June 6, 1929; Richmond *News Leader*, June 5, 1929.

STITH, WILLIAM (1707-1755), historian, was born in Henrico County and educated at Oxford. In the year of his graduation (1727/28) he was ordained an Anglican priest. While serving in Henrico Parish, near Varina, Virginia, he wrote the one book for which he is remembered: *The History of the First Discovery and Settlement of Virginia* (1747). He relied on the earlier histories of Captain John Smith (*q.v.*), Robert Beverley (*q.v.*), and the minutes of the Virginia Court. He also had access to the records of the London Company. The *History* covers the Colony's history from the beginning through 1624.

BOOK: *The History of the First Discovery and Settlement of Virginia*, 1747.

REFERENCES: J. B. Hubbell, *The South in American Literature, 1607-1900*, 1954; Louis D. Rubin, Jr., ed., *A Bibliographical Guide to the Study of Southern Literature*, 1969.

STRACHEY, WILLIAM (c.1567-1620), chronicler, wrote "A True Reportory of the Wracke, and Redemption of Sir Thomas Gates," published first by Samuel Purchas in *Purchas His Pilgrims* in 1625. It was written, however, soon after William Strachey's arrival in Virginia, May 23, 1610, and was a letter vividly describing a storm at sea which blew the ship *Sea Adventure*, their pinnace, away from the other ships and caused it to be wrecked on the Bermudas. The voyagers set to work immediately to build two small ships in which to continue their voyage.

When Sir Thomas Gates sailed for England in July, 1610, he took the letter with him. It is thought that William Shakespeare subsequently became familiar with the contents of the letter and used them in writing his play, *The Tempest*.

Strachey remained in the Jamestown Colony a little more than a year (some accounts say three years), as its first secretary. When he returned to England, he edited the first code of laws for the colony of Virginia. He also wrote two parts of *The Historie of Travaile into Virginia Britannia, Expressing the Cosmographie and Comodities of the Country, Together with*

the Manners and Customes of the People. This project was abandoned because of the lack of a publisher. In 1849 the Hakluyt Society published the
manuscript written in 1618. (M.M.C.)

REFERENCES: Francis C. Rosenberger, *Virginia Reader*, 1948; J. B.
Hubbell, *The South in American Literature 1607-1900* (bibliography), 1954.
Louis D. Rubin, Jr., ed., *A Bibliographical Guide to the Study of Southern
Literature*, 1969. See also Swem's *Virginia Historical Index*, Vol. 2, 1936.

STREET, MARY DALLAS (1885-1951), editor, short story writer, and
novelist, was born in Richmond and was educated there in Miss Ellett's
School. In 1921 she became one of the founding editors of Richmond's
"little" magazine, *The Reviewer*. Her efforts in its behalf are acknowledged
by Emily Clark (*q.v.*) in *Innocence Abroad* (1931). She spent part of her
year in New York, close to the many magazines to which she contributed
and another part at Warm Springs, Virginia. Her sketches for *The Reviewer*
are perhaps better known than her two novels.

BOOKS: *Summer's End*, 1936; *Christopher Holt*, 1946.

REFERENCES: Emily Clark, *Innocence Abroad*, 1931; Gerald Langford,
ed., *Ingénue Among the Lions*, 1965; Maurice Duke, "*The Reviewer:* A
Bibliographical Guide to a Little Magazine," *Resources for American Literary
Study*, Vol. 1, No. 1 (Spring 1971).

STROTHER, DAVID HUNTER ["Porte Crayon"] (1816-1888), was
born in Martinsburg, Virginia (now West Virginia) and inherited from his
father, clerk of Berkley County and veteran of the War of 1812, a love of
literature, art, and music befitting a country gentleman of that day. His
innate talent for sketching brought him under the tutelage of Samuel F. B.
Morse (1836) at New York University. When his master abandoned painting
for telegraphy two years later, his pupil struck out for the frontier and
toured Kentucky, Illinois, and Indiana, painting dignitaries en route to pay
his way. Beginning in 1840, he began to study in Europe, varying periods
in Paris, Rome, and Florence with tours through the Apennines. These
trips produced thirteen sketches which were published in the Martinsburg
Gazette.

Upon returning to America, he fell into the pattern of spending his
winters in New York illustrating books, magazines, and religious tracts and
his summers doing portraits in Virginia. In 1853 he was commissioned by
Harper's Magazine to write and illustrate a series of articles on the Falls of
the Blackwater. These were eventually followed by books in a similar vein:
*Virginia Illustrated, North Carolina Illustrated, A Winter in the South, A
Summer in New England,* and *The Mountains.* These brought him perhaps
greater fame than any Virginia writer enjoyed at the time.

Finding secession abhorrent, he served the North during the Civil War.
He subsequently returned to his family at Bath, West Virginia, to face
thirteen years of obscurity, his style of writing and illustrating being now

out of vogue. In 1879 he began six years' service as Consul General to Mexico, and finally died in Charles Town, West Virginia.

He is remembered mainly as a precursor to the Local Color movement, having fictionalized such characters as the Southern Negro and the Appalachian mountaineer. (C.D.E.)

BOOKS: *Illustrated Life of General Winfield Scott, Commander-in-chief of the Army in Mexico*, 1847; *Virginia Illustrated*, 1857; *The Old South Illustrated* (ed., with introduction by Cecil B. Eby, Jr.), 1959.

REFERENCES: *Library of Southern Literature*, Vol. 11; Burke and Howe, *American Authors and Books 1640-1940*, 1943; J. B. Hubbell, *The South in American Literature 1600-1900*, 1954; William Couper, *History of the Shenandoah Valley*, Vol. 2, 1952; *American Heritage*, Vol. 6, No. 2 (Feb., 1955), Cecil D. Eby, Jr., *"Porte Crayon": The Life of David Hunter Strother*, 1960; Louis D. Rubin, Jr., ed., *A Bibliographical Guide to the Study of Southern Literature*, 1969.

STUART, DABNEY (1937-   ), is a native of Richmond. He was graduated from Davidson College and attended Harvard as a Woodrow Wilson fellow. Now an associate professor at Washington and Lee University, he spends a great deal of time on his poetry, two collections of which have been published. In a recent interview in the Richmond *Times-Dispatch* (see below), he made a statement which characterizes his work: "Nothing is uninspiring. Objects, people, no matter who they are. Anything seems to be a fit subject for a poem." This belief perhaps accounts for the success his work has met with on the American literary market. He considers "Goshen Pass: Winter," "The Maury River," and "The Fisherman" three of his best efforts.

BOOKS: *The Diving Bell*, 1964; *A Particular Place*, 1969.

REFERENCES: Richmond *Times-Dispatch*, April 19, 1970 and Nov. 15, 1970.

STYRON, WILLIAM (1925-   ), novelist, states: "I was born in Newport News, Virginia, 11 June, 1925.

"I attended Duke University where I came under the influence of Dr. William Blackburn, who encouraged me to write. I think my favorite writers at that time were Wolfe, Fitzgerald, Hemingway, the Elizabethans, and Flaubert, who teaches one to control both style and emotions. I was bitten deeply by the Faulkner bug, too, but have subsequently tried (and I think succeeded) pruning away the Faulkner influence in my work.

"I am married, have three children, and live in Litchfield County, Connecticut, in serene farm country which, at least so far, has proved conducive to work.

"I have long since ceased expatiating on any 'philosophy' of writing, since past experiences have proved that I usually put my foot in my mouth. My present theory (my theory or theories fluctuate) is simply that a writer either has talent or he hasn't, but that all the talent in the world is to no avail unless the writer is willing to take the risk and work until the sweat pours out, day after day.

"I don't consider myself a 'Virginian' writer, or even a 'Southern' writer. I have great respect for what the South has produced in literature, but I don't believe that the region has any monopoly upon writers. Perhaps I say this because I have not lived in the South since I was a boy, but I do think that the great danger now—in regard to Southern writing in general—is a specious and chauvinistic regionalism. A writer is where he comes from—true—but more so what he is and where he's been."

BOOKS: *Lie Down in Darkness*, 1951; *The Long March*, 1956; *Set This House on Fire*, 1960; *The Confessions of Nat Turner*, 1967.

REFERENCES: Louis D. Rubin, Jr., ed., *A Bibliographical Guide to the Study of Southern Literature*, 1969.

SWEM, EARL GREGG (1870-1965), librarian, historian, bibliographer, and editor, was born in Belle Plains, Iowa, and was graduated from La-fayette College in Pennsylvania. But like Lester Cappon (*q.v.*) he spent much of his life in Williamsburg working on a bibliographical source which would facilitate the study of his adopted state's history. The four-volume *Virginia Historical Index* (1934-36) has become an indispensable tool for students of Virginia history. It has come to be known as simply "Swem's Index" or "Swem" and is a monument to Dr. Swem's career as librarian at the College of William and Mary. However, it should be noted that his published works fill an entire bibliographical volume, which was compiled by James A. Servies (see below).

BOOK: *Virginia Historical Index*, 1934-1936.

REFERENCES: *The Virginia Librarian*, Vol. 12, No. 2 (Summer 1965); James A. Servies, comp., *Earl Gregg Swem: A Bibliography*, the College of William and Mary, 1960.

TABB, JOHN BANISTER (1845-1909), poet, was born of a planter family in Amelia County. His poor vision necessitated education by tutors at home. He was, however, able to serve on a blockade runner during the Civil War. Imprisonment at Point Lookout, Maryland, in 1864 brought him into contact with and under the influence of Sidney Lanier. Through their friendship, Tabb began to write poetry.

After the War he studied both music and theology, expecting to become an Episcopalian priest. But his interest in Roman Catholicism led him to membership in that church and he was graduated from the Catholic St. Charles College in Maryland in 1875. In 1884, he was ordained a priest, though he never held a parish. Instead, he returned to St. Charles, where he remained an English teacher for the rest of his life. Here, too, he did most of his writing, even after his blindness (1908). His poetry is most properly called metaphysical, resembling that of the Americans Edward Taylor and Emily Dickinson as well as the school of Donne.

BOOKS: *Poems,* 1894; *Lyrics,* 1894; *Bone Rules: Or, Skeleton of English Grammar,* 1897; *Child Verse,* 1899; *Later Lyrics; The Rosary in Rhyme,* 1904; *Quips and Quiddits: Ques for the Qurious,* 1907; *Later Poems,* 1910; *The Poetry of Father Tabb* (ed. by Francis Edward Aloysius Litz), 1928; *Best Poems,* (ed. by Litz) 1957.

REFERENCES: James D. Hart, *Oxford Companion to American Literature,* 1965; *Virginia Cavalcade,* Vol. VI, No. 1 (Summer 1956); Kunitz and Haycraft, *American Authors, 1600-1900,* 1938; Gordon Blair, *Father Tabb, Poet, Priest, Soldier, Wit: Memories and Impressions of a Personal Friend,* 1940; F. E. A. Litz, *Father Tabb: A Study of His Life and Works,* 1923; Louis D. Rubin, Jr., ed., *A Bibliographical Guide to the Study of Southern Literature,* 1969. See also Swem's *Virginia Historical Index,* Vol. 2, 1936.

TAYLOR, ELKANAH EAST (Mrs. E. Jordan Taylor) (1888-1945), poet, critic, and editor, was educated at Sweet Briar College and at the College of William and Mary. From early childhood she contributed poetry to magazines, and she remained an active force for poetry in Virginia during her mature life. In 1926, she founded *Will-o'-the'Wisp,* and served as its editor until 1935. Her lyrics were collected several times, most notably, perhaps, in *Candles on the Sill* (1927).

BOOKS: *Whispering and Other Poems,* 1919; *Dust and Flame,* 1923; *Candles on the Sill,* 1927.

REFERENCES: *Who's Who,* 1944, 1945; Richmond *Times-Dispatch,* Aug. 8, 1945.

TAYLOR, JOHN ["JOHN TAYLOR OF CAROLINE"] (1753-1824), essayist, was born either in Orange or in Caroline County, Virginia. In any case, he was reared by Edmund Pendleton in Caroline, and after attending the College of William and Mary, studied law under Pendleton. After serving in the Revolution, he was a Delegate to the Virginia legislature. He supported the Jeffersonian goals of a broadened franchise and religious freedom and helped significantly in Jefferson's election in 1800. He was more violently anti-Federalist than Jefferson, however, and wrote a scorching reply to John Adams' *Defense of the Constitutions of Government of the United States of America,* which had condemned the idea of a natural aristocracy. His most famous writings, however, were his essays written for a Georgetown newspaper over the pseudonym *Arator,* and issued in book form in 1813. While defending the ideals of Jeffersonian Democracy and the old agricultural order, these essays also contain much practical agricultural lore. They were obviously written by one who knew both areas intimately and practised them religiously.

BOOKS: *Arator: Being a Series of Agricultural Essays, Practical and Political,* 1813; *An Inquiry into the Principles and Policy of the Government of the United States,* 1814; *Construction Construed, and Constitutions Vindicated,* 1820; *Tyranny Unmasked,* 1822.

REFERENCES: J. B. Hubbell, *The South in American Literature, 1607-*

1900, 1954; Maurice Duke, "John Taylor of Caroline, 1753-1824: Notes Toward a Bibliography," *Early American Literature*, Vol. VI, No. 1 (Spring 1971); Louis D. Rubin, Jr., ed., *A Bibliographical Guide to the Study of Southern Literature*, 1969.

TAYLOR, ROBERTA NEWTON (1895-1970), poet, was born and educated in Norfolk, Virginia. She specialized in music, but in later years found expression through poetry. Her poems have appeared in various periodicals. She is a member of the Poetry Society of Virginia and has participated for two summers in the Writers' Workshop of the New York University Summer School at Chautauqua, New York.

A grand-daughter of a Virginia bishop, she celebrates the history and traditions of her native state through many of her poems. Her book, *Blue Heron*, is illustrated by her daughter-in-law, Nancy Atcheson Taylor, and has a foreword by Nancy Bird Turner (*q.v.*), distinguished poet of Virginia. (B.D.)

BOOKS: *Blue Heron*, 1952; *The Place Called Morning*, 1959.

REFERENCES: Margaret H. Carpenter, *Virginia Authors' Yearbook*, 1956, 1957, 1958.

TERHUNE, MARY VIRGINIA HAWS [MARION HARLAND] (1830-1922), a writer of fiction and non-fiction, used the name Marion Harland, a pseudonym which became famous in the years following her publication of *Commonsense in the Household: A Manual of Practical Housewifery* (1871). Skeptical about its ability to make money, one New York publisher refused the manuscript. Scribner's, who did publish it, was surprised when the book sold over 100,000 copies. It was followed by further books and articles on etiquette, cooking, meal planning, cooking by gas and other household subjects.

Mrs. Terhune's household articles were much sought after by magazines and newspapers. The articles also gave impetus to the "woman's magazine," found in commercial magazine racks today.

In addition, the author wrote travel books, biographical studies, and twenty-six novels. Romantic, sentimental, and moralistic, her novels were set mainly in the South before and during the Civil War. John Reuben Thompson (*q.v.*), editor and author, who read her first novel, *Alone*, when it was submitted to a Richmond publisher, advised against publishing it except at the author's risk. The book subsequently sold more than 100,000 copies.

Popular as her novels were, they are not the writing by which she will be remembered. It is her pioneer work in the field of home economics that gives firmness to her reputation as a writer. (M.M.C.)

BOOKS: *Breakfast, Luncheon, and Tea*, 1875; *The Art of Cooking by Gas*, 1896; *Marion Harland's Complete Cook Book*, 1903; *Marion Harland's Complete Etiquette*, 1914; *Alone*, 1854; *The Hidden Path*, 1898; *True as Steel*, 1872; *A Gallant Fight*, 1888; *Judith*, 1883; *His Great Self*,

1892; *Dr. Dale* (with her son, Albert Payson Terhune), 1900; *The Car-ringtons of High Hill*, 1919; *Loitering in the Pleasant Paths*, 1880; *The Home of the Bible*, 1896; *Where Ghosts Walk*, 1898; *Charlotte Brontë at Home*, 1899; *William Cowper*, 1899; *John Knox*, 1900; *Hannah More*, 1900; *Marion Harland's Autobiography*, 1910.

REFERENCES: *Who's Who in America*, Vol. 12, 1922-23; *Dictionary of American Biography*, Vol. 18, 1936; *Who Was Who in America*, Vol. I, 1943; Burke and Howe, *American Authors and Books 1640-1940*, 1943; J. B. Hubbell, *The South in American Literature, 1607-1900*, 1954; *Marion Har-land's Autobiography*, 1910.

THOMPSON, JOHN REUBEN (1823-1873), lecturer, editor, and poet, was born in Richmond. After attending schools in Richmond and in East Haven, Connecticut, he attended the University of Virginia. Following a short legal practise, he became owner and editor of the *Southern Literary Mes-senger*, which was to become one of the leading Southern periodicals of its day. He brought before the public such new authors as Hayne, Timrod, and James Barron Hope. He was a friend of Poe and delivered numerous lectures on "The Genius and Character of Edgar Allan Poe." He was a poet in his own right, achieving fame with "Ashby," "Music in the Camp," "The Battle Rainbow," and "The Burial of Latane."

BOOKS: *Education and Literature in Virginia*, 1850; *Across the Atlantic*, 1856; *Poems of John R. Thompson*, ed. with a biographical sketch by John S. Patton, 1920; *The Genius and Character of Edgar Allan Poe*, ed. by J. H. Whitty and J. H. Rindfleisch, 1929.

REFERENCES: J. B. Hubbell, *The South in American Literature 1607-1900* (bibliography), 1954: Kunitz and Haycraft, *American Books and Authors 1600-1900*, 1938; Louis D. Rubin, Jr., ed., *A Bibliographical Guide to the Study of Southern Literature*, 1969. See also Swem's *Virginia Historical Index*, Vol. 2, 1936.

TRIGG, EMMA GRAY WHITE (1890-   ), writer of light opera and verse, was born in Norfolk, but moved to Richmond in 1907. Her literary activity includes two collections of verse and the books and lyrics of three operettas, one of which is *To Have and to Hold*, based upon the Mary Johnston (*q.v.*) novel by the same title. She is also quite active in social and civic affairs.

BOOKS: *After Eden*, 1937; *Paulownia Tree*, 1969.

REFERENCES: Richmond *Times-Dispatch*, Jan. 8, 1950; Norfolk *Vir-ginian-Pilot*, Jan. 9, 1955; Margaret H. Carpenter, *Virginia Authors' Year-book*, 1957.

TROUBETZKOY, ULRICH (1914-   ), non-fiction writer and poet, was born in Hartford, Connecticut. Her undergraduate training was completed at the University of Chicago, where she studied with Thornton Wilder. She did graduate work at Columbia and at Cornell. Her professional activities have been numerous—free-lance writer; foreign correspondent; art, drama, and book critic; magazine and newspaper editor and wildlife specialist.

She was well known as editor of *Virginia Cavalcade* and as a member of the editorial staff of *Virginia Wildlife*. She was the first regular art critic for the Richmond *Times-Dispatch*. She has won wide acclaim as a poet, having published several collections and won numerous awards, among them the Arthur Davison Ficke Memorial Award for sonnet sequences; Poetry Society of America monthly and annual awards; and the Jamestown Award of the 350th Anniversary Commission. She also holds numerous honorary and professional memberships.

BOOKS: *Out of the Wilderness*, 1957; *Richmond: City of Churches*, 1957; ed., *Significant Addresses of the Jamestown Festival*, 1958; *Poetry Party, 1961-1962*, 1962; *Bluebonnets and Blood*, 1968; *Sagamore Creek*, 1969.

REFERENCES: Margaret H. Carpenter, *Virginia Authors' Yearbook*, 1956, 1957, 1958.

TUCKER, GEORGE (1775-1861), political economist and miscellaneous writer, was born in Bermuda and came to Virginia in 1795, where he was educated at the College of William and Mary. After he was graduated, he studied law under the direction of St. George Tucker *(q.v.)*, a distant relative, and then practiced in Richmond and Lynchburg. Later he was a member of the Virginia legislature, and was elected to Congress three times. On retirement he became Professor of Moral Philosophy at the University of Virginia, by appointment of Thomas Jefferson. He served in this position for twenty years.

After retiring from teaching in 1845, Tucker settled in Philadelphia, where he continued to study and write. Three of his books were published after he was eighty. In 1860-61, the winter following the death of his third wife, he travelled extensively through the South and observed the growing tension. Although he was an opponent of slavery, he could not sympathize with either the Southern extremists or the Northern sentimentalists and ardent reformers.

His books include two novels as well as history, biography, and writing on political economy. His literary reputation rests primarily on his writings in the field of economics. (C.H.H.)

BOOKS: (probable author) *Letters From Virginia*, 1816; *Essays on Various Subjects of Taste, Morals and National Policy, By a citizen of Virginia*, 1822; *The Valley of the Shenandoah*, 1824, 1970; *A Voyage to the Moon*, 1827; *The Life of Thomas Jefferson* (2 vols.), 1837; *The Laws of Wages, Profits and Rent Investigated*, 1837; *The Theory of Money and Banks Investigated*, 1839; *Progress of the United States in Population and Wealth in Fifty Years*, 1843; *The History of the United States from Their Colonization to the End of the Twenty-Sixth Congress in 1841* (4 vols), 1856-57; *Political Economy for the People*, 1859.

REFERENCES: Kunitz and Haycraft, *American Authors 1600-1900*, 1938;

J. B. Hubbell, *Virginia Life in Fiction*, 1922; J. B. Hubbell, *The South in American Literature 1600-1900* (bibliography), 1954; T. A. Emmet, *An Account of the Tucker Family of Bermuda*, 1898; P. A. Bruce, *History of the University of Virginia*, 1920-22; *Proceedings of the American Philosophical Society*, 1865; *Daily Richmond Enquirer*, April 13, 1861. Louis D. Rubin, Jr., ed., *A Bibliographical Guide to the Study of Southern Literature*, 1969. See also Swem's *Virginia Historical Index*, Vol. 2, 1936.

TUCKER, NATHANIEL BEVERLEY (1784-1851), novelist, writer of non-fiction, and editor, was the son of St. George (*q.v.*) and Frances (Bland) Tucker, and the half brother of John Randolph of Roanoke. He received his early education from tutors and later attended the College of William and Mary. He was graduated in 1801, after which he studied and then practiced law.

After spending some time with John Randolph (whose antipathy toward slavery he could not share), fighting in the War of 1812, and living seventeen years in Missouri, he returned to Williamsburg in 1833.

In 1834, he became Professor of Law at the College of William and Mary, a position his father had once held. He felt the necessity of being heard, but instead of running for office, he preferred to use his influence in essays in the newspapers and contributions to such magazines as the *Southern Literary Messenger* and the *Southern Quarterly Review*. At one time he contemplated a literary career, but abandoned it when his novels did not make a profit. His hope was that he could find some fulfillment of his ideas by impressing them on his pupils.

Beverley Tucker was a friend of Thomas Willis White, the owner of the *Southern Literary Messenger*. In addition to contributing his own writing to the magazine, he read manuscripts and occasionally wrote reviews. (M.M.C.)

BOOKS: *George Balcombe*, 1836; *The Partisan Leader: A Tale of the Future*, 1836; *Gertrude*, serialized in the *Southern Literary Messenger* from September, 1844, to December, 1845.

REFERENCES: J. B. Hubbell, *The South in American Literature 1607-1900* (bibliography), 1954; Frances Coleman Rosenberger, *Virginia Reader*, 1948; James D. Hart, *Oxford Companion to American Literature*, 1965; Mildred L. Rutherford, *American Authors*, 1899; Louis D. Rubin, Jr., ed., *A Bibliographical Guide to the Study of Southern Lliterature*, 1969. See also *Swem's Virginia Historical Index*, Vol. 2, 1936.

TUCKER, ST. GEORGE (1752-1827), poet, writer of non-fiction, and editor, was born in Bermuda. With his older brothers, Thomas Tudor and Nathaniel, he came to the American continent in 1771. St. George became a student at the College of William and Mary and studied law with George Wythe. After spending some time in Berumda, he returned to Virginia, served in the Revolution, and in 1778 married Mrs. Frances (Bland) Randolph, the mother of young John Randolph of Roanoke. Henry St. George and Nathaniel Beverley (*q.v.*) were the sons of Frances and St. George Tucker.

After the Revolution the elder Tucker practiced law, and in 1790 succeeded George Wythe as Professor of Law at the College of William and Mary. His first wife had died in 1788, and in 1791 he married Mrs. Lelia (Skipwith) Carter. In 1804, he resigned from his teaching position. He had been a judge of the general court of Virginia from 1788 and was elected to the supreme court of appeals of the state in 1803. In 1813 President Madison appointed him judge of the Federal District court of Virginia in which position he remained until 1827.

Tucker's disapproval of slavery is manifested in *A Dissertation on Slavery: With a Proposal for the Gradual Abolition of it, in the State of Virginia,* a selection of college lectures, published in book form in 1796. His was not an uncommon view of the time.

His five-volume annotated edition of *Blackstone's Commentaries,* published in 1803, was considered the authority on the subject. He added in the appendix, "View of the Constitution of the United States," a discussion upholding the sovereignty of the state, and a note "On the State of Slavery in Virginia," condemning the existence of slavery in the nation.

Professor Tucker associated with a group of people in Williamsburg who, like the Hartford Wits, delighted in writing light verse and occasional essays. Some of their writing was published in William Wirt's series, "The Old Bachelor," which appeared first in the Richmond *Enquirer* but later was published in book form.

Several of Tucker's longer patriotic poems were published; his shorter poems, however, were never collected, although he did write to the Philadelphia publisher Mathew Carey about collecting them. (M.M.C.)

BOOKS: *Liberty: A Poem on the Independence of America,* 1788; *The Probationary Odes of Jonathan Pindar,* 1796; *A Dissertation on Slavery,* 1796, 1861; ed., *Blackstone's Commentaries,* 1903.

REFERENCES: Francis Coleman Rosenberger, *Virginia Reader,* 1948; J. B. Hubbell, *The South in American Literature, 1607-1900* (bibliography), 1954; James D. Hart, *Oxford Companion to American Literature,* 1965; Mrs. Geo. P. Coleman, ed., *Virginia Silhouettes,* 1934; Mary Haldane Coleman, *St. George Tucker: Citizen of No Mean City,* 1938; *Virginia Law Register,* Vol. I, No. 11 (March 1896); *Virginia Cavalcade,* (Autumn 1955). Louis D. Rubin, Jr., ed., *A Bibliographical Guide to the Study of Southern Literature,* 1969. See also Swem's *Virginia Historical Index,* Vol. 2, 1936.

TURNER, NANCY BIRD (1880-1971), poet, author of juveniles and non-fiction, was born in Boydton, Virginia. She summarizes her early influences as follows: "the simple, unforgettable charm of childhood spent in the country, mostly in old rural rectories of Virginia and Maryland, the religious education I received, and the impact on my young mind of the beauty of the Bible."

She was educated first at home and then at the Hannah Moore Academy

116   VIRGINIA AUTHORS

(the Maryland Diocesan school for girls). Her career has included editorial work on the staffs of *The Youth's Companion* and of Houghton Mifflin, as well as a busy schedule of public readings. Though she has much to say on the subject of a philosophy of writing, the core is contained in her own terse statement: "If the person has talent, it is bound to show itself, even entirely without aid, sooner or later. There is, though, one great help to be drawn on—familiarity with the most beautiful poetry of our literature. But anyone with a poetic talent will have the familiarity anyway; it will be automatic. The poetry in the Bible is a tremendous inspiration."

BOOKS: *A Riband on My Rein,* 1929; with Sidney Gunn, *The Mother of Washington,* 1930; *Star in a Well,* 1935; *Silver Saturday,* 1937; *In the Days of Young Washington,* 1931; *Ray Coon to the Rescue,* 1931; with Gertrude Nichols, *The Hopskips,* 1940; *Sycamore Silver,* 1942; *Zodiac Town,* 1921; *Magpie Lane,* 1927; *When It Rained Cats and Dogs,* 1946; *Poems, Selected and New,* 1965.

REFERENCES: Richmond *Times-Dispatch,* Sept. 18, 1949; Margaret H. Carpenter, *Virginia Authors' Yearbook,* 1956, 1957.

TURPIN, EDNA (1867-1952), author, co-author, or editor of more than forty books, was born at "Echo Hill," a plantation in Mecklenburg County. Later she lived in Richmond and then in New York. For many years she worked for a publishing company, editing school books and writing in her spare time. She has at least thirteen imaginative books to her credit and thirty-two texts. A born storyteller, she wrote many of her books for children. *Littling of Gaywood* was reprinted as a Williamsburg book. Her vivid presentation of history makes *The Story of Virginia* a good introduction to Virginia history. (M.M.C.)

BOOKS: *Honey Sweet,* 1911; *Happy Acres,* 1913; *Peggy of Roundabout Lane,* 1917; *Treasure Mountain,* 1920; *The Old Mine's Secret,* 1938; *Whistling Jimps,* 1922; *Echo Hill,* 1933; *Three Circus Days,* 1935; *Lost Covers,* 1937; *Zickle's Luck,* 1938; *Littling of Gaywood,* 1939; *The Story of Virginia,* 1949.

REFERENCES: Richmond *Times-Dispatch,* Sept. 25, 1949; *Booklist,* Oct., 1935; *Christian Science Monitor,* July 25, 1938; *Horn Book,* May 14, 1938.

TYLER, LYON GARDINER (1853-1935), writer of non-fiction, was born at "Sherwood Forest," Charles City County, Virginia, and educated at the University of Virginia. He practiced law in Richmond, and in 1887 became a member of the House of Delegates. From 1888 to 1919 he was President of the College of William and Mary which, under his leadership, became non-sectarian and coeducational. From his own resources he published the *William and Mary Quarterly* (1892-1919), and upon retirement continued to edit the periodical as *Tyler's Quarterly Historical and Genealogical Magazine* until his death. He was author of numerous books on Virginia history.

BOOKS: *The Letters and Times of the Tylers,* 1884-96; *Parties and Patronage in the United States,* 1891; *The Cradle of the Republic,* 1900,

1906; *England in America*, 1904; *Williamsburg: The Old Colonial Capital*, 1907; *Narratives of Early Virginia*, 1907; *History of Virginia from 1763-1861*, 1924; *Ripples of Rhyme*, 1933; ed., *Men of Mark in Virginia*, 1906-1909; ed., *Encyclopedia of Virginia Biography*, 1915.

REFERENCES: John Elias Hobeika, *The Sage of Lion's Den*, 1948; *Dictionary of American Biography*, Vol. 19, 1936; *Men of Mark in Virginia*, 1906-09. See also Swem's *Virginia Historical Index*, Vol. 2, 1936.

VALENTINE, BENJAMIN BATCHELDER (1862-1919), poet, was a native of Richmond, who did some work in poetic composition, as well as some along other literary lines. A volume of his dialect poems. *Ole Marster and Other Verse*, was published in 1921. Probably the best known of his poems is "In Old Virginia," first printed in 1893. (C.H.H.)

BOOK: *Ole Marster and Other Verses*, 1921.

REFERENCES: Armistead C. Gordon, Jr., *Virginian Writers of Fugitive Verse*, 1923. See also Swem's *Virginia Historical Index*, Vol. 2, 1936.

WALSH, CHAD (1914-   ), has described his career as that of "writer, college professor, and priest, which I suppose indicates my combination of interests." He has been quite active in all three of these areas. He was born in South Boston, Virginia, and attended Marion College, the University of Virginia (B.A., 1938), and The University of Michigan (M.A., 1939; Ph.D., 1943). Most of his teaching career has been spent at Beloit College in Wisconsin and he has been a Fulbright lecturer to Italy and Finland. In addition to founding the *Beloit Poetry Journal*, he has written a good deal of poetry and much criticism on the subject (e.g. *Doors into Poetry* (1962)). He is an ordained priest in the Episcopal Church, and several of his titles are in the realm of religion (e.g. *C.S. Lewis: Apostle to the Skeptics* (1949); and the popular drama, *Campus Gods on Trial* (1953)).

BOOKS: *Stop Looking and Listen: An Invitation to the Christian Life*, 1947; *C. S. Lewis: Apostle to the Skeptics*, 1949; *The Factual Dark*, 1949; *Campus Gods on Trial*, 1953; *Knock and Enter*, 1953; *Eden Two-Way*, 1954; *Faith and Behavior*, 1954; *Behold the Glory*, 1956; *Nellie and Her Flying Crocodile*, 1956; *The Rough Years*, 1960; *The Personality of Jesus*, 1961; *Doors into Poetry*, 1962; *From Utopia to Nightmare*, 1962; *The Story of Job*, 1963; *The Psalm of Christ*, 1963; *The Unknowing Dance*, 1964; *Today's Poets*, 1964; *Garlands for Christmas*, 1965; *The Honey and the Gall*, 1967; *The End of Nature*, 1969.

REFERENCE: *Contemporary Authors*, 3.

WASHINGTON, BOOKER T. (1859-1915), writer of non-fiction, was born in Franklin County, Virginia, south of Roanoke. At thirteen he entered the Normal and Agricultural Institute set up in Hampton to help Negroes who had recently been freed. During his three years there he supported himself by working as a janitor. After leaving the Institute, he taught at Malden, Virginia, and then took eight months further training in the Wayland Seminary in Washington, D. C. At twenty he returned to Hampton Normal and Agricultural Institute as a teacher and helped found a night school where pupils were encouraged to develop their natural skills and follow their natural tendencies.

The young educator was under thirty when he became the first principal of the new Normal and Industrial Institute at Tuskegee, Alabama. His assets were a $2000 grant from the Alabama Legislature and the use of an old shanty and a church. By persistence he was able to construct a kiln in which his pupils could make bricks that they would later use to build the Institute's needed buildings. In ten years' time they built thirty-six buildings.

An indefatigable writer in the cause of Negro education, Booker T. Washington's most famous piece of writing is his autobiography, *Up From Slavery*, which has been reprinted numerous times. (M.M.C.)

BOOKS: *The Future of the American Negro*, 1899; *Sowing and Reaping*, 1900; *Up From Slavery*, 1901; *Character Building*, 1902; *Working with the Hands*, 1904; *Putting the Most Into Life*, 1906; *Frederick Douglass*, 1907; *The Negro in Business*, 1907; *The Story of the Negro*, 1909; *My Larger Education*, 1911; with R. E. Park, *The Man Farthest Down*, 1912; ed., *Tuskegee and Its People*, 1905.

REFERENCES: E. J. Scott and Lyman Beecher Stowe, *Booker T. Washington: Builder of a Civilization*, 1916; E. D. Washington, *Selected Speeches of Booker T. Washington*, 1932; A. P. Stokes, *Tuskegee Institute: The First Fifty Years*, 1931. See also Swem's *Virginia Historical Index*, Vol. 2, 1936.

WATKINS, LUCIAN BOTTOW (1879-1921), poet, was born and educated at Chesterfield, Virginia. He later attended the Virginia Normal and Industrial Institute at Petersburg and became a teacher until World War I. As a result of his service abroad, his health was impaired, and he died in 1921. (M.M.C.)

BOOKS: *The Old Log Cabin*, 1910; *Voices of Solitude*, 1903.

REFERENCES: James Weldon Johnson, *The Book of American Negro Poetry*, 1922, 1931; Robert Thomas Kerlin, *Negro Poets and Their Poems*, 1935.

WEDDELL, ALEXANDER WILBOURNE (1876-1948), historian and diplomat, was a native of Richmond. Though he held a law degree (from George Washington University), he served in various diplomatic posts from 1908 until 1946. An avocational historian, his major contribution is *Virginia Historical Portraiture* (1930), published in a limited editon. He served as president of the Virginia Historical Society and was a founder of the Virginia Museum of Fine Arts.

BOOKS: *Virginia Historical Portraiture*, 1930; *Richmond, Virginia, in*

Old Prints, 1737-1887, 1932; *Portraiture in the Virginia Historical Society,* 1945; *A Description of Virginia House,* 1947.
REFERENCES: *Who Was Who,* 2, 1943-1950.

WEEMS, MASON LOCKE (1759-1825), writer of non-fiction and Episcopal clergyman, better known as "Parson Weems," was born in Ann Arundel County, Maryland. He was admitted to the priesthood by the Archbishop of Canterbury, and served several parishes in Maryland.

In July, 1795, after his marriage to Frances Ewell, he moved to her home in Dumfries, Virginia. In 1806 he built "Bel Air" as a home for his family. For a time he was rector of Pohick Church, but most of his life was spent as an itinerant bookseller, wandering up and down the Atlantic seaboard from New York to Savannah, selling the books of Mathew Carey and other publishers.

Though he helped promote the sale of John Marshall's *Washington,* his fame rests chiefly on his own book, *The Life and Memorable Actions of George Washington,* which appeared in 1800. This work subsequently ran through seventy editions, making it one of the great best sellers of the early nineteenth century. The first edition was a twelve-page pamphlet; the second, an octavo pamphlet of eighty-two pages.

With the eleventh edition in 1811, the biography was fully developed. It was this edition that made Weems's reputation as a writer and added considerably to the fortunes of his printer. Weems first recounted the hatchet and cherry tree story in the edition of 1816. Later and more scholarly historians regard the story as fanciful. Weems's claim to be Washington's pastor was based upon his brief rectorship of Pohick Church. (M.M.C.)

BOOKS AND PAMPHLETS: *Hymen's Recruiting Sergeant,* 1799; *The Philanthropist,* 1799; *The Patriot,* 1802; *God's Revenge Against Murder,* 1807; *God's Revenge Against Gambling,* 1810; *God's Revenge Against Adultery,* 1815; *The Drunkard's Looking Glass,* 1812; *God's Revenge Against Duelling,* 1820; *The Bad Wife's Looking Glass,* 1823; *The Life and Memorable Actions of George Washington,* 1800; *Life of General Francis Marion,* 1809; *Life of Dr. Benjamin Franklin,* 1815; *Life of William Penn,* 1822.

REFERENCES: Duyckinck, *Cyclopedia of American Literature,* 1855; *Dictionary of American Biography,* 1928-37; Kunitz and Haycraft, *American Authors, 1600-1900,* 1938; Fred L. Pattee, *First Century of American Literature 1770-1870,* 1935; Paul Leicester Ford and Emily Ford Skeel, *Mason Locke Weems* (3 vols.), 1928-29; W. G. Simms, *Views and Reviews in American Literature,* 1945; J. B. Hubbell, *The South in American Literature 1607-1900,* 1954; Warrenton, (N. C.), *Reporter,* July 8, 1825.

WERTENBAKER, CHARLES CHRISTIAN (1901-1955), editor, author, foreign correspondent, was born in Lexington, Virginia. He was a student at the University of Virginia during 1919-21, took a year for newspaper work, and then returned to the University for the years 1923-25.

He was associated with *Time, Life,* and *Fortune* magazines for many years, mainly as a foreign correspondent. In 1944 he covered the European invasion for *Time* magazine. He was the author of nine books and many articles.

For several years before his death he had lived in Ciboure, France. (M.M.C.)

BOOKS: *Boojum*, 1928; *Peter the Drunk*, 1929; *Before They Were Men*, 1931; *To My Father*, 1936; *A New Doctrine for the Americas*, 1941; *Invasion*, 1944; *Write Sorrow in the Earth*, 1947; *The Barons*, 1950; *Death of Kings*, 1954.

REFERENCES: *New Yorker*, Dec. 26, 1953; *Saturday Review*, Jan. 16, 1954; *Newsweek*, Jan. 17, 1955; *Time*, Jan. 17, 1955; *Reporter*, Jan. 27, 1955, *Newsweek*, Mar. 18, 1957; *Death of a Man*, 1957; *Look*, 21:41-2, Mar. 19, 1957.

WERTENBAKER, GREEN PEYTON ["Green Peyton"] (1907-   ), writer of non-fiction, was born in Charlottesville, Virginia, to a family whose association with the University of Virginia extended back to appointments by Jefferson. He attended there 1924-25 and 1927-29. After working as a Richmond reporter, a free-lance writer, and as editor of *Fortune* (1933-38), as Southwest News Bureau Chief of *Life* and *Time*, and as Combat Information Officer in the Navy during the War, he received a Rockefeller Fellowship (1947) to write *America's Heartland*. He became a free-lance writer in 1949.

BOOKS: *Black Cabin*, 1933; *Rain on the Mountain*, 1934; *5,000 Miles Towards Tokyo*, 1945; *San Antonio: City in the Sun*, 1946; *For God and Texas: The Life of P. B. Hill*, 1947; *America's Heartland: The Southwest*, 1948; *The Face of Texas*, 1961; *Fifty Years of Aerospace Medicine*, 1968.

REFERENCE: Richmond *Times-Dispatch*, Feb. 13, 1949.

WERTENBAKER, THOMAS JEFFERSON (1879-1966), historian, was born in Charlottesville and received three degrees from the University of Virginia (Ph.D., 1910). From 1910 to 1936 he was a professor of history at Princeton and held various visiting professorships thereafter. One of the most distinguished historians Virginia has produced, he was honored with honorary degrees from the College of William and Mary and Oxford. Colonial American history was his special interest, and his trilogy of books—*Virginia Under the Stuarts* (1948); *Patrician and Plebeian in Virginia* (1910); *and The Planters of Colonial Virginia* (1922) (published together (1958) as *The Shaping of Colonial Virginia*), represents the importance of his contribution.

BOOKS: *Patrician and Plebeian in Virginia*, 1910; *Virginia Under the Stuarts*, 1914; *The Planters of Colonial Virginia*, 1922; *The Middle Colonies*, 1938; *The Old South*, 1942; *The Golden Age of Colonial Culture*, 1942; *Torchbearer of the Revolution: The Story of Bacon's Rebellion*, 1942; *The Puritan Oligarchy*, 1947; *Father Knickerbocker Rebels*, 1948; *The Shaping of Colonial Virginia*, 1958.

REFERENCES: *Contemporary Authors*, 7-8; Richmond *Times-Dispatch*, April 25, 1966.

WILDER, ROBERT INGERSOLL (1901-   ), novelist, playwright, script writer, and short story writer, was born in Richmond and attended Stetson and Columbia Universities. After working in various capacities on the New York *Sun*, he went to Hollywood in 1948. Here he has written scripts for several movies (e.g. *The Big Country*, which starred Gregory Peck and Jean Simmons). He is also author of a number of plays (e.g. *Stardust* (1930)); one of them—*Flamingo Road* (1943)—was turned into a movie. His short stories have appeared in many magazines, including the *New Yorker* and *Smart Set*.

BOOKS: *God Has a Long Face*, 1940; *Out of the Blue*, 1943; *Flaming Road*, 1943; *Written on the Wind*, 1945; *Mr. G. Strings Along*, 1946; *Bright Feather*, 1948; *Wait for Tomorrow*, 1950; *And Ride a Tiger*, 1951; *Autumn Thunder*, 1952; *The Wine of Youth*, 1955; *The Sun is My Shadow*, 1958; *Plough the Sea*, 1961; *Wind from the Carolinas*, 1964; *Fruit of the Poppy*, 1965; *The Sea and the Stars*, 1967.

REFERENCE: *Contemporary Authors*, 13-14.

WILLIAMS, FRANCES LEIGH (1909-   ), historian, biographer, and novelist, was born in Richmond and early in her career (1927-35) worked on the *News Leader* there. She then worked for two years as research assistant to Douglas Southall Freeman (*q.v.*) She subsequently worked as a dealer in fashions and as a hotel manager. The latter vocation was reflected in her novel *Welcome to Dunecrest* (1955). She is perhaps best known for her biographies: e.g. *Matthew Fontaine Maury: Scientist of the Sea* (1963) and *Plantation Patriot: A Biography of Eliza Lucas Pickney* (1967).

BOOKS: *Historic Richmond: Her Story and Her Spirit*, 1936; *They Faced the Future*, 1951; *Welcome to Dunecrest*, 1955; *The Shawnee Tomahawk*, 1958; *Matthew Fontaine Maury: Scientist of the Sea*, 1963; *Prologue to the Future*, 1965; *Ocean Pathfinder: A Biography of Matthew Fontaine Maury*, 1966; *Plantation Patriot: A Biography of Eliza Lucas Pinckney*, 1967.

REFERENCE: *Contemporary Authors*, 13-14.

WILLIAMS, REBECCA YANCY (1899-   ), writer of non-fiction, was born in Lynchburg, Virginia, but has lived for many years in Richmond. Though she has done book reviews for Virginia publications, her chief works have been book-length studies of Virginia history and biography. Perhaps the best known of these is *The Vanishing Virginian*, which was made into a movie and shown in many parts of the world during the 1940's.

BOOKS: *The Vanishing Virginian*, 1940; *Carry Me Back*, 1942.

REFERENCES: *Webster's Biographical Dictionary*; R. Yancey Williams, *Carry Me Back*, 1942; Manuscript Collection of Biographies of Lynchburg Writers at the Jones Memorial Library, Lynchburg, Va.; Richmond *Times-Dispatch*, Dec. 12, 1948.

122   VIRGINIA AUTHORS

WILSON, JAMES SOUTHALL (1888-1963), historian, biographer, educator and editor, was born at Bacon's Castle, Virginia. After being educated at the College of William and Mary (B.A., 1904), the University of Virginia (M.A., 1905), and Princeton (Ph.D., 1906), he returned to teach at William and Mary. However, it was at the University of Virginia, where he became Edgar Allan Poe Professor of English in 1916, that he made his most lasting contributions. In addition to his numerous publications on Poe (e.g. *Facts About Poe* (1926)), he is remembered as the founder of the *Virginia Quarterly Review*, which began in the spring of 1925. From its founding to the present, it has been recognized as one of the major reviews in America.

BOOKS: *Alexander Wilson: Poet, Naturalist*, 1906; *Facts About Poe*, 1926.

REFERENCES: *Virginia Quarterly Review* (Autumn 1963); Richmond *Times-Dispatch*, June 27, 1963.

WILSON [THOMAS] WOODROW (1856-1924), writer of non-fiction, was born in Staunton, Virginia. After education at Princeton (M.A., 1879) and at Johns Hopkins (Ph.D., 1886), he taught at Bryn Mawr and Princeton and was elected president of the latter in 1902. In 1911 he became Governor of New Jersey and in 1912 President of the United States. Promising neutrality, he was re-elected in 1916, changed policy in 1917, and brought America into war and signed the peace treaty in 1918. He became a permanent invalid in 1919, while on a speaking tour promoting the League of Nations. His writings are in the areas of history, political science, and biography.

BOOKS: *Congressional Government: A Study of American Politics*, 1885; *The State: Elements of Historical and Practical Politics*, 1889; *An Old Master and Other Political Essays*, 1893; *Mere Literature and Other Essays*, 1896; *A History of the American People* (5 vols.), 1902; *Constitutional Government in the United States*, 1908; *The New Freedom*, 1913; *Division and Reunion, 1829-1889*, 1893; *Robert E. Lee*, 1924; *The Wilson Reader*, ed. by Frances Farmer, 1956.

REFERENCES: James D. Hart, *The Oxford Companion to American Literature*, 1965; Ray Stannard Baker, *Woodrow Wilson and the World Settlement* (3 vols.), 1922; Ray Stannard Baker, *Woodrow Wilson's Life and Letters* (8 vols.), 1927-39; William Edward Dodd and Ray Stannard Baker, eds., *The Public Papers of Woodrow Wilson*, 1925-27; Col. Edward Mandell House, *The Intimate Papers of Colonel House* (4 vols.), 1926-28. See also Swem's *Virginia Historical Index*, Vol. 2, 1936.

WIRT, WILLIAM (1772-1834), lawyer, writer, unwilling politician, and orator, was a literary force during the years he lived in Virginia. In Richmond he gave stimulus to a group of young lawyers and journalists who contributed their essays to Richmond newspapers, notably the *Enquirer*.

The Letters of an English Spy is a collection of Wirt's essays that proved their popularity by going through ten editions. In portraits of prominent Virginians he mildly criticized current foibles.

"The Old Bachelor" series of about thirty-three numbers was published mainly in 1811. Wirt and some of his friends wrote about politics, oratory, morals, education, and other subjects suited, they thought, to instruct and improve their readers. The satiric portraits that Wirt delighted in writing were sometimes mistaken for attacks on the subjects, a purpose far from his thoughts. The series was published in book form in 1814 and again in 1818.

Sketches of the Life of Patrick Henry (1817) took twelve years to write. Material was hard to find, and reports from people who had known Patrick Henry were contradictory. The famous speeches had to be reconstructed since Henry did not write his speeches. Wirt used the recollections of such men as Jefferson *(q.v.)*, St. George Tucker *(q.v.)*, and Judge Tyler to reconstruct the "Give Me Liberty, or Give Me Death" speech of March 23, 1775. The speech was given in indirect discourse, except for the famous quotation.

The book was first published in 1817 and received varying criticism. Wirt himself was dissatisfied with it. It was popular, however, and by 1860 had gone through fifteen editions. (M.M.C.)

BOOKS: *The Letters of a British Spy*, 1803; *The Old Bachelor*, 1814; *Sketches of the Life and Character of Patrick Henry*, 1817.

REFERENCES: John Pendleton Kennedy, *Memoirs of the Life of William Wirt* (2 vols.) 1849, 1850; J. B. Hubbell, *The South in American Literature 1607-1900* (bibliography), 1954. Louis D. Rubin, Jr., ed., *A Bibliographical Guide to the Study of Southern Literature*, 1969. See also Swem's *Virginia Historical Index*, Vol. 2, 1936.

WOLFE, THOMAS KENNERLY ["TOM WOLFE"] (1931-   ), was born in Richmond and attended St. Christopher's School there. After graduation from Washington and Lee (B.A., 1951) and Yale (Ph.D., 1957), he embarked on a career as a journalist and free-lance writer which has brought him distinction. While working on an article for *Esquire* magazine, which he did not have time to finish, he started typing out his notes and saw emerging a style which was telegraphic in its syntax and contained many comments made in contemporary idiom, many of them a single word or phrase. These characteristics parallelled those of the "pop-art" movement, and he has continued to write in this vein, having dubbed his new-found mode "the wowie!" style. His first book-length effort was *The Kandy-Kolored Tangerine-Flake Streamline Baby* (1965). His work has met with mixed reaction. Some have called it faddish, but the more serious critics have seen his serious attempt to get at exact meanings by presenting current cultural phenomena in the informal language of the age in which they occur.

BOOKS: *The Kandy-Kolored Tangerine-Flake Streamline Baby*, 1965; *The Electric Kool-Aid Acid Test*, 1968; *The Pump House Gang*, 1968; *Radical Chic and Mau-Mauing the Flak Catchers*, 1970.

REFERENCES: *Commentary*, Fall, 1969; *Saturday Review*, March 23,

1968; *Esquire,* Nov. 1967; *Newsweek,* Jan. 31, 1966; *Vogue,* April 15, 1966; Richmond *Times-Dispatch,* Aug. 18, 1971.

WOOLFOLK, JOSIAH PITTS ["JACK WOODFORD"] (1894-1971), novelist, critic, and writer of non-fiction, was born in Chicago and educated at Northwestern. He subsequently became a master telegrapher. His ability to compose rapidly in this medium carried over into his fiction writing: he claimed he could write a 1,200-word short story within an hour without corrections. Because he frequently wrote under pseudonyms (e.g. "Gordon Sayre" and "Howard Kennedy" in addition to "Jack Woodford"), it is rather difficult to determine the entirety of his output; however, estimates run as high as sixty books and innumerable stories and movie scripts. One of the books written in Richmond (where he had relatives) was *The Evangelical Cockroach* (1926), a representative satire said by a reviewer to have been written "by a disciple of the Mencken-Nathan school." He was more famous, however, for books on how to write, best known of which was *Trial and Error* (1933). He wrote in Chicago, Texas, and Hollywood, but returned to Richmond in 1954, where he stayed until 1962, at which time he was committed by a court order to Eastern State Hospital, where he died in May, 1971.

BOOKS: *Evangelical Cockroach,* 1926; *Sin and Such,* 1930; *Find the Motive,* 1932; *City Limits,* 1932; *The Loud Literary Llamas of New York,* 1950.

REFERENCES: *Who's Who,* 1954, 1955; Richmond *News Leader,* June 17 and 19, 1971.

WORMELEY, CARTER, W. (1874-1938), poet, was born in Richmond and worked there on the staff of the *Richmond Journal* and as a publicity official for the Commonwealth. Though circulated in numerous newspapers during his lifetime, his poems were never collected. However, when they appeared, they served as witty and at times incisive commentaries on contemporary personalities and events. So well were they appreciated that the General Assembly named Wormeley Virginia's Poet Laureate in 1936 with the provision that the title not pass to a successor. Many of his poems were political, his last line being "and send regards to Jim," referring to James A. Price, who was then Governor.

REFERENCES: Richmond *News Leader,* Aug. 25, 1938.

WRIGHT, WILLARD HUNTINGTON ["S. S. VANDINE"] (1888-1939), art critic, editor, journalist, and writer of detective fiction, was born in Charlottesville, Virginia. He studied English literature at Harvard and art in Munich and Paris with the idea of becoming an artist. He also considered being a symphony orchestra conductor.

After working as a literary critic for the Los Angeles *Times* and as editor of *Smart Set,* he wrote a novel (*A Man of Promise* (1916)). This was unsuccessful, and it was not until the mid-1920's, during recovery from a nervous breakdown, that he wrote a long synopsis for three mystery novels and was commissioned by Scribner's to write them. The first, *The Benson Murder Case* (1926), was an immediate success. It was followed by eleven others.

The detective-protagonist of these, Philo Vance, is said to resemble the author both in appearance and personality. Mr. Vance is bored, languid, or erudite as the case demands.

BOOKS: With H. L. Mencken and George Jean Nathan, *Europe After 8:15*, 1914; *What Nietzsche Taught*, 1915; *Modern Painting*, 1915; *The Creative Will*, 1916; *Informing a Nation*, 1917; *Misinforming a Nation*, 1917; *The Future of Painting*, 1923; *The Benson Murder Case*, 1926; *The "Canary" Murder Case*, 1927; *The Greene Murder Case*, 1928; *The Bishop Murder Case*, 1929; *The Scarab Murder Case*, 1930; *The Kennel Murder Case*, 1932; *The Dragon Murder Case*, 1933; *The Casino Murder Case*, 1934; *The Garden Murder Case*, 1935; *Philo Vance Murder Cases*, 1936; *The Kidnap Murder Case*, 1936; *The Powwow Murder Case*, later called *The Gracie Allen Murder Case*, 1938; *The Winter Murder Case*, 1939; ed., *The Great Detective Stories*, 1927.

REFERENCES: *Who Was Who in America*, Vol. 1, 1942; *Who's Who in America*, Vol. 20, 1938-39; *Dictionary of American Biography, Supplement Two*, Vol. 22, 1958; Kunitz and Haycraft, *Twentieth Century Authors*, 1942; Howard Haycraft, *Murder for Pleasure: The Life and Times of the Detective Story, 1941*.

5.95

William Byrd ①

George Mason ②

Thomas Jefferson ③

A Brief Chronology of Virginia Writers

Captain John Smith 1580-1631
Jamestown

Robert Beverley 1673-1722
King and Queen County

William Byrd 1674-1744
Westover - Charles City Co.

George Mason 1725-1792
Gunston Hall - Fairfax Co.

George Washington 1732
Mount Vernon   1799

Patrick Henry 1736-1799
Ashland

Thomas Jefferson 1743-1826
Monticello

James Madison 1751-1836
Montpelier - Orange County

James Monroe 1758-1831
Ash Lawn

John Randolph of Roanoke
Roanoke   1773 - 1833

Wm Holmes McGuffey
Charlottesville 1800-1873

Wm Alexander Caruthers
Lexington   1802-1846

Edgar Allan Poe 1809-1849
Richmond

George Wm Bagby 1821-1883
Buckingham County

John Esten Cooke 1830-1886
Winchester

Marion Harland (M.V. Terhune)
Amelia County   1830-1922

John Banister Tabb 1845 1909
Amelia County

Thomas Nelson Page 1853
Ashland   1922

Woodrow Wilson 1856-1914
Staunton

Booker T. Washington
Hampton   1859-1915

John Fox Jr. 1863-1919
Big Stone Gap

Mary Johnston 1870-1936
Buchanan

Ellen Glasgow 1874-1945
Richmond

Sherwood Anderson 1876
Marion   1941

Willa Cather 1876-1947
Winchester

James Branch Cabell
Richmond   1879-1958

Douglas S. Freeman 1886 1953
Lynchburg

John Dos Passos 1896-1970
Westmoreland County

Clifford Dowdey 1904-
Richmond

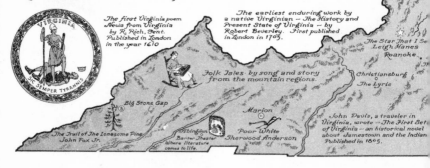

VIRGINIA
SIC SEMPER TYRANNIS

The first Virginia poem News from Virginia by R. Rich, Gent. Published in London in the year 1610

The earliest enduring work by a native Virginian — The History and Present State of Virginia — by Robert Beverley. First published in London in 1705.

The Star That I See Leigh Hanes Roanoke

Folk Tales - by song and story from the mountain regions.

Christiansburg The Lyric

Big Stone Gap ⑧

Marion ⑪

The Trail of the Lonesome Pine John Fox Jr.

Abingdon Barter Theater Where literature comes to life.

Poor White Sherwood Anderson

John Davis, a traveler in Virginia, wrote — The First Settlers of Virginia — an historical novel about Jamestown and the Indians. Published in 1805.

A Literary Map of The

John Fox Jr. ⑥

Amélie Rives ⑨

Mary Johnston ⑩

Sou

A Literary Map of the Commonwealth of Virginia printed originally in 1957 by The Virginia Association of Teachers of English.